Using
WordStar

**Versions 5, 5.5
and 6**

CW01563929

Using WordStar

Versions 5, 5.5 and 6

Alan Balfe

HEINEMANN
NEW·TECH

Heinemann Newtech
An imprint of Heinemann Professional Publishing Ltd
Halley Court, Jordan Hill, Oxford OX2 8EJ

OXFORD	LONDON	MELBOURNE
AUCKLAND	SINGAPORE	IBADAN
NAIROBI	GABORONE	KINGSTON

First published 1989
Second edition 1990

© Alan Balfe 1989, 1990

British Library Cataloguing in Publication Data
A CIP catalogue record for this book is available from
the British Library

ISBN 0 434 92386 9

Produced by SC&E Morris Computer Services,
Bodenham, Hereford

Printed and bound in Great Britain by
Biddles Ltd, Guildford and King's Lynn

Contents

Contents

Contents

9

Contents

PART 9   PROFINDER

APPENDICES

Preface

It is just a year since I wrote *Using WordStar 5* but during that time the computer industry, as always, has moved on dramatically, with improvements and new products coming thick and fast. On the hardware front, a year ago the best-value computers available were the 80286-based 12 MHz machines, with 1 Mb of RAM and EGA monitors. Today the best value machine is an 80386 (or an 80386SX) running at 25 MHz, with 4 Mb of RAM and, at the very least, a VGA monitor. The curious thing is that in terms of price, in real terms the two machines cost the same.

Twelve months ago I was using a 24-pin dot matrix printer – I couldn't afford a laser – but since then the price of printers has fallen considerably and I now use a PostScript printer which cost very little more than a top quality dot matrix did a year ago. In fact, it is in the area of printers that there has been the greatest amount of change, with new products appearing almost weekly.

Because of all this change, WordStar (which used to be called MicroPro) have revamped and updated their world-renowned program. First we had WordStar 5.5. Actually this was very little different to WordStar 5 in terms of capabilities; however, WordStar rewrote just about every printer driver that the program included – most especially it provided true PostScript compatibility to take advantage of the printers that were then beginning to become prevalent. (If you try using the PostScript driver that comes with WordStar 5 you get an error message because the driver is incorrect!)

The latest release is WordStar 6.0. This now includes the largest range of printer drivers to be found in any word-processing program. I haven't actually counted them but according to the PR blurb, WordStar now supports just about every printer available on the market today. WordStar 6.0 was also the first word processor to provide support for the new Hewlett-Packard Laserjet

III with its scalable fonts. You can now use any point size you want from 4-point, which is the minimum size that is actually legible, all the way up to 999-point, which will produce letters that are 13.875 inches tall. (You don't get many of them onto a page!) However, the core of the program remains the same but now there are a host of extras. Over the past year I have continued to use WordStar; personally I find that the program is so simple and easy to use that it is still the best for my needs.

This book is intended primarily for those who are new to WordStar; it covers all the aspects of the WordStar program, up to and including WordStar 6, from the initial installation through to producing complex documents and mail-merging them. It has separate chapters about the related programs which are included with WordStar: MailList, TelMerge, PC-Outline, Inset and Pro-Finder.

It has purposely been written in a light, conversational style – rather than as a reference book – but that doesn't mean that you can't skim-read it. The layout is such that you can find anything you want within seconds. I hope that you will enjoy reading it as much as I enjoyed writing it.

Alan Balfe

June 1990

PART ONE

Getting started

SECTION 1
Welcome to WordStar Professional

Mention word processing to anyone, especially if they own and use a PC or AT on a regular basis, and ask them to give you the name of the first such program that pops into their head. In at least 50% of cases the program they will name will be WordStar. To a great many people WordStar *is* word processing and the program has a huge and devoted following.

WordStar has been around as long as there have been Personal Computers and the first version of the program was released to coincide with the launch of Big Blue's original machine. These days there are a huge range of word processors available, for a wide range of machines. Just as any spreadsheet has to provide compatibility with *Lotus 1-2-3* to be taken seriously, so any word processor worth its salt has to be capable of loading and saving WordStar-compatible files.

WordStar has become so synonymous with word processing over the years, and with computers in general, that its hot-key combinations have been incorporated into a host of other software; for example, *Sidekick, PC-Outline* and *Procomm* to name just three. The hot-key combinations use the standard alphanumeric keys in combination with the **Ctrl** or **Alt** keys to produce a range of effects. For instance **Ctrl-K B** marks the start of a block while **Ctrl-K K** marks the end of it, **Ctrl-Q F** is used to find words or phrases and **Ctrl-O C** is used to centre text. On the actual WordStar program it is possible to 'program' a total of forty-eight of these combinations into the function keys so that you have a wide range of effects readily at hand at the touch of a button. In addition you can have a total of thirty-six macros programmed, which are accessed using the **Esc** key. The main benefit of all this is that it saves you time, leaving you to get on with composing the document.

■ SECTION 1
Welcome to WordStar Professional

WordStar is highly complex, so much so that it was one of the first programs to have specially designed training sessions created for it by third party interests – and such courses are still run to this day. But once you have mastered the program you are unlikely to ever use another word processor.

So why the updated version? Basically, because any piece of software can never be perfect – people's aspirations, needs and desires are constantly changing as they want more and more from any program. This is especially true with word processors; almost daily they acquire more of the features that had previously only been available on DTP packages. Eventually the two types of program will become a single organism (probably within the next five years) – a Word Publisher that will allow you to create a document with a host of typefaces, graphics, cartoons, illustrations and text. However, that is in the future. What does WordStar offer its users today?

In a nutshell – choice! You can now run the program with the old style on-screen menus or the new pull-down ones. You can produce an on-screen graphical display of what your document will look like in true WYSIWYG and have up to twenty-one pages displayed at any time, albeit that this will only give you an overall impression. The dictionary – a proper English one and not just the standard American one – comes complete with more than 220,000 words and you can add extra ones as necessary. The thesaurus can provide synonyms for the same number of words and will provide you with fifty-plus possible alternatives – and give you a definition of each one. One minor disappointment with this is that the thesaurus uses American spellings – 'colour' spelled as 'color' – so you need to run the dictionary to correct them! The reason is that the two sub-programs were written by different companies and just incorporated into the overall package.

15

SECTION 1
Welcome to WordStar Professional

When it comes to producing a hard copy of a document WordStar is in a league all of its own. It will support a vast range of printers, including laser and PostScript ones. The program allows you to configure up to 100 different printers and you can use any one of them at any time. You can even custom design your own specialised printer interface and store it as a printer device.

WordStar Professional comes complete with two other integrated programs, *MailList* and *TelMerge*. The former is a specialised database that allows you to store personal details of people and/or companies for incorporation into documents at a later stage. It also has a pre-designed form for inventory control. You cannot, unfortunately, redesign either form but they will suffice for most simple form letters and reports.

The latter program is a complete E-mail communication program, on a par with the best dedicated programs that are available on the market today. All you need is a Hayes-compatible modem and you can use WordStar to communicate around the world.

Also bundled with the rest is *PC-Outline*, the ideas organiser from Brown Bag Software. Unfortunately this cannot be accessed from within WordStar unless it is running in memory-resident mode.

However there is a price to be paid for all the raw power that the complete suite of programs give you. The necessary files take up more than 4.5 megabytes of disk space and WordStar uses nearly all of the memory available under the MS-DOS 640 Kb limit. Theoretically you can run the program on a twin floppy machine but who would want to – you would lose so many capabilities that you might as well not bother.

This tells you who the program is intended for: anyone who is seriously into producing text, such as journalists, writers and

SECTION 1
Welcome to WordStar Professional

business users. It is not really meant for home users who will produce the odd letter to Aunt Sarah once a quarter. But, if you can afford it then get it, because it really is one of the best word processors you will ever use and as new versions are released the cost of updating your old version is very low.

But that is enough about the glories of WordStar. This book is about using the program, from the original installation right through to producing columned output, mailmerge, telecommunications, Outline and ProFinder. Along the way it will explore the intricacies of using the program to produce specific effects. Because of the sheer size of the program it will be assumed throughout the book that you are using a hard-disk computer.

■ SECTION 2
Notational conventions used in this book

Throughout the book you will come across keystrokes, dot commands, MS-DOS commands, etc. that have to be input at some stage. Here are a few notes about the way that they will appear in the text.

Key names

The names of keys will always appear in **bold** as they are written on the keyboard. Thus Escape appears as **Esc**, Control as **Ctrl**, Alternative as **Alt**, Return as **Enter**, etc. Similarly the function keys appear as **F1**, **F2** and so on. Note that individual letters will appear in upper case because that is the way they are written on the keyboard.

Key combinations and sequences

Where it is necessary for you to press a number of keys together they will appear in the text in bold, joined by a hyphen. Thus **Ctrl-K F** means that you hold down **Ctrl** and **K** at the same time, before releasing them and pressing **F**.

If the keys are intended to be pressed sequentially they will appear in bold but without hyphens. Thus **Esc K Enter** means you first press **Esc** and release it, then press **K** and release it and finally press **Enter** and release it.

Direction keys

The arrow keys are always referred to by their direction of action, again in bold: **Up**, **Down**, **Left** and **Right**. The remaining cursor keys will appear as they are on the keyboard; for example, **PgUp** and **Home**.

■ SECTION 2
Notational conventions used in this book

Entering commands

Throughout this book anything that you are intended to type verbatim will appear in bold. For example, when it comes to customising the program you have to enter **WSCHANGE** – the name of the sub-program that allows you to change the shipped defaults – and you enter the program name as it appears in bold.

MS-DOS commands will also appear in bold; for example, **COPY A:*.***. Where you are required to supply a word or filename in a command it will appear in standard round brackets. For instance **MD C:**(DIRECTORY) means that you enter 'MD C:\' and then a directory name.

■ SECTION 3
Installing the program

Throughout this book I shall refer to WordStar as a generic title, rather than to individual versions of the program. However, any specific differences between the versions will be mentioned. The one major difference between the versions is that WordStar 5 has no installation routine, whereas 5.5 and 6 do.

There is a golden rule in computing that you never work from the original disks, they should only be used for making copies. Normally you would have to copy all of the WordStar disks before using them but, because in this case you will copy them directly to the hard disk, you may break the rule. Besides which WordStar 5 comes on 12 disks, 5.5 comes on 20 but Version 6 uses 22 360 Kb 5¼" disks! BUT be very careful when handling the disks that they do not get damaged in the process.

WordStar 5 installation

WordStar 5 has no installation routine, so your only option when installing the program is to create the sub-directory and copy the disks manually. Boot up the computer, open the packet of disks and have them ready. Once the system prompt appears on the screen enter DIR C: to find out if you have enough room for all the WordStar 5 files. You must have at least 4,640,768 bytes free – preferably more – or the program will not fit on your hard disk. If you have less than this you will have to make room somehow. The alternative is to be very selective about which files you include on your disk and that is outside the scope of this book.

Once you are certain there is enough room on your disk, ensure that you are in the root directory and then enter MD C:\WS5 to make a directory that will hold all of the files. WordStar 5 needs to run from a directory called WS5, at least initially, to be able to work properly. Once the directory is created, enter CD \WS5 to move into it.

■ SECTION 3
Installing the program

Place one of the master disks into drive A, close the catch and enter COPY A:*.*. This will copy all the files from the floppy disk into the WS5 directory on your hard disk. Once the files have been copied, replace the floppy disk with the next in the suite and press **F3**, followed by **Enter**. (**F3** causes the last string of characters entered on the keyboard to reappear.) Carry on doing this until all the master disks have been copied.

Replace the master disks in their pack and put them somewhere safe, preferably in a dark, cool and dry place. You should not need to use them again, unless you somehow corrupt the files that are now on your hard disk.

WordStar 5.5 and 6 installation

With the advent of WordStar 5.5, MicroPro, as they then were, included an installation routine which is selective. That is, it allows you to install only those parts of the program which you actually want and along the way it tells you how much space you need on your hard disk to use each element. The same routine is also used for WordStar 6. Because of this you can actually install WordStar 6 in much less space then you would need for WordStar 5. What you install is largely dependent on what hardware – especially printers – you are using or will want to use. However, hard disk space is normally at a premium, so you will want to use as little as possible. In what follows I am assuming that you want to install the core of WordStar, the main associated programs and just one printer driver. Even so, you need at least 4 Mb of disk space available – you won't use it all but it is better to have too much than too little.

1 Boot up the computer and verify that you have enough disk space by entering DIR C: – assuming that you are going to install the program on drive C.

2 Insert the disk labelled *Installation Customisation* into drive A and then enter **A:** to log onto the drive.

3 Enter **WSSETUP**. Read the first screen and then press **F10**.

4 You will be asked to verify that you are copying from drive A onto drive C. If you are using an alternative drive just enter the corresponding letter. Finally you have the option of changing the directory in which WordStar 6 will be installed. By default this is \WS but you can change it to anything you want, e.g. \WS6. When you have made the changes, or accepted the defaults, press **F10** again to begin the installation.

5 Select those elements of the program that you want to install. Move the highlighting bar, using the cursor keys, and then press + to nominate an element for installation. If

```
                         Add or Remove Features

Press F10 to install features marked with +. To add or remove other features,
move highlighting and press + or -. (To change a directory, highlight the
feature and press F3.) Press F10 when finished indicating all changes.

  ■ WordStar                              C:\WS6
  ■ Dictionaries                          C:\WS6
  ■ Advanced Page Preview                 C:\WS6
  ■ PostScript                            C:\WS6
  ■ Inset                                 C:\WS6\INSET
  ■ MailList                              C:\WS6\MAILLIST
  ■ TelMerge                              C:\WS6\TELMERGE

  Description: Main program files for word processing. (1157K)
  Directory: \WS6

┌ Directions: ─────────────────┬──────────────────────────────────┐
│  F1 = Help                   │     PgUp/PgDn = Move between pages │
│  + - = Add/delete item       │                                  │
│  F10 = Finished              │  ↑ ↓ ← →, Home, End = Move highlighting │
│  Esc = Abandon changes       │         F3 = Change directory     │
└──────────────────────────────┴──────────────────────────────────┘
```

WordStar 6 installation screen

you make a mistake just press '–' to de-select it. Note that you *must* install WordStar itself – which is a bit of a pain if you want to install something extra later.

You can also change the directory names for any of the elements you want installed. Move the highlighter to the item and press **F3**. Then simply enter the new directory and/or sub-directory. Note that you cannot change the drive – just the directories. Personally, I always change the directory names for the various elements, e.g. Inset goes into \WS\INSET, MailList goes in \WS\MAILLIST, etc.

Hard disk requirements
To install WordStar itself you will need a minimum of 1157 Kb, which includes the program, all the overlays, help files, etc.

The Dictionaries and Thesaurus need another 544 Kb. I would advise you to install these because WordStar has the best Dictionary and Thesaurus of any word processor I have ever seen. Together they include over 220,000 words and when you consider that the Oxford English Dictionary contains 250,000 you can see that WordStar is very comprehensive.

The Advanced Page Preview, which needs 415 Kb, allows you to see one or more pages on screen as they will appear when printed. Page Preview is absolutely essential, especially if you are using a PostScript printer. WordStar itself is character-based, not WYSIWYG ('What You See Is What You Get'), and that means that what you normally see on the screen is rarely, if ever, exactly what you will get on paper. Whenever you select a different font, for instance, the on-screen characters do not change; you can only see the difference with Page Preview or when you actually print the page.

■ SECTION 3
Installing the program

If you are going to use a PostScript printer you must also install the PostScript element of WordStar – the printer driver itself is not sufficient – but this only takes up 43 Kb of disk space.

Inset is the screen capture and editing program that allows you to 'photograph' the image on screen and then incorporate it into a WordStar document. The program also allows you to extensively edit and manipulate the image. Inset needs 667 Kb of disk space, which is rather a lot, but you can cut this right down later as you will see. If you are not going to be incorporating graphic images then you do not really need the program.

MailList is the program that allows you to produce a database of names and addresses, which can be used in conjunction with WordStar itself to produce personalised letters. It will also allow you to do a number of special things that cannot be done in the word processor itself, such as conditional printing. You will need 147 Kb of space for the program.

TelMerge allows you to use WordStar and a modem to provide interactive communications between computers, such as logging onto BT Gold or Prestel. Again, whether or not you install this program is dependent on whether or not you use electronic mail. If you do want to include it you will need 75 Kb of disk space.

PC-Outline, which is on Page 2 of the installation screens (just press the **Down** key from TelMerge), is an ideas organiser produced by Brown Bag Software. It is not a word processor or even a text editor but for formatting ideas it is superb. (For instance, I use it to plan the contents of my books.) The program is not really part of WordStar, although it can read and write WordStar-format files, and so it normally goes into a directory of its own. It needs 122 Kb of space.

■ SECTION 3
Installing the program

ProFinder, again, is not part of WordStar. It is actually a simple, easy-to-use file-management utility which is very useful for organising files on your disk. If you decide to install it you will need 256 Kb of space.

Star Exchange allows you to convert files from one format to another, for example from WordStar to Microsoft Word and vice versa. Unfortunately the program needs nearly 1 Mb of disk space. Thus the program is only worth installing if you have a number of files to convert. (If you have updated from WordStar 2000 then you should definitely install the program because the format used in WordStar 2000 is different to that used in WordStar 6.)

The Printer Database is huge – it will consume nearly 2.5 Megabytes of disk space – because it includes the device drivers for every printer that WordStar is capable of working with. You definitely do not need to install this if you have only one or two printers. The database makes installing additional printers very quick and easy, although personally I find that it is better to do this from WSCHANGE (see later). As you continue the installation WordStar will allow you to install a single printer.

Completing the installation
Having made your selections press **F10** to begin the installation. At various points the program will prompt you to swap the disks as the elements you selected are copied to the hard disk. The length of time this takes depends on your computer and the speed of the drives. On average it takes about 15 minutes to install everything except the Printer Database. (A tip: when the main installation has finished and it says 'Remove the disk and press F10 to continue', re-insert the Installation disk at the same time.)

Having installed the main program and the sub-elements, the installation then allows you to begin the customisation of the program. Note that this is only a very basic thing – the real customisation comes later.

1 Select the monitor type you will be using. The first three possibles will all produce 23 lines by 80 columns, i.e. large chunky characters. However if you have an EGA screen you can elect to have 43 lines displayed, while on VGA you can have 50 lines. The reduction in size of the characters simply means that you can see more of a whole page at a glance.

2 To install a printer you will need the correct disk. Press **F10** after installing the monitor and you will be presented with a screen telling you what printers are installed: i.e. none and hence it is blank.

3 Enter the name of your printer; remember you can only use eight characters. You will be taken to the next screen, which allows you to select the actual printer. WordStar provides drivers for just about every major printer type. However, it cannot provide drivers for every individual model, so you may well have to install the model that your printer emulates. For example, my StarScript PostScript printer has to be installed as an Apple LaserWriter. Be warned: the layout of the printer installation could be much better than it is. If you select the wrong type of printer and so access the wrong disk, you then have to press **Esc**. This does not take you back one step as you expect – instead it cancels the printer installation completely!

4 The final thing that the installation program allows you to do is to add the new directory you have just created to your AUTOEXEC.BAT file if you wish. You should do so or you may find that parts of the program won't work at all, let alone correctly.

5 Once the installation is completed, remove the disk from the drive and put it back in its envelope. Store the master disks somewhere safe, cool and dark. Now reboot your machine so that the new path is operable.

While the installation program that comes with WordStar 5.5 and 6 is better than nothing it is not the most user-friendly installation you will ever encounter. Most especially, the printer section is ridiculous. You may well find that you have to re-install the program a second, or even a third time before you get everything you want copied. Don't worry if the printer you want is not installed at this point, it is actually easier to install printers using WSCHANGE, as you will see later.

Amongst the collection of disks there is also one labelled *Tutor*. This is not copied as part of the normal installation. Instead you have to copy the disk contents to the WordStar directory by hand.

Removing unwanted files

Once the machine has rebooted log into the WordStar directory using **CD** (directory name) and then enter **DIR/W**. You should find that you have about 100 files in the main directory, assuming you have put the associated programs in their own sub-direc-tories, and you are using around 4 to 4.5 Mb of disk space. A number of these files are superfluous and can be deleted.

1 Enter **DIR *.DOC**. You will find there are five such files. They are intended to be examples for you to play with; DIARY.DOC, for example, is a wonderfully American tirade about visiting London. You should read each of them at least once but then you can delete them all to recover 16 Kb.

SECTION 3
Installing the program

2 Enter DIR *.PS, if you installed PostScript. There are eight files. Of these you must keep, at the very least, WSPROL.PS and WSPROL2.PS. The others can be safely deleted to recover 20 Kb.

3 You can also delete the following:

BOX is just a box made of Extended ASCII characters.

384K.PAT can be deleted, providing you have at least 1 Mb of memory. The file is a special patch that allows WordStar to run in limited memory. However, if you have less than 1 Mb of RAM you should not be using WordStar in the first place because it is very memory-hungry.

DRAFT.PDF is a printer driver for a generic printer. You can safely delete this because you will install the correct driver for your own printer.

KSPEED.PAT is another patch. This one changes the speed of the keyboard response.

PATCH.LST gives a listing of the hexadecimal codes used for various functions. As a user of WordStar you are probably more concerned with using the program than in how it works (I know I am) and so you can delete this file.

Deleting these five files will give you back 92 Kb of disk space. By deleting all the files mentioned above you get back a total of 128 Kb – not a lot but there is more to come.

4   Log into the directory that contains Inset – e.g. **CD INSET** – and enter **DIR/W**. You will find there are 114 files and most of them are unnecessary.

5   Enter **SETUP**. This will display a message telling you that Inset has not been set up yet.

6   Select the monitor type, e.g. EGA. Simply move the highlighter and then press **Enter**. This part of the program will provide a default – which is generally correct.

7   Next, select the printer type you will be using. There is a long list of possibles. Move the highlighter using the cursor keys and then press **Enter** to select the one you want.

8   Having made your main selection you will then be presented with a list of 19 possible options. The first and third you have just selected.

The **Graphics Mode**, item B, really only applies if you are going to be using software that does not write directly to the video RAM, e.g. Lotus 1-2-3. Nonetheless you will find that the default setting works adequately.

Item D, **Colour/BW**, applies to the printer, not the monitor.

The remaining settings are self-explanatory and the defaults are largely determined by the hardware you are using. To change any of them just press the item letter, make your selection and then press **Enter** to come back to the main menu. When you have finished, press **F10**.

9 Having returned to MS-DOS and the system prompt you should now enter DIR/W again. This will list all the printer drivers that Inset supports. As you have just selected one, and set Inset to work with it, you can now delete all the extraneous drivers until all that remains is the one you installed. All the printer drivers have an extension of .PRD. Deleting the extras will recover around 100 Kb of disk space.

10 Similarly, you can now delete all the unwanted monitor drivers. These are all programs in their own right and have the extension .EXE. Delete all the ones that are not what you installed. Again this will give you back some 43 Kb of disk space. (Don't delete the files called I20C, I20F or I20S as these are needed by Inset itself.)

All the files with the extension .PIX are the sample picture files. Those with the extension of .INF are information files for the program. Deleting the superfluous files should save you some 140 to 150 Kb of disk space. Add to that the savings from before and you will have reduced the total disk burden by around 275 Kb. This does not sound like much but that is the size of the files. The actual disk space could be as much as four times that, depending on the type of hard disk you are using. The actual amount you save depends on the number of sectors – portions of the disk – that are allocated to a cluster (the minimum file space).

That's the end of the installation and you are now ready to begin customising WordStar to your own personal preferences.

WordStar 5 can be configured in an almost unlimited range of methods, options and styles, or you can use it as it is. However, this is unlikely to be as you want; some of the shipped defaults are a little peculiar and the layout of the function key commands as they are preset means that it is too easy to accidentally lose your work instead of saving it. There are two ways in which you can configure the program: a simple generic way and a more complex but highly individual method.

```
                    Main Installation Menu

 A   Console.........................Choose your monitor.

 B   Printer.........................Choose your printer.

 C   Default printer.................Choose a default printer.

 D   Computer........................Choose operating system and disk
                                     drives on your computer.  Check the
                                     CONFIG.SYS and AUTOEXEC.BAT files.

 E   Dictionaries....................Specify location of the dictionaries.

 F   Help level......................Specify pull-down or classic menus.

 X   Finished with installation.


 Enter your menu selection...      ? = Help
                                   For detailed changes, run WSCHANGE.
```

WINSTALL Main Installation Menu (WordStar 5)

To do the former make sure that you are in the correct directory – that is, the one that contains all the WordStar files – and then enter **WINSTALL**. This is the simple configuration program and it allows you to set the broad parameters by which the program will operate. Using the program is very simple because it is largely menu-based. However, it uses a layered approach and it is quite easy to forget where you are within it. At any time, pressing **Esc** will cancel the current operation and take you up one layer, so that if you get stuck just keep pressing this key until you return to the main menu screen. By definition this program cannot provide a highly personalised version of WordStar for you as it sets only the broad parameters.

Once the first screen appears just follow the on-screen instructions. Type **WS** as this is the name of the WordStar program and then press **Enter** twice. (If you want to name the configured program something else you must enter the new name when prompted.) The Main Installation Menu will then appear, as shown in the figure above.

To select any of the menu options you need only press the letter that is shown beside each option. The program also provides on-line help that is context-sensitive – that is, it relates to what you are currently doing – at every stage. To activate this facility just press **?** and sub-menus bearing additional information will pop up.

Console

The first option available is **Console**. (The word is a hang-over from the early days of computing when computers only had a keyboard and printer for inputting and outputting information. These days, console refers to the monitor and the keyboard.) To activate the option press **A** and a second menu will appear bearing four further options.

A) Monitor Selection

This allows you to select one out of five possible options. If you are using any IBM-compatible monitor you will probably get the best results by setting the monitor selection to *A – Using RAM directly*. This works on most monitors and is faster than the ROM BIOS method.

If you have only a CGA monitor you may get better results by selecting B. The CGA monitor is prone to producing 'snow' – a scattering of interference lines – on the screen. WordStar have therefore created a special screen driver to remove this.

D – EGA 43 line display works very well. The text is sharp and easy to read and it produces less Moire patterns than the standard 25-line display. Once you have finished with WordStar your monitor will default back to the standard display.

Similarly the VGA 50-line display gives the best results on a VGA monitor.

Once you have set the monitor of your choice press **X** to return to the Main Installation Menu.

B) How underlined text will appear

This provides you with three possible choices and you may select whichever you are most comfortable with. However, setting how the text will appear is much better done using WSCHANGE, which is covered in Part Two.

C) Soft space and soft tab display

WordStar 5 can be used to produce a document that is fully justified; that is, both the left and the right-hand margins line up. It does this by placing *soft spaces* between the standard spaces so that the words spread out across the line. You can have these soft spaces appearing as ordinary spaces but it makes things easier if you set them to something else. This option allows you to do just that. By turning the soft spaces on you will get a small dot appearing wherever there is a soft space.

D) Video attributes

This only allows you to set one of three pre-defined options and unless you have an MDA or Hercules monitor fitted to your computer you will be better off setting them by using WSCHANGE.

Once you have finished with the Console options press **X** to return to the Main Installation Menu.

Installing a printer

The second option that WINSTALL provides allows you to install a printer, out of a selection of 88. When you select this option another program, called PRCHANGE, is activated and it is this which actually configures the printer drivers. To use the program properly you must know what printer you have or intend using. If your printer does not appear on the list of possibles you must know which of them it emulates. For instance the Citizen HQP-40 does not appear on the list but because it emulates the Epson

LQ-800 you would select this instead. To select the printer just follow the instructions on the screen. Once you have finished press **X** to return to the Main Installation Menu.

Having installed your printer(s) you must now select the one that will serve as the default; that is, the one that will normally be used for producing hard copies. This is what the third line of the Main Installation Menu does. It allows you to select one of the printers you have installed as your main printer. Whenever you create a document within WordStar 5 the program will automatically assign the default printer to that document; for example, the possible typefaces and fonts are dependent on the printer. If you don't set a default you will have to select a printer for every document *and* set it each time you want to produce a hard copy.

Checking the computer

Item D on the Main Installation Menu is probably the most important one of all. The first option is vitally important because it tells the WordStar program which disks you will be using, and hence where the files are stored. You *must* put your hard disk as the first drive – don't place them in alphabetical order – because the first drive will become the WordStar default! After inputting each drive letter you will be asked if it is a floppy drive or not.

Another thing that this option does is allow you to ensure that your computer is configured properly to run WordStar by checking, and if necessary altering, your CONFIG.SYS file. The reason for this is that you must have a line saying **FILES=20** (or more) for the program to work satisfactorily. WINSTALL can check CONFIG.SYS for you – which is much easier than having to rewrite the file. You can also use this option to add the WordStar 5 directory to your **PATH** command so that the program can be run from any directory on your disk. If you do not do this you will be unable to access some of the sub-programs, except when you are in the WS5 directory!

Providing that you have named the WordStar directory as WS5 you can ignore item E, otherwise you must tell the program where it can find its dictionary and thesaurus files. Again this is easier to do using WSCHANGE.

Setting the Help Level

The final option of the WINSTALL menu lets you select the Help Level (see Section 7).

■ SECTION 6
Installing WordStar 6 with WINSTALL

Under WordStar 6, WINSTALL now activates various sub-programs rather than doing everything itself, as was the case with WordStar 5. You simply move the highlighter to the area you want to change and press **Enter**; you will be taken to a new menu. If you encounter any problems just press **F1** to activate the on-line help facility.

When the program is activated it will bear a highlighter overlaying the **Install a monitor** option. This is identical to that which you used as part of the installation and so can be ignored.

```
                              WINSTALL

         Install a monitor
         Modify or install a printer (PRCHANGE)
         Set basic editing defaults
         Add or remove a feature
         Customize WordStar (WSCHANGE)
         Add fonts to custom database (LSRFONTS)
         Save and return to DOS




     (C) Copyright 1990 WordStar International Corporation. All rights reserved.

  Directions:
    F1 - Help
                              Start typing name = Find matching name
                                 ↑ ↓, Home, End = Move highlighting
    Esc - Quit without saving              ◄──┘ = Select
```

WINSTALL Main Installation menu (WordStar 6)

The second option, **Modify or install a printer**, allows you to do exactly what it says. When this option is selected WINSTALL retreats into the memory and another program called PRCHANGE is loaded and run. (You can run this program independently of either WINSTALL or WSCHANGE.) Modifying the printer set-up is not recommended and is unnecessary. However, you can use this

37

```
                        Set Basic Editing Defaults
          Help level
          Default paragraph style
          Initial logged directory
          Default printer
          Check CONFIG.SYS file
          Modify AUTOEXEC.BAT file
          Return to WINSTALL Menu




  Directions:
    F1 - Help
                                  Start typing name = Find matching name
                               ↑ ↓ ← →, Home, End = Move highlighting
    Esc - Previous screen                      ◄─┘ = Select
```

Set Basic Editing Defaults Menu

facility to install additional printer drivers – but you will need the master disks if you have not installed the Printer Database.

Set basic editing defaults brings up another menu. The first option is to 'Set the Help Level' (see Section 7).

Default paragraph style allows you to create a style that will be applied automatically to all new documents. In WordStar 5 you could select a default font but that was all; in WordStar 6 you can effectively define a complete default page, including the fonts, margins, tabs, line spacing and print attributes. WordStar comes complete with nine predefined styles. The normal default is Body Text, which therefore does not appear on the menu, but you can select any of the other eight. At this point you cannot define alternative styles – you can only do that from within a document in WordStar itself. A major problem with selecting a default style is that you don't know what they are. Granted you have the style names but there is no way to find out what these contain until you run the WordStar program itself.

Initial logged directory allows you to specify a directory or sub-directory that WordStar will automatically log onto whenever the program is run. Simply move the highlighter to here, press **Enter** and then enter the full path to the directory you want to use. The directory must be created before you run the program, if it does not already exist.

Default printer allows you to select one of the printers you have installed as the one for which all documents will be configured. As the printer driver contains details of the fonts available, this effectively means that choosing a particular printer will allow you to use only those fonts that are available for that printer.

Check CONFIG.SYS will examine your CONFIG.SYS file to find out how many FILES you have set. For WordStar to work correctly you must have a minimum of **FILES=24**. WINSTALL can check for this and modify your CONFIG.SYS automatically if necessary.

Modify AUTOEXEC.BAT simply adds the WordStar directory to your PATH statement, or creates a PATH statement if one does not already exist. The WordStar directory must be on the path in order for the program to be able to find the various overlays that it uses.

Add or remove a feature on the WINSTALL main menu activates that part of the installation program which installs chunks of the WordStar program. Quite simply, it means that you can use this to change the major parts of WordStar without having to re-run the WSSETUP program off the master disks.

Customise WordStar will activate WSCHANGE, the major Word-Star configuration program. We will cover that in detail in a while and so ignore it here.

Add fonts to custom database is to be used only if you have extra fonts to be added to the printer drivers. These apply only to Hewlett-Packard fonts and PostScript fonts (which you must have available on a separate disk and which must have the extension .AFM).

The final option allows you to save the changes you have made and return to MS-DOS and the system prompt. Once you have done so you should reboot the computer – especially if you have modified CONFIG.SYS and/or AUTOEXEC.BAT.

■ SECTION 7
Setting the help level

WordStar provides you with two basic methods of operation: pull-down menus or classic menus. The former is one of the new features of the program, while the latter is the one most familiar to long-time users. As the program is shipped, it is set for the new method but you can change this using WINSTALL. The type of menu you choose is a matter of personal choice; for myself I prefer the classic menu as it is actually easier and more informative than the pull-down menu.

There are five possible levels of help available when you are using WordStar; which you choose will depend on you.

Level 4 is the new pull-down menus. If you select this you will not be able to see the function key labels on the screen when using the program, although you can still use the classic keystrokes. With this option selected you get a list of the possible menus, with their initial letters highlighted, along the top of the screen. To activate any of the pull-down menus you press **Alt** together with the corresponding letter of the menu.

Level 3 is the first of the classic menus. It allows you to have the main Edit Menu on screen at all times, which occupies the top nine lines of the screen. This contains details of the other available sub-menus. To activate one of them you press **Ctrl** and the initial letter of the one you want. In addition you get the function key labels on the bottom two lines of the screen.

Level 2 is similar to Level 3 but turns off the main Edit Menu. This level leaves the function key labels, so that you can use nearly the entire screen for a document.

Level 1 just provides you with the function key labels; none of the menus will appear and you have to remember all the possible keystroke combinations.

■ SECTION 7
Setting the help level

Finally, Level 0 turns all the menus and the function key labels off so that you have the entire screen available for a document.

For a complete beginner Level 3 is probably the best as it provides the most information. Once you have finished with the installation, pressing **X** from the Main Menu will save your specification to the disk. It takes some time so don't be alarmed if nothing appears to be happening for a while.

You can create a number of different versions of the program by running WINSTALL and naming each version differently, but remember that each one will occupy over 150 Kb of disk space.

■SECTION 8
Inset

Inset is a memory-resident program that will allow you to create simple graphics any time you wish. It is available with WordStar 5.5 and 6 only. The quality of the graphics will depend very much on the screen driver that you install; EGA or VGA will give very high quality whereas CGA yields substantially poorer graphics. Once you have created the image you store it on disk as a file and you can then include it in any document you create within WordStar. One problem with the program, however, is that it is very memory-hungry and it will substantially reduce the amount of RAM you have available.

As we have already covered installing the program, we will just concentrate on using it here. You can use Inset in two ways: either as a standalone memory-resident program or as part of WordStar. In both cases the program will be loaded into memory, with the resulting hassles that brings. To unload it from RAM, regardless of which way you loaded it, you must log into the directory that contains the program and then enter **RI**.

From within WordStar you activate the program by pressing **Ctrl-P &**. This works providing certain conditions are met:

■   You have enough memory available to run Inset.

■   You have told WordStar where to find the necessary program files, using WSCHANGE.

■   The file called SETUP.COM has not been deleted.

■   Inset has already been loaded into RAM.

If you want to use just the screen-capture facility you should load Inset using **INSET/C**.

■ SECTION 8
Inset

Once the program has been activated, its menu bar will appear along the bottom of the screen. This bears the main commands as follows:

■ **View** simply allows you to look at any image that currently exists as a PIX file; a number of these are supplied as samples.

■ **Save** writes the captured or created file to the disk and applies the extension .PIX.

■ **Modify** allows you to alter an image and it contains a number of sub-options:

    –   **Clip** allows you to change the boundaries of an image. When you import a graphic the area within the boundaries is imported. By changing the boundaries you can increase, decrease or otherwise clip the image.

    –   **Rotate** allows you to turn the image, horizontally or vertically.

    –   **Expand** changes the size of the image.

    –   **Ink** changes the colour of the ink in the image.

    –   **Pass** determines the number of passes that will be used by the printer to produce a hard copy of the image. This only applies to dot matrix printers.

    –   **Border** turns the outline border of the image on or off.

– **Status** allows you to view the changes you have made and/or the degree of those changes.

– **NoMenu** turns off the menu bar until you press another key.

■ **Edit** allows you to edit an image. The screen will only appear if you are in text mode.

■ **Print** does just that, but it also includes sub-options which control various aspects of the printing.

■ **Output** also controls some aspects of the printing. Any changes you make here will also be carried forward to become the new defaults for the Inset program itself.

■ **Help** provides an overview of the help. The program provides brief, context-sensitive help through all the commands and sub-options – providing you have not deleted the help file.

PART TWO

Using WSCHANGE

■ SECTION 9
What is it?

WSCHANGE allows you to customise WordStar in very fine detail. It controls all the major, and many of the minor parameters by which the program appears and works. The program itself is only 818 bytes but the main overlay it uses is just over 48 Kb and it can also call in other programs and overlays as necessary. This part of the book describes the WordStar 6 version of WSCHANGE; earlier versions were very similar.

WSCHANGE is probably the most complex and involved customisation program that you will ever encounter but the degree of control that it allows is second to none. If you are new to WordStar it is very easy to get lost in the complexity of the program; even some seasoned users have difficulty with this. The important thing to remember is that you can always get back to the beginning by pressing **Esc** – this will terminate the current operation and/or return you to the previous level.

```
                         WSCHANGE Main Menu

A  Console......Monitor                Function keys        Video attributes
               Monitor patches        Keyboard patches

B  Printer......Choose a default printer
               Change printer name    Printer defaults     Printer interface

C  Computer.....Disk drives           Operating system     Memory usage
               WordStar files         Directory display    Patches

D  WordStar.....Page layout           Editing settings     Help level
               Spelling checks        Nondocument mode     Indexing
               Shorthand              Merge print          Miscellaneous

E  Patching.....General patches       Reset all settings   Auto-patcher

X  Finished with installation
 ──────────────────────────────────────────────────────────────────
   Enter your menu selection...       F1 - Help
                                      ^C - Quit and cancel changes
```

WSCHANGE Main Installation Menu

■ SECTION 9
What is it?

Once the program is loaded you will be presented with the Main Installation Menu (see the figure above), which is the heart of the program. WSCHANGE is arranged in 'logical' elements or steps. Selecting any option will move you down the structure to the next element, and so on until you reach the actual parameter that you want to change. Once you have made the alteration you move back up to the Main Menu by reversing your path. Because the program is so complex we will examine it in separate parts, as they appear on the Main Installation Menu.

A map of the WSCHANGE options is given in Appendix XII.

Console is an old word in computer terminology. Originally it referred to the keyboard and printer interface between the human world and the computer, in the days before monitors. These days console refers to the keyboard and the monitor. Selecting the first option on the Main Installation Menu will bring up the screen shown below; from here you can customise the interface between the program and yourself.

```
                      Console Menu
A  Monitor............Monitor selection     Monitor name
                      Screen sizing

B  Function keys......Define keys           Onscreen Labels

C  Video attributes   Screen display
                      (colors, bold...)

D  Monitor patches.....Special characters   Cursor control
                      Video attributes      Save colors and attributes
                      Cursor sizing

E  Keyboard patches....Function keys        Save function keys

X  Finished with this menu

┌──────────────────────────────┬──────────────────────────
  Enter your menu selection...  │   F1 = Help
```

WSCHANGE Console Menu

A) Monitor

a) Monitor selection
Allows you to select one of five possible monitors. Select the monitor type that could be connected to your computer. The one you choose will affect how the editing screen appears on the monitor.

A) IBM PC compatible (includes EGA & VGA)
If you have a standard IBM-compatible monitor then you should select this option. It will work with any monitor on a machine that is IBM-compatible, including Hercules. However, because this is a generic selection you may find that your monitor suffers from snow (interference lines) – if it does, then you will have to install the monitor as something else.

B) IBM PC CGA compatible
This is slower than the previous selection and is intended to be used only on CGA monitors, though it will work with EGA and VGA screens.

C) IBM PC ROM compatible
This is the slowest possible choice but it will remove virtually all the snow from the screen. You should select this option if your monitor is less than 100% IBM-compatible.

D) IBM PC EGA compatible with 43 lines
This works only with EGA and VGA monitors – don't try it on a CGA. The characters are clear and well-defined and because you have 43 lines you can have almost two-thirds of a page on screen at any one time. Once you have finished with WordStar the screen returns to the standard 23-line display.

E) IBM PC VGA compatible with 50 lines
On a VGA screen you can use this selection; it provides 50 lines on screen and the characters are roughly half the size of normal. However, they are very clear and it does mean that you have nearly a full page displayed on screen. Again, the monitor returns to 23 lines when you terminate WordStar.

F) Reset all IBM screen and function key defaults
This will cancel any changes in the monitor and function keys you have set and return WordStar to the shipped defaults.

b) Monitor name
Allows you to display the name, using up to 37 characters, of the monitor that you have selected. The name will then appear every time that the program is run at the start-up screen. However it disappears once the program proper loads.

c) Screen sizing

1) Height
Enter a value for the number of lines of text that will be displayed on the editing screen. The value will be automatically updated if you select either the EGA 43 or VGA 50-line display.

2) Width
Enter a value for the number of characters that will be displayed in ten pitch (10 characters to the inch) across the screen. Word-Star 5 does not have a provision for defining the screen display in terms of 12 pitch or more. The ruler line will always be shown for 10 pitch even though this will not necessarily match.

3) Horizontal scroll width
Defines the number of columns that the cursor will scroll if the text being entered goes off the right-hand edge of the editing screen.

■ SECTION 11
Programming the keys

B) Function keys

This option allows you to change the shipped default of the function key settings. These keys – only up to ten of them, not the twelve that are available on an AT-compatible keyboard – can be used by themselves, or in conjunction with **Ctrl**, **Alt**, or **Shift**. This allows a total of forty combinations, to produce certain effects on screen. There is no on-line help available with this section of the program – you have been warned!

As the program is shipped the **Alt-function key** settings produce some of the IBM Extended ASCII character set (see Appendix IX) so that you can draw boxes in a document. However, if your printer is not capable of printing these then there is not much point in having them – but they are quicker than having to use **Alt** and the character's denary value.

To change any of the key settings move the cursor to whichever you want to change and then press **Enter**. At the bottom of the screen the definition of what is already programmed into the key(s) will be displayed and you will be asked if you want to change it. Pressing **N** leaves things as they are, while **Y** allows you to input your own string. How you set the keys is your own problem but to give you some ideas here are the settings that I use:

F1	**Ctrl-Q L**	Spell check the document from the current cursor position to the end.
F2	**Ctrl-Q J**	Activate thesaurus to provide synonyms for the word beginning at the current cursor position.
F3	**Ctrl-P B**	Begin or end bold text printing effect.

53

F4	**Ctrl-P Y**	Begin or end italic text printing effect.
F5	**Ctrl-A T**	Delete to the left from current cursor position to next blank space.
F6	**Ctrl-T**	Delete to right from current cursor position to next blank space.
F7	**Ctrl-Q S**	Move to extreme left of the current line.
F8	**Ctrl-Q D**	Move to extreme right of the current line.
F9	**Ctrl-O D**	Hide control characters so that only their effects show on screen.
F10	**Ctrl-K S**	Save current document to disk and then resume editing.

All these settings will be shown on the bottom line of the key function labels across the base of the screen.

Shift-F1	**Ctrl-J**	Context sensitive help activation.
Shift-F2	**Ctrl-U**	Undo the last delete operation.
Shift-F3	**Ctrl-K B**	Mark the beginning of a block.
Shift-F4	**Ctrl-K K**	Mark the end of a block.
Shift-F5	**Ctrl-K Y**	Delete the marked block.
Shift-F6	**Ctrl-K V**	Move previously marked block to the current cursor position.

SECTION 11
Programming the keys

Shift-F7 Ctrl-K C   Copy the previous marked block to current cursor position.

Shift-F8 Ctrl-P K   Mark word or phrase as an index item for later use.

Shift-F9 Ctrl-O P   Activate Page Preview for current document.

Shift-F10 Ctrl-K D   Save current document and return to opening menu.

These settings are shown on the top line of the function key labels at the base of the screen. As you can see, the settings are roughly laid out in two sets. The **Shift-function key** combinations are mainly block commands, while the pure function keys are mainly orientated towards text manipulation.

Ctrl-F1   Ctrl-Q F   Search document and find a particular word.

Ctrl-F2   Ctrl-Q A   Search document, find a particular word and replace it with another.

Ctrl-F3   Ctrl-Q I   Move directly to the specified line number or page number. This is extremely useful if you are using long documents, such as the chapter of a book, because you can navigate through the pages very quickly.

Ctrl-F4   Ctrl-P N   Set normal typeface.

Ctrl-F5   Ctrl-P S   Set or terminate underline printing.

■SECTION 11
Programming the keys

The remaining **Ctrl-function key** combinations are not used because they would not necessarily save any time, the other functions I use each consists of two keystrokes anyway, so programming them into the function keys saves no time.

C) Video attributes

This allows you to 'design' the on-screen colours that will be used on the text editing screen and the program in general, for example to select the colours for the menus and help messages.

a) Select colours individually
Allows you to select the colours in which the text and the various print options – bold, italics, underline, etc. – will appear on screen. As you change each one an example of how it will appear is given at the right-hand side of the screen.

b) Colour display default
Set the program to display the print options using a pre-programmed selection of colours. This will cancel any other selection that has been made.

c) Monochrome display default
Used if you have an MDA or Hercules monitor attached.

d) Shipped default
The settings programmed by WordStar.

SECTION 13
Further monitor customisation

D) Monitor patches

This menu includes the following: Define Special Characters, Cursor Control, Video Attributes, Save selected Colours, Set Cursor Size for CGA monitors, Set Cursor Size for all other monitors. In order to change any of these you must use hexadecimal – see the manual for full details.

a) Special characters

1)	DEL display string
2)	Soft hyphen display
3)	Begin block marker
4)	End block marker
5)	Box drawing characters
6)	Tab (ASCII 09) mask

b) Cursor control

1)	Cursor movement delay
2)	Delay value for auto-realignment
3)	Cursor sizes

c) Video attributes

1)	Video Attributes subroutine
2)	Colours
3)	Reverse bright/dim

d) Save colours

Allows you to save the current screen colour settings in a disk file. This can later be used by the auto-patcher routine to automatically set the program the way that you want it to appear. This is the only option under this heading that does not require a hexadecimal input.

SECTION 13
Further monitor customisation

e) Cursor size for CGA monitors
1)   Thin cursor during insert mode
2)   Block cursor during insert mode
3)   Thin cursor during overtype mode
4)   Block cursor during overtype mode
5)   Thin cursor after WordStar
6)   Block cursor after WordStar

f) Cursor size for all other monitors
1)   Thin cursor during insert mode
2)   Block cursor during insert mode
3)   Thin cursor during overtype mode
4)   Block cursor during overtype mode
5)   Thin cursor after WordStar
6)   Block cursor after WordStar

■ SECTION 14
Keyboard responses

E) Keyboard

Sets various parameters for the function keys and saves them if required. Again the values must be input as hexadecimal numbers, except for option (c) below.

a) Function keys
1)   Size/delay for function key burst
2)   Function key lead-in character
3)   Edit Menu translation table
4)   Opening Menu translation table
5)   Prompt translation table
6)   Type-ahead flush control
7)   On-screen function labels

b) Keyboard repeat rates
1)   Short delay before inserting
2)   Long delay before inserting
3)   Fast rate for inserting text
4)   Slow rate for inserting text
5)   Short delay before deleting
6)   Long delay before deleting
7)   Fast rate for deleting text
8)   Slow rate for deleting text

c) Save function keys
Having gone to all the trouble of redefining the various keys, a job that can take quite a while, you now want to be able to save them in a separate file in case of accident. The file should be backed up onto another disk for safe keeping. This option allows you to save the function key settings onto your hard disk in the WordStar sub-directory. You will need to use the MS-DOS COPY command to make the backup when you have finished with the complete installation.

■ SECTION 15
Installing printers

When you install a printer the WSCHANGE program loads another program called PRCHANGE which does the actual installation. It is possible to run this second program independently – without using WSCHANGE – by moving into to the WordStar sub-directory and then entering **PRCHANGE**. Once the program is loaded, by either method, you will be presented with another menu, as shown in the figure below. This provides you with five basic options but, as with installing the console, each option leads to numerous others.

```
                          Printer Menu

  A  Choose a default printer

  B  Change printer name on sign-on screen

  C  Printing defaults

  D  Printer interface...Printer busy handshaking    Printer subroutines
                          Background printing

  X  Finished with this menu




  Enter your menu selection...        | F1 - Help
```

Printer Installation Menu

■ SECTION 16
Choosing a default printer

A) Choose default printer

Choose one of the installed printers to be the default. This is the printer information that will be selected automatically and thus it determines what fonts and typefaces you will be able to use. Once you have loaded a document you will be able to change the printer selection by using **Ctrl-P** = to load an alternative set of fonts.

B) Change printer name

The name of the default printer appears on the initial WordStar screen as the program is loaded. With this option you can choose the printer name that will appear. For instance you might have selected a printer emulation – Epson LQ-800 – but want the name of the actual printer – Citizen HQP-40 – to appear on the screen.

C) Printing defaults

Select what the default printing effects will be. There are three
basic selections: ON, OFF and DIS. The latter is the abbreviation
for 'Discretionary'; in other words you select the effect from within
a document instead of having it loaded as the default.

```
                   Printing Defaults Menu #1

A  Print nondocument as default................OFF        PNODOC
B  Bidirectional printing......................ON          .bp
C  Letter quality printing (NLQ)...............DIS         .lq
D  Microjustification..........................DIS         .uj
E  Underline blanks............................OFF         .ul
F  Proportional spacing........................DIS         .ps
G  Normal character font.......................No font name
H  Alternate character font....................No font name
I  Strikeout character........................."-"         STKCHR
J  Line height (1440ths/inch)..................240         INIEDT+40
K  Sub/superscript roll (1440ths/inch).........90          .sr

2  Printing Defaults Menu #2
X  Finished with this menu


    Enter your menu selection...        F1 - Help
```

Printing Defaults Menu #1

1a) Print non-document as default
If this is turned to ON the various print-effect commands embedded in a document will be printed out as they appear, not as
the effects.

1b) Bidirectional printing
Specifically applies to a daisywheel printer; all dot matrix printers
these days are capable of this action. It allows the print head to
work in both directions, providing that it is capable of doing so.

1c) Letter quality printing

This gives the best quality printing but is much slower and noisier than draft printing.

1d) Micro-justification

Allows the justification to be based on the actual size of the paper rather than the size of the characters. Again this will only work providing your printer is capable of doing so.

1e) Underline blanks

When something is printed out underlined you have the option of having the spaces between the words underlined or not by adjusting this selection.

1f) Proportional spacing

Again this is dependent on the printer.

1g) Normal character font

You can select any of the fonts that are available for the default printer as a default font. You simply select the font name and then, depending on the type of printer, select either a pitch or a point size for the font. This will then become the normal font for all documents. One word of caution: the font does not appear on screen, only on the Page Preview and on the printed copy. This means that you continue to use normal characters on the screen because WordStar is not WYSIWYG ('What You See Is What You Get').

1h) Alternate character font

Once you are within WordStar itself, pressing **Ctrl-P A** will allow you to change the font quickly and easily – but only to the one you select here. It is worth selecting an alternative for a number of reasons. For instance, I normally use Palatino 11-point on my PostScript but that means that the text runs off the edge of the screen because of the size. Therefore I selected Zapf Dingbats 11-point as the alternative. The Dingbats are graphics characters and they have a much higher pitch than Palatino. When I am writing on screen I use the alternative font, so that all the words are visible on the screen; before I save the document I remove the alternate font so that it prints correctly.

1i) Strikeout character
Selects the character that will be used for strikeout. Normally set to the hyphen '-'.

1j) Line height (1440ths/inch)
The depth of the lines as they appear on your printer is controlled by this option. The number is a multiple of $\frac{1}{1440}$ths of an inch. Thus to obtain the standard six lines to an inch the value entered here should be 240.

1k) Sub/superscript roll (1440ths/inch)
Allows you to define how far up and/or down the sub- and superscript characters will appear relative to the standard characters. Again the value is entered as a multiple of $\frac{1}{1440}$ths of an inch.

2a) Print page numbers
Depending on what you are using the word processor to do you will either want the page numbers to appear or not. For instance, if you are mainly writing single-page letters then you are unlikely to want them to have the number '1' at the bottom of each page. On the other hand, if you are writing a long letter or some other many-sheeted document then the page numbers may be necessary. Decide which you want and then set it here. You can always turn the page numbers off within a document by entering a dot command (.op) at the beginning.

■ SECTION 17
Default printing

```
                    Printing Defaults Menu #2
A   Print page numbers..........................ON          .op
B   Kerning.....................................ON          .kr
C   Load Inset at print-time....................ON          I INSET

1   Printing Defaults Menu #1
X   Finished with this menu




Enter your menu selection...        F1 - Help
```

Printing Defaults Menu #2

2b) Kerning

This is a very old term from the days of typesetting using lead
print. Normally any character occupies a distinct 'block' and these
are lined up side by side to produce the lines of text. However,
some characters can be packed tighter than this because of the
shape of the letters. For instance, the letter A has a downward
sloping line on the right-hand side, and the letters V and W have
an upward sloping line on the left-hand side. Therefore when you
put A and V side by side the lines complement each other; this
means that the two letters can be squeezed together so that they
take up less room. They also look better as a result. On most laser
printers – though not all – you can kern the letters in this way by
turning this option on. To the best of my knowledge no dot matrix
printer will allow kerning.

2c) Load Inset at print-time

Inset is the graphics capture and handling program now supplied with WordStar. If you have incorporated graphics into a document you will have to load the Inset program in order to be able to print them. You can run Inset either as memory-resident or as an independent program. If you do the latter you must load the program to print the graphic. The program will be loaded and then the printing occurs.

■ SECTION 18
Printer interface

D) Printer interface

a) Printer busy handshaking
Tells WordStar how it will interact with the printer and what delay it will use before it informs you that the printer might be jammed or off-line.

b) Printer subroutines
Allows you to change the input/output routines that the computer will use to send and/or receive characters from the printer. The values must be entered in hexadecimal.

c) Background printing
WordStar gives you the option of having a document printed concurrently; that is, you can be printing one document whilst working on another at the same time. The advantage to this is that you are not locked out of the computer while the printer is busy.

■ SECTION 19
Computer options

This set of options allows you to tailor your computer and Word-Star, so that the two will interact properly in the way that you want them to. It is probably the most important part of the entire installation routine and it is vital that you get it right.

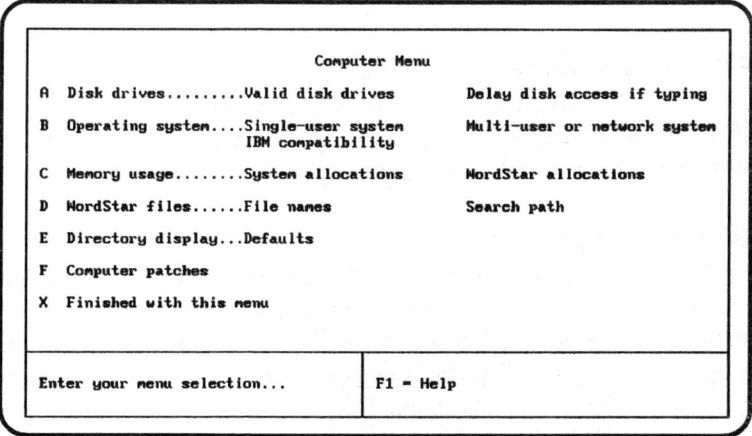

Computer Menu

A) Disk drives

This designates the disk drives on your computer that WordStar will use and as such they must be input in the correct order. The first drive that you input must be the hard disk that holds the WordStar files. You will be prompted to tell the computer whether each drive letter that you input is a floppy drive or not; get it wrong and you will have to start again by cancelling the current operation and then selecting this option again. You can enter as many disk drives as you have available, up to the limit of twenty-six that is imposed by MS-DOS.

■ SECTION 19
Computer options

B) Operating system

All this does is set the program to operate as a single-user system – that is, on a single computer – or on a network.

a) Single-user system
Sets the WordStar program so that it will be used on a stand-alone machine, i.e. a self-contained single computer.

b) Multi-user system
Allows you to set WordStar to work on a network.

c) IBM compatibility
Because there are so many IBM-compatible machines and IBM clones around it was necessary to include this extra option. It contains five possible sub-options that allow you to take advantage of just how compatible your computer is. You can change these if you wish, but I suggest that you leave them alone until you have tried WordStar first. Only if you experience any hardware problems should you try changing the settings here.

■ SECTION 20
Allocating memory

C) Memory usage

Defines how WordStar will use the available memory, how it will set the size for the dictionaries and thesaurus, macros, etc. This option includes nineteen different possible selections, on two menus.

1a) WordStar RAM resident
If the Random Access Memory of your computer is large enough then you have the option of making the entire program memory resident (though why you would want to do so is beyond me). The problem with doing this is that you will then not be able to get any on-line help because the overlays won't work. In addition the program will still need to access the disk for the spelling check and the shorthand macros.

1b) Main dictionary to RAM
You can speed up the spell-checking operation by loading the main dictionary - all 220,000 words of it - into the RAM. However, the buffer that you specify must be large enough to take it all.

1c) Speller, thesaurus, hyphenator memory usage
WordStar permits you to allocate memory to the dictionary and thesaurus in a number of different ways. You select the appropriate method under this heading. The best possible choice is to have them all in separate memory areas, if you have the room to do it.

1d) Main spelling dictionary buffer
The amount of memory that the computer allocates for the main dictionary. The standard setting is 46 Kb but it can be less than this if you wish. It does not need to be more, as the main spelling dictionary cannot be increased in size; it is a fixed length. Only the personal dictionary can be enlarged.

■ SECTION 20
Allocating memory

1e) Personal dictionary buffer

How big is your personal dictionary going to be? WordStar allows you to increase the number of acceptable words used for the spell-checking routine by creating a separate personal dictionary. This contains the words which you wish to have included but that do not appear in the main one: most notably locations and specialised terms, but also a large number of plurals.

Whenever you run a spelling check the document will first be checked, word by word, against the main dictionary. If it encounters a word that is not in this dictionary then the program will check the word against the contents of the personal dictionary. Only after having checked both 'books' will the program prompt you with an error if it cannot find the suspect word. In every case you will have the option of adding the unknown word to your personal dictionary.

As this file grows you will need to allocate additional space to it but a good initial value is about 5 Kb; this will store some 850 average length-words.

1f) Messages and menus buffer

The default for this is 4 Kb and it should provide sufficient space for most uses. As you have only a limited amount of memory in the first place you should be wary of allocating it in chunks that are larger than necessary. Again, the amount of memory needed for this facility is unlikely to increase so you might as well use the default settings.

1g) Text spillover

Whenever you create or modify a document it is actually read into and then held in the computer's memory while you work on it. However if the document is very large – for example, the chapters of this book – then only part of it is held in memory at any one time – the remainder is held in a temporary file on disk, the *spillover*.

Under this option you can specify how many records – chunks of 128 bytes – will be used for this spillover. However, the program has the facility to decide for itself. By setting the value to zero the program will handle any and all spillovers automatically.

1h) Shorthand buffer size

WordStar has a facility that allows you to create up to thirty-six shorthand macros, using the twenty-six letters and ten digits. These are strings of text and/or commands that are accessed and then placed in a document by pressing **Esc** and then the appropriate character. They can be extremely useful as they provide a shortcut to entering commonly-used text and commands and each one can be up to 64 characters long. For instance, in the course of writing this book I use the word 'WordStar' frequently and so I have programmed it into a macro. Thus, whenever I need the word I just have to press **Esc 1** and it appears at the current cursor position.

This option allows you to specify the amount of memory that will be used for storing the macros in terms of records, which are 128 bytes each. I have it set to 10, allowing me a total of 1280 possible characters. I rarely use 64 characters for any macro and thus this amount will allow me sufficient room to create all the macros that I need.

1i) Dot command buffer

The default value, 2000 bytes, to which this is set should be sufficient for the majority of needs as it will not need any more memory than this.

■ SECTION 20
Allocating memory

2a) Unerase buffer

Although you may delete text from within a document it is not actually obliterated immediately. Instead it is stored in a temporary buffer, so that if you have erased it accidentally it can be restored. Obviously you can only restore the last block of text that has been erased. The value specified is the maximum number of bytes – characters – that can be restored in one operation. Again, this is a chunk of the memory that is being used so it pays not to make it too large; on average, a value of 500 bytes should be sufficient. If you are erasing more than 500 characters at a time then there are more efficient and useful methods of doing so, as you will see later.

2b) Text editor memory

This refers to the amount of memory that is used for storing a document (actually, the one that you are working on). You can input any value from 4 Kb to 64 Kb, depending on the type of documents you will be creating. Once this value has been set any document that is larger than the value will produce spillovers. As these are stored in temporary files on disk, making the Text Editor Memory too small will force the program to access the disk continually, thus slowing down the operation of the program. As the program is actually geared to work with documents of up to 64 Kb, you might as well set the value to that and have done with it.

2c) Header and footer size

No, this does not refer to football – it applies to elements of a document. For most people they will never be used and so the default size can be left as it is.

2d) Merge print

Merge printing is used particularly when you want to produce form letters under MailList (described later). In fact, many people will probably not use the facility. It is geared much more to business users than to individuals. However if you do want to use the facility then you must allocate sufficient memory to allow the process to work. The default value of 4 Kb should be sufficient for most needs.

2e) Number of menu font definitions

The default value of 100 means that you may use up to this number of separate fonts within any document – providing your printer is capable of producing that many.

2f) Number of font family definitions

In this case a *font* is defined as a typeface and its printing effects. Thus 'Roman 10', 'Roman 10 Bold' and 'Roman 10 Italic' are all regarded as different and therefore separate fonts. The default value is 20. In practice most printers will not be able to produce this number but it is as well to have an excess rather than a deficiency.

2g) Proportional space data tables

In order to produce a document with proportional spacing the WordStar program must have information about how to do so. This option allows you to set the number of tables of information about this. The default setting is 2.

2h) PDF buffer size

This refers to the definitions that are created whenever you install a printer, and how large each definition file will be on the disk. The default setting of 16 refers to records – that is, 128 bytes – and you are unlikely to need to change it.

2i) Footnote buffer size

Whenever you create a footnote it is not actually placed in the document until you save it. Instead it is stored temporarily in memory and then added later. This option allows you to define how large the temporary buffer will be. The default setting is 8 records – 1 Kb – and if you need to increase it beyond this value then you are not using footnotes!

2j) Endnote buffer size
This is similar to footnotes, above, and refers to the amount of memory allocated to the buffer used to store endnotes. The default value of 2 – 256 bytes – should be sufficient for the majority of users.

■ SECTION 21
Finding the files

D) WordStar files

This series of options allows you to customise very precisely how the WordStar program will work by defining its search path and organising its overlays. You have a total of 24 choices spread over three menus. The first menu deals primarily with the names of the overlays that the program will use. The use of overlays reduces the amount of memory that is required to run the program, because they are only loaded when needed and then discarded once you are finished with them.

```
                        WordStar Files Menu #1
  A  Define default search path...................0BB9        DEFPTH
  B  Reassign drive and path for all WordStar files
  C  Messages and menus file......................C:WSMSGS.OVR(1)
  D  Indexer exclusion list file..................C:WSINDEX.XCL(1)
  E  Shorthand storage file.......................C:WSSHORT.OVR(1)
  F  Help overlay.................................C:WSHELP.OVR(1)
  G  Paragraph styles library file................C:WSSTYLE.OVR(1)
  H  TelMerge from Additional Menu................C:TELMERGE.EXE(5)
  I  MailList from Additional Menu................C:WSLIST.COM(6)

  2  WordStar files menu #2
  3  WordStar files menu #3
  4  WordStar files menu #4
  X  Finished with this menu


  Enter your menu selection...      F1 - Help
```

WordStar Files Menu #1

1a) Default search path
As it arrives, WordStar is set to default to a specific sub-directory. In other words, it will look for all of its related files within this directory. However, if you have stored the program in a different directory you will need to change the default search path so that

it can find the necessary files. You may specify up to three separate paths if you wish.

1b) Reassign drive and path

Allows you to change the drive and path in a similar way to (1a) above.

1c) Messages and menus file

Refers to the overlay file – the default is named WSMSGS.OVR – that will be used by the program to find the various on-screen messages and prompts that it needs. If you change the name of the overlay you will have to inform WordStar of the new filename by using this option.

1d) Indexer exclusion list

WordStar has a built-in facility that will allow you to index a document automatically – well, almost. The facility is not of much use to a home user, perhaps, but if you are using the program to write books it becomes almost essential. To include a word in the index you use the key sequence **Ctrl-P K** to mark the word or phrase in the document and then run the indexer from the main menu later, after you have saved the document.

To speed up this operation you can preset the indexer to automatically exclude certain words – which is what this option does. The excluded words are normally stored in a file called WSINDEX.XCL but if you have changed it – for instance, because you are writing two vastly differing types of documents and so need two exclusion files – you will need to inform WordStar of the new filename.

1e) Shorthand storage file

Allows you to change the name of the file that is used to store the macros. Again you are only likely to need to do this if you are writing widely differing types of documents and hence need more than one file. By default the file is called WSSHORT.OVR.

1f) Help overlay

Tells the program the name of the file that stores the help overlays. By default it is WSHELP.OVR.

1g) Paragraph style library file

This simply tells WordStar where to find the list of defined library styles. As it is shipped WordStar includes nine paragraph definitions but you can change these, as you will see later. The filename is shown at the right-hand side of the screen followed by a number in brackets; this latter is the path that will be used to find the file. Unless you have changed the location of the file you should leave it alone.

1h) TelMerge from Additional menu

Tells WordStar where the necessary file is stored in the same way as above. As you installed the program, so WordStar automatically assigned the correct path to the file.

1i) MailList from Additional menu

As above but applied to MailList, the name and address database.

WordStar Files Menu #2

This menu is again concerned with the names and locations of the various files for each function. As they appear on screen they are correct, including the locations that are a result of the installation.

```
                      WordStar Files Menu #2
A    Spelling checker overlay......................C:WSSPL000.OVR(2)
B    Main spelling dictionary file.................C:SPLMN000.DCT(2)
C    Personal spelling dictionary file.............C:PERSONAL.DCT(2)
D    Foreign language dictionary (if required).....C:SPLIN000.DCT(2)
E    Thesaurus overlay file........................C:WSTHS000.OVR(2)
F    Thesaurus dictionary..........................C:THESR000.DCT(2)
G    Thesaurus definitions overlay.................C:DEFIN000.DCT(2)
H    Advanced Page Preview work files..............C:????????.CRT(3)
I    Advanced Page Preview file....................C:PREVIEW.OVR(3)
J    Location of FONTID.CTL for Page Preview........C:FONTID.CTL(3)


1    WordStar files menu #1
3    WordStar files menu #3
4    WordStar files menu #4
X    Finished with this menu


Enter your menu selection...          F1 - Help
```

WordStar Files Menu #2

```
                      WordStar Files Menu #3
A    Hyphenation overlay...........................C:WSHYP000.OVR(1)
B    Main data file for hyphenation................C:HYPMN000.DCT(1)
C    Index file for hyphenation....................C:HYPIN000.DCT(1)
D    Printer description files.....................C:????????.PDF(1)
E    Printer overlay files.........................C:????????.OVR(1)
F    Print from keyboard template file.............C:KEYBOARD.MRG(1)
G    Inset program for print-time loading..........C:INSET.EXE(4)
H    Graphics files directory display..............12A1        GRPHMK
I    Graphics files file extension.................129C        GRPHFT

1    WordStar files menu #1
2    WordStar files menu #2
4    WordStar files menu #4
X    Finished with this menu


Enter your menu selection...          F1 - Help
```

WordStar Files Menu #3

■ SECTION 21
Finding the files

WordStar Files Menu #3

This menu is again concerned with the names and locations of the various files for each function. As they appear on screen they are correct, including the locations that are a result of the installation.

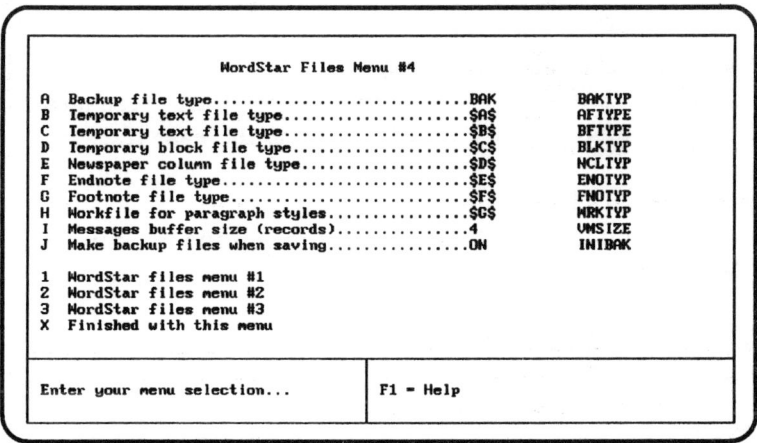

```
                    WordStar Files Menu #4
A    Backup file type.............................BAK        BAKTYP
B    Temporary text file type....................$A$        AFTYPE
C    Temporary text file type....................$B$        BFTYPE
D    Temporary block file type...................$C$        BLKTYP
E    Newspaper column file type..................$D$        NCLTYP
F    Endnote file type...........................$E$        ENOTYP
G    Footnote file type..........................$F$        FNOTYP
H    Workfile for paragraph styles...............$G$        WRKTYP
I    Messages buffer size (records)..............4          VMSIZE
J    Make backup files when saving...............ON         INIBAK

1    WordStar files menu #1
2    WordStar files menu #2
3    WordStar files menu #3
X    Finished with this menu


Enter your menu selection...        F1 - Help
```

WordStar Files Menu #4

WordStar Files Menu #4

This menu determines the non-specific files.

a) Backup file type
When saving files from WordStar you have the option of overwriting existing files, which means you have no backup, or renaming the old file and then saving the new one to the old name. Use this option to tell WordStar what extension should be used for the old

81

files. By default it is BAK but it can be anything else, other than the reserved words of course.

b) to h)

This concerns the internal temporary files that WordStar uses as a result of its operation. As the files are only temporary – i.e. they vanish once the main program is terminated – there is not need to make any changes here.

i) Message buffer size (records)

By default this is set to 4. It is used to hold the messages that WordStar displays. I have never needed to increase the size.

j) Make backup files when saving

This is the option that allows you to turn on the backup facility; by default it is on.

■ SECTION 22
The directory

E) Directory display

Allows you to set the default settings for the directory display that appears at the start of the program.

```
                    Directory Display Menu
A  Display file directory.......................ON        INIDIR
B  Directory in alphabetical order..............ON        DIRSRT
C  File types excluded from directory..........0D1C        NOTYPE
D  Filenames that are shown....................0E04        DIRFIL
E  Initial directory log-on....................0CE2        INILOG
F  Show space remaining on disk.................ON        DSPACE
G  Show size of each file.......................ON        SHOSIZ
H  Show files with changing drive/dir..........OFF        SDIRFL
I  Display file directory at filename prompts...ON        DIRSIZ

X  Finished with this menu



Enter your menu selection...        F1 - Help
```

WordStar Directory Usage Menu

a) Display file directory
Again this is a toggle switch. It allows you to be presented with a list of the files in a directory, except those contained in the exclusion list (item (c) below). If set to OFF then you will not be able to see which files are in the directory. In effect, it provides a small measure of security should anyone else be likely to use your computer.

b) Directory in alphabetical order
If set to ON then the files will be displayed in alphabetical order. Any files with numbers will be shown first, in numerical order,

then the alphabetical files and finally any that use other characters.

If you turn the option OFF then the files will be displayed as they appear on the disk.

c) Files excluded
Some of the files on your disk you will not want to see, because they are program files, for instance, or otherwise unchangeable. By using this option you can specify which file extensions will not be shown. By default you cannot see the various overlays and dictionary files.

d) File names that are shown
Allows you to specify which files, other than those included in the exclusion list, will be displayed. Normally set to '????????.???' so that you can see them all.

e) Initial directory log on
WordStar can be pre-programmed to log onto a specific directory on loading. If do not want your documents to be stored in the WordStar directory – the default setting – but would rather have them in a separate sub-directory you will need to inform the program of this fact by using this option.

It makes sense to have all your documents in one directory – for example, called DOCUMENT – and then have additional sub-directories within this that hold related files. For instance: PRIVATE, for your personal correspondence; CLIENTS, holding letters to your customers; RELEASES, to hold press releases and publicity material. Each of these directories would be contained within the main DOCUMENT directory. By having WordStar log onto this directory as a matter of course you will save a lot of time, as you will not have to navigate through your disk to find the files that you want.

f) Show space remaining on disk
At the Opening Menu of the program you will be shown a list of the files and/or directories in the default directory. For each file you will also be shown the size, in Kb. By setting this option to ON you can also see at a glance how much space you have remaining on the disk for additional files.

g) Show size of each file
If you do not want to know the size of the files then turn this option OFF; otherwise, the size of the files is given in kilobytes.

h) Show files when changing drive/dir
By default this is OFF. As you change drive or directory from the Opening Menu, so the display of filenames in the original directory vanishes.

i) Display file directory at filename prompts
This applies to the main file menus of the program. When you are opening a file menu – for example, when printing – you can have the full path to that directory and/or file displayed by turning this option ON, or do without it by turning it OFF.

■SECTION 23
Computer patches

F) Computer patches

Sets the various strings and subroutines that the program will use. The default settings should suffice. To make changes to any of the settings you must enter the values in hexadecimal.

■ SECTION 24
WordStar settings

Having customised the computer and peripheral devices it is now time to begin to customise the program itself – all of which is controlled from this menu.

```
                        WordStar Menu

A   Page layout........Page size and margins     Headers and footers
                       Tabs                      Footnotes and endnotes
                       Stored ruler lines        Paragraph styles

B   Editing settings....Edit screen, help level  Typing
                       Paragraph alignment       Blocks
                       Erase and unerase         Lines and characters
                       Find and replace          WordStar compatibility
                       Paragraph numbering       Line numbering

C   Other features......Spelling check           Nondocument mode
                       Indexing                  Shorthand (key macros)
                       Merge printing            Miscellaneous
                       Char conversion patches

X   Finished with this menu

Enter your menu selection...        F1 - Help
```

WordStar Menu

A) PAGE LAYOUT

This menu controls the effective format of the page as it will appear both on screen and on the printer.

A) Page size and margins

On older versions of WordStar these settings were done by inputting lines and columns, but WordStar will allow you to input the values in terms of inches. Depending on how you feel about measurements this is either a hindrance or a great advance. (Actually, the best method would be if you could use both but, unfortunately, you don't have that option.) The trouble is that if you get the sizes wrong then the result will not be as you expect. For instance, the page number may appear at the head of the following page instead of at the base of the one to which it refers.

Unfortunately the only way that you can check that you have got it right is to change some of the settings and do a test print, then go back and change the settings again until you get it right. The values given below are the ones that I use which produce pages of proper length on my Citizen HQP-40 printer using A4 fanfold.

a) Page length
The page length will affect the number of lines you have on a page, at the rate of six to the inch. Fanfold A4 paper is 11¾" but if you input this size here you will find that the text overflows to the next page because it doesn't allow any room for headers and footers. By trial end error I have found that a size of 11" works best; that is, allowing 66 lines per page.

b) Top margin
You are unlikely to ever want to print out on the very first line of a piece of paper, and so you must set a top margin. This is the number of lines that the printer will skip whenever it prints at the head of the page. There is no standard but a useful amount is half an inch (or three lines).

c) Bottom margin
As with the top of the paper, so with the base. You are unlikely to want to print to the very extreme and so need to set the bottom margin. I use a setting of 1.33" because it works. Setting it to less than this causes the page number to drop to the next page.

d) Header margin
The header margin is the number of lines that will be used for header notes (surprise, surprise!) and the value that you input

must not exceed that used for the top margin. A value of 0.33", or two lines, works well.

e) Footer margin

As above, but at the base of the sheet of paper. Again the value must not be greater than the bottom margin. Set it to the same as the header margin unless you intend writing documents with a lot of footnotes.

f) Page offset on even page

You can make WordStar print out at any point on the paper. For instance, most A4 fanfold will actually accommodate more than 80 characters and if you were to print from the extreme left-hand edge you would end up with a margin on the right. Besides this, you are unlikely to ever use all 80 characters for a document; 65 looks much better. Thus you would set this value to define the offset margin on the left-hand side of the paper. If you are using 65 characters you would enter 0.8" here so that the text will be centred on the paper.

g) Page offset on odd page

WordStar will allow you to offset either the even numbered pages or the odd numbered pages. To set the former enter a value in (f) above, to the set the latter enter a value here. To centre the text properly on all pages the value will need to be entered on both options.

h) Left margin

Having set how the text will appear on the sheet you now need to decide how many characters across you will customarily use on a document. (In a sense this option should appear before the previous two – it would be more logical.)

```
                    Page Sizing and Margins Menu

A   Page length........................11.00"      INIEDT+18  .pl
B   Top margin.........................00.50"      INIEDT+14  .mt
C   Bottom margin......................01.33"      INIEDT+16  .mb
D   Header margin......................00.33"      INIEDT+1F  .hm
E   Footer margin......................00.33"      INIEDT+21  .fm
F   Page offset on even page...........00.80"      INIEDT+24  .poe
G   Page offset on odd page............00.80"      INIEDT+26  .poo
H   Left margin........................00.00"      RLRINI     .lm
I   Right margin.......................06.50"      RLRINI+2   .rm
J   Paragraph margin (-1 for none).....(none)      RLRINI+4   .pm

X   Finished with this menu




Enter your menu selection...        ? = Help
```

Page Sizing and Margins Menu

The margin referred to here does not apply to the printing, as you might expect, but rather to the number of characters that the editing screen will be offset. Thus to use the entire screen enter a value of zero; you can always change it within a document by using the dot commands, which we will cover later.

i) Right margin
This refers to the right-hand edge of the editing screen. As WordStar is designed to work with characters of 10 pitch this means that you get 10 characters to an inch. Thus you can define how many characters you want to have by entering a value based on this figure. I use a value of 6.5", which would normally give 65 characters across the page. However, I use 12 pitch as the default, because I think it looks better, so I actually get 78 characters to a line. (Unfortunately the ruler line still only shows 65 characters!)

j) Paragraph margin

You can make the program automatically offset all paragraphs if you wish by entering a value here. If you would prefer not to then you must enter -1 which will turn the facility off.

B) Headers and footers

a) Print page numbers

Do you want the page numbers to appear or not? If the former, toggle this setting to ON, for the latter turn it OFF.

b) Position of page numbers

If you do decide to print the page numbers you can have them appear in any column that you wish by entering a value here. To have them appear in the centre enter -1.

c) Initial page numbers

Again, you can change this so that the first page you print out will be numbered whatever you wish.

C) Tabs

a) Regular tabs

You can define the tab stops – very useful for skipping across a document – by entering values in inches here. The tabs will be shown on the ruler line as exclamation marks.

b) Decimal tabs

As above, you enter the values in inches. If you use decimal tabs they will appear on the ruler line as hash marks.

■ SECTION 24
WordStar settings

D) Footnotes and endnotes

Selecting this option will bring up two additional menus, the first covering footnotes and the second dealing with endnotes. Within both you can select which font will be used for producing the notes; what will be the reference mark within the main body text; how they will appear; and how large the buffer will be.

E) Stored ruler lines

This option allows you to create up to ten ruler lines and select which one will be used as the default.

F) Paragraph styles

a) Library of paragraph styles
This is identical to the setting you made under the Computer Files Menu, *D) WordStar Files Menu #1, Item G.*

b) Default paragraph style
By default WordStar is set to work with a style called Body Text, the exact specifications of which depend on your printer and the page layout you have set. There are also an additional eight paragraph styles that you can select from. However – and this is a major fault – you cannot tell what the styles contain until you run WordStar itself. Thus you are better off not changing this until after you have run the main program and examined the styles and/or created you own personal preference.

c) Temporary file extension
This is simply the name of one of the temporary files WordStar will use in conjunction with the paragraph styles.

■ SECTION 24
WordStar settings

d) Storage buffer size
This allows you to specify the amount of space allocated for holding the paragraph styles you create. The default setting allows you to create more than 50 styles.

G) Units of measurement

WordStar can now work with different units of measurement, although the way that it uses them is sometimes a bit strange. You can select Inches, Centimetres or Points for the various options and mix them up any way you like. (A point is $\frac{1}{72}$ of an inch.) I have found that the best settings, for my own use, are:

Horizontal units – Centimetres
Vertical units – Centimetres
Line height units – Points
Font size units – Points

■ SECTION 25
More defining

B) EDITING SETTINGS

This option allows you to adjust a vast number of settings that control the editing screen. It includes seventeen sub-menus plus additional sub-sub-menus. However, we are only going to cover the main headings or this book would be huge!

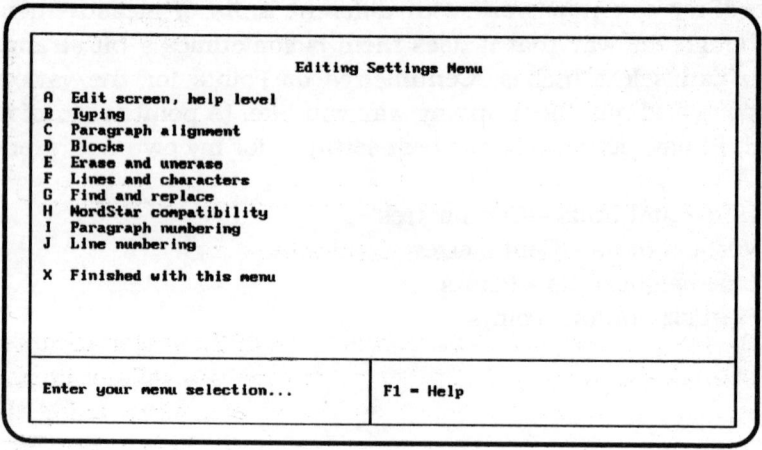

```
                            Editing Settings Menu
    A   Edit screen, help level
    B   Typing
    C   Paragraph alignment
    D   Blocks
    E   Erase and unerase
    F   Lines and characters
    G   Find and replace
    H   WordStar compatibility
    I   Paragraph numbering
    J   Line numbering

    X   Finished with this menu



    Enter your menu selection...        F1 - Help
```

Editing Settings Menu

A) Edit screen, help level

Sets the help level, status line, soft space display, etc. Consists of three sub-menus plus additional ones.

1a) Help level
The help level can be any one of five possibles. Which you choose is likely to be influenced by whether you are a new user of WordStar or if you have used the program in any of its previous incarnations.

■ SECTION 25
More defining

```
                    Edit Screen, Help Level Menu #1
  A  Help level...................................2        INIHLP  ^jj
  B  Display function keys at help level 4........OFF      LABHP4
  C  Status line..................................ON       INISTA
  D  Status line filler character................." "      STFILL
  E  Soft space display..........................OFF       INIEDT+0D
  F  Soft space character......................... · FA    SOFTSP
  G  Page break character.........................─ C4     SOFTSP+1
  H  Binding space character......................■ FE     SOFTSP+2
  I  Snaking column character.....................■ F8     SOFTSP+3
  J  Column break character.......................═ CD     SOFTSP+4
  K  Dot leader character.........................","      SOFTSP+5
  L  Print control display........................ON       INIEDT+3 ^od

  2  Edit Screen Menu #2
  3  Edit Screen Menu #3
  X  Finished with this menu
 ┌──────────────────────────────────┬──────────────────────────┐
 │ Enter your menu selection...     │ F1 = Help                │
 └──────────────────────────────────┴──────────────────────────┘
```

Edit Screen, Help Level Menu #1

Level 4 is the new *pull-down menus* – one of the major advances of this release. If you select this setting then you will not be able to see the function key labels on the screen when using the program, although you can still use the classic keystrokes. With this option selected you get a list of the possible menus, with their initial letters highlighted, along the top of the screen. To activate any of the pull-down menus you press **Alt** and the corresponding letter of the menu together: for example, **Alt-P** to get the Print Controls Menu.

Level 3 is the first of the *classic menus*. It allows you to have the main Edit Menu on screen at all times, which occupies the top nine lines of the screen. This contains details of the other available sub-menus. To activate one of them you press **Ctrl** and the initial letter of the one you want: for example, **Ctrl-P** for the Print Controls Menu. In addition you get the function key labels on the bottom two lines of the screen.

■ SECTION 25
More defining

Level 2 is similar to Level 3 but turns off the main Edit Menu and leaves the function key labels, so that you can use nearly the entire screen for a document. This is probably the best setting possible because it is the middle course and hence the simplest.

Level 1 provides you with just the function key labels. None of the menus will appear and you have to remember all the possible keystroke combinations to activate any of them. Alternatively you could access the on-line help continually until you get used to the program.

Finally, Level 0 turns all the menus and the function key labels off so that you have the entire screen available for a document. This is not recommended for someone who is new to the program.

1b) Display function keys at help level 4
Normally the function key settings only appear at help level 1 to 3 but by turning this setting on you can also have them appear at level 4.

1c) Status line
This is a line that appears at the top of the editing screen and it contains a list of information. In order, it tells you the name of the current document; the page number, line number and column of the cursor; the current mode (for example, Insert); whether paragraph alignment is on or off; and finally whether the justification is on or off.

However, you do not have to have the status line displayed. This option allows you to toggle the setting.

1d) – 1k)
These options define various characters used for special effects. Use the default settings.

■ SECTION 25
More defining

1l) Print control display

Because WordStar is not true WYSIWYG the text will always appear as standard, except on the Page Preview. The only way that you can tell if you have changed font is because the names will appear in brackets whenever they are activated. These print controls do not occupy any space in the printed text but they appear to do so on the screen, so they can push the text to one side. By toggling this option you can turn the appearance of these characters off or on.

```
                      Edit Screen, Help Level Menu #2
 A   Ruler line..................................ON          INIEDT+5   ^ot
 B   Default onscreen function key labels........ON          FUNLAB
 C   HMI (1800ths) units for ruler line.........180          RLUNIT
 D   VMI (1440ths) units for line height........240          INIEDT+40
 E   Hard return ending character................"<"         SCMARK
 F   Soft return ending character................" "         SCMARK+1
 G   Long line character........................."+"         SCMARK+2
 H   End of file character......................."^"         SCMARK+3
 I   Overprint line character...................."-"         SCMARK+4

 1   Edit Screen Menu #1
 3   Edit Screen Menu #3
 X   Finished with this menu


 Enter your menu selection...      │  F1 - Help
```

Edit Screen, Help Level Menu #2

2a) Ruler line

This simply turns the ruler display on or off. If you are using a dot matrix printer with 10 pitch then having the ruler displayed is useful. However if you are using anything else then the ruler is effectively useless.

■ SECTION 25
More defining

2b) Default onscreen function key labels
This turns on or off the labels which occupy the bottom two lines of the screen (regardless of the number of lines you are using). The labels will be whatever you set them to be when you defined the function keys.

The remaining options, and those on Menu #3, are simply various characters used for specific tasks. The defaults should not need to be changed.

B) Typing

Controls the various parameters that will have an effect on how fast the editing screen will function.

```
                              Typing Menu
  A   Word wrap at right margin....................ON      INIEDT+1 ^ou
  B   Insert characters...........................ON      INIEDT+2 ^v
  C   Fast typing display pause....................0       DFAST
  D   Fast typing page/line/column delay..........10       UPDLY
  E   Disk access pause............................0       DDISK
  F   Automatic backspace characters.............0C4A      AUTOBS
  G   Scroll speed.................................0       INIEDT+9

  X   Finished with this menu




  Enter your menu selection...        ? - Help
```

Typing Menu

a) Word wrap
WordStar, as with many other word processors, is intended to make the production of text documents simple and easy. One way in which this is done is by having the cursor wrap around automatically at the right-hand end of the line – instead of waiting for you to do it manually.

b) Insert characters
This sets the default choice for whether the insertion of characters is set to ON or not. With it turned OFF you will have to toggle into Insert mode whenever you need it and then out again. (It is curious that people who use word processors frequently usually have this

■ SECTION 26
Setting the speed

default setting ON, whereas those who use them only infrequently use Overwrite mode.)

c) Fast typing display pause
It takes time to insert text into a document, whether it is being created or edited, and this setting allows you to define how fast that insertion will be. The lower the value the shorter the pause will be.

e) Disk access pause
By setting this to zero you will reduce the disk access pause to a minimum and thus speed up the action of the program.

g) Scroll speed
Again, with this set to zero the speed with which the program works and displays pages will be increased.

```
                    Paragraph Alignment Menu
A   Right-justification..........................ON      INIEDT ^oj
B   Line spacing.................................1       INIEDT+8 ^os
C   Auto-hyphenation.............................ON      INIEDT+4 ^oh
D   Characters before auto-hyphenation...........5       HYMAX
E   Auto-align...................................ON      INIEDT+0E
F   Delay value for auto-alignment...............500     DALIGN
G   Watch progress of ^QU alignment..............OFF     RFINTR

X   Finished with this menu




┌──────────────────────────────────┬──────────────────────┐
│  Enter your menu selection...     │   F1 - Help          │
└──────────────────────────────────┴──────────────────────┘
```

Paragraph Alignment Menu

C) Paragraph alignment

a) Right justification

If you look at any book – this one for instance – you will see that the text down the right-hand margin is all aligned. In other words, it is fully right justified. It is standard practise to do this with books but it is fairly rare with other documents. However, you may want to produce your text in this fashion. To do so turn this setting ON. If you leave it OFF then the text will appear as normal. The program forces the text to be justified by inserting 'soft spaces' between the words so as to spread them out across a line.

b) Line spacing

You will want most text to be single line spaced, the way that it normally appears in a newspaper or book, but you can have any spacing that you wish. Just enter the value here and this will become the default. You can always change it within a document by using a dot command.

c) Auto-hyphenation
WordStar provides you with an option to wrap entire words or to split them, by a user-defined amount, and conjoin the split with a hyphen. Use this option to select whichever you want.

d) Characters before auto-hyphenation
If you set the previous setting to ON you must now decide how many characters you will use to break a word. The value you input here will be the default for the break. Hence if you set it to 5 and you then had a word like 'automatic' appearing at the end of the line, the word would be split into 'auto-matic': the first part on one line and the second on the next one.

e) Auto-align
The default setting is ON so that the text will automatically align itself to the other settings.

f) Delay before auto-alignment
Input a value for the pause between the insertion of characters and the realignment of the existing ones.

g) Watch progress of ^QU alignment
Whenever you change font or move the margins, the document must be realigned to allow for this. The quickest way is to press Ctrl-Q U, i.e. realign the whole document. This process takes time, especially if you have the screen updated as the alignment takes place. By turning this setting off, the default, the alignment is speeded up and you will only see the finished result.

■ SECTION 28
Blocks and erasing

D) Blocks

This controls the default settings for how blocks of text will be dealt with. The first option allows you to turn the column mode, which produces newspaper-style columns, on or off. We will cover the use of columns later in the book.

Items (c) and (d) define the markers that are used to mark the beginnings and ends of the blocks.

E) Erase and unerase

a) Maximum characters unerasable
You can define how large the unerase buffer is by entering a value here. If you make it too big you may find that you do not have enough memory for other aspects of the program. When you erase blocks of text within a document they are stored in this buffer so that they can be restored if necessary. If the block is too big to fit into the buffer you will be prompted with a message telling you so.

b) Unerase single characters
Normally the unerase buffer will only store blocks of text that have been marked and then deleted. However, single characters that have been removed using Del can also be stored in the buffer by turning this setting to ON. Remember that each erasure will automatically overwrite the contents of the buffer and so you can only restore the text that was last deleted.

The other settings, (c) and (d), control the action of the Del key and the cursor.

More defaults

F) Lines and characters

The three sub-menus of this option control the major characters that will be used by the program. The first two, in particular, allow you to define those characters, such as punctuation marks, that will be included as parts of words for the purposes of spell-checking and word jumping. Most of the settings should be left as the defaults with which they are shipped.

```
Characters that are currently considered part of a word are marked with a "*".

 00  ^@    10  ^P    20       *30 0     40 @    *50 P     60 `    *70 p
 01  ^A    11  ^Q    21 !     *31 1    *41 A    *51 Q    *61 a    *71 q
 02  ^B    12  ^R    22 "     *32 2    *42 B    *52 R    *62 b    *72 r
 03  ^C    13  ^S    23 #     *33 3    *43 C    *53 S    *63 c    *73 s
 04  ^D    14  ^T    24 $     *34 4    *44 D    *54 T    *64 d    *74 t
 05  ^E    15  ^U    25 %     *35 5    *45 E    *55 U    *65 e    *75 u
 06  ^F    16  ^V    26 &     *36 6    *46 F    *56 V    *66 f    *76 v
 07  ^G    17  ^W   *27 '     *37 7    *47 G    *57 W    *67 g    *77 w
 08  ^H    18  ^X    28 (     *38 8    *48 H    *58 X    *68 h    *78 x
 09  ^I    19  ^Y    29 )     *39 9    *49 I    *59 Y    *69 i    *79 y
 0A  ^J    1A  ^Z    2A *      3A :    *4A J    *5A Z    *6A j    *7A z
 0B  ^K    1B  ^[    2B +      3B ;    *4B K     5B [    *6B k     7B {
 0C  ^L    1C  ^\    2C ,      3C <    *4C L     5C \    *6C l     7C |
 0D  ^M    1D  ^]   *2D -      3D =    *4D M     5D ]    *6D m     7D }
 0E  ^N    1E  ^^    2E .      3E >    *4E N     5E ^    *6E n     7E ~
 0F  ^O    1F  ^_    2F /      3F ?    *4F O     5F _    *6F o     7F ▲

Enter a 2-digit character code (or M for more, Press ◄┘ when done)...
```

Characters that are part of words

G) Find and replace

Sets the default find and replace options.

H) WordStar compatibility

Versions 5, 5.5 and 6 are the latest releases in a long line of word-processing programs from WordStar International (formerly

```
                    WordStar Compatibility Menu
A  ^H moves left (not erase left)..............OFF    CTLHFL
B  ^^ (same as ^6) case toggle.................OFF    CASEFL
C  DEL erases left (not at cursor)..............OFF    DELFLG
D  Cursor stays in column 1 at marker...........ON    BLKFLG
E  No extra soft lines at paragraph end........OFF    LSPFLG
F  Esc acts like ^R and ◄┘.....................OFF    ESCFLG
G  Automatically fill out last record...........ON    SETEOF
H  ^QX goes to right side of screen.............ON    QUXFLG
I  Classic commands at Opening pull-down menu...OFF    PULFLG
J  Dot commands automatically put into file.....ON    USEDOT

X  Finished with this menu



Enter your menu selection...        ? - Help
```

WordStar Compatibility Menu

MicroPro) and as such they use certain commands and control sequences that are different to earlier versions. Using this menu you can reset your version to be more like these previous versions – for example, Release 4 – if you wish. However, if you are a new user of the program then it is suggested that you leave them as they are shipped.

I) Paragraph numbering

This allows you to define the way in which WordStar will number paragraphs, if you enable the option. Normally you would not want the paragraphs numbered, unless you are writing a tabulated and formal report, and so you would not need to change the defaults.

SECTION 29
More defaults

J) Line numbering

Allows you to select the font that will be used for line numbering and set the various parameters which this facility will use. In the production of normal text documents you are unlikely to ever use this facility.

■ SECTION 30
Odds and sods

C) OTHER FEATURES

This section is really a catchall for those things that do not fit elsewhere and also to tidy up the loose ends.

```
                        Other Features Menu

        A   Spelling check
        B   Nondocument mode
        C   Indexing
        D   Shorthand (macros)
        E   Merge printing
        F   Character conversion patches
        G   Miscellaneous

        X   Finished with this menu




        Enter your menu selection...     ? = Help
```

Other Features Menu

A) Spelling check

Allows you to name the spelling check overlay, the main dictionary, the thesaurus overlay and the personal dictionary file. The major element that it allows you to alter is the way in which the dictionaries and thesaurus are handled. If you have sufficient memory it is well worth placing them all into separate chunks of memory.

This option also allows you to set the size of the memory buffer that will be used to hold the main dictionary, in kilobytes. If you make this too large then you will be unable to run the spelling check because there will be insufficient room for the overlay.

B) Non-document mode

This module allows you to set the non-document defaults. For instance you can have all documents treated as pure ASCII files and thus not be able to produce any print effects and special characters. However if you want to produce standard kinds of documents, complete with printing effects, then you should set the defaults to OFF.

C) Indexing

This allows you to modify the index exclusion list and set how the indexing feature will work.

D) Shorthand

Defines the file that will be used to store the macros by name and size. Also sets the formats for the date, time and numbers.

E) Merge printing

Modifies the settings that will be used for merge printing (for example, in conjunction with MailList).

F) Character conversion patches

Sets the defaults for the patches. The values must be entered as hexadecimal.

■ SECTION 30
Odds and sods

G) Miscellaneous

a) Sign-on message
When WordStar is booted up it displays the various copyright notices and then tells you what monitor and printer it has been installed for. You can also make it display a short message if you want. Enter the text of the message here and it will appear every time the program is loaded.

b) Longest delay
The value entered here determines how long the sign-on message will be visible. If you do not want it to be shown enter zero and it will disappear so fast that you won't be able to see it!

c) Medium delay
This determines how long the pause will be between you asking for a menu and it actually appearing.

d) Shortest delay
The final delay deals with how fast a document will be realigned after text has been inserted.

h) Size of other window
WordStar will allow you to have two windows open at the same time, each containing whatever document you wish. You can then move text back and forth between the two easily and quickly. This option allows you to enter a default size for the second window.

i) Auto-backup
Theoretically this option allows you to automatically save your documents if the computer has been idle for a period of time. The value you enter is the time in seconds. Once the computer has not detected an input from the keyboard in that time then the

document currently on screen will be backed up automatically. However, I have never been able to get it to work!

j) Go to top of page

Once you are in WordStar you can move to any page of a long document by pressing **Ctrl-Q I**. Normally the cursor will then appear at line 1, column 1 of the target page; this is the default setting. However, if you turn the setting off then the cursor appears at the first printable character on the target page.

k) Language default

WordStar needs to know what language you are speaking, and hence what you will be writing. As you install the program it will read the information from the CONFIG.SYS file and set its language support to whatever COUNTRY you have specified there. However, you can change this to another language with this option.

l) Current code page support

Code pages are a feature of MS-DOS 4.0 and are much too complex to go into here. Suffice to say that if you have changed the code page you are using you will also need to inform WordStar of the pages you will be running under.

■ SECTION 31
Patching it up

The final option on the Main Installation Menu is entitled 'Patching'. It allows you to create a patch file that will be used by the program on booting up so that the settings you have defined will become the operable defaults.

A) Auto-patcher

The auto-patcher is that part of the program that will read in the settings you have made, providing that you have saved them into a non-document (pure ASCII) file. You can use this facility to read in the changes that you have made to the program so that they are operable immediately.

B) Save settings

This is the option that allows you to save your changes. Simply enter a filename and the program will do the rest for you.

C) Reset all settings

If you find that all the changes which you have made don't work the way that you wanted, but you do not want to go back and change them all one at a time, you can use this facility to return everything to the original shipped defaults. Be warned – this will wipe out every single change that you have made. The option provides you with a prompt to ensure that you do want to delete the changes.

PART THREE

Starting the program

■ SECTION 32
Booting up

To run the program all you need to do is enter **WS** – providing that you have added the sub-directory to the PATH on your AUTOEXEC.BAT file, either manually or by using the facility in either of the installation programs.

If you have not added it to the PATH, you will have to enter **CD** followed by the WordStar sub-directory name to move into the correct directory and then enter **WS** to activate the program. You must move into the directory first or the program will be unable to find the necessary overlays and files – for example, the dictionaries and help. If it cannot do so then you will find that many of the facilities of the program will not be available to you.

Once the program has loaded, and after presenting you with the various copyright notices, you will be presented with the Main Menu, as shown below

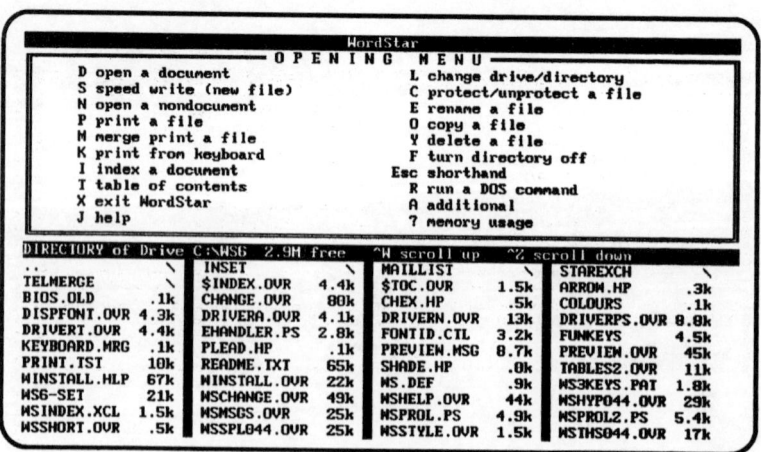

WordStar 5 Main Menu

■ SECTION 32
Booting up

This is divided into three basic parts. The first twelve lines make a neat box that contains the major commands. Immediately below this is a single line that informs you of the directory you are logged into and how much disk space you have available for additional files. The rest of the screen – or as much of it as you have specified in WSCHANGE – is used to contain a directory of the files, arranged in four columns, that already exist in that directory. If you have set the display to alphabetical then the display will show the sub-directories first, then any files that are named using numerals, next are the alphabetical files and finally are those whose names have another character as their initial letter. Otherwise the files and directories will be shown as they occur on the disk.

To activate any of the major commands all you need do is press the corresponding letter beside each one; for example, to terminate

```
┌────────────────────────────── WordStar ──────────────────────────────┐
│ ══════════════════════ O P E N I N G   M E N U ═══════════════════════│
│   D open a document               L change drive/directory            │
│   S speed write (new file)        C protect/unprotect a file          │
│   N open a nondocument            E rename a file                      │
│   P print a file                  O copy a file                       │
│   M merge print a file            Y delete a file                      │
│   K print from keyboard           F turn directory off                │
│   I index a document            Esc shorthand                         │
│   T table of contents             R run a DOS command                 │
│   X exit WordStar                 A additional                        │
│   J help                          ? memory usage                      │
│ ─────────────────────────────── H E L P ──────────────────────────────│
│ For help with a command on the Opening Menu, press the key that corresponds│
│ to it. To view or change the help level, press the F1 or J key now.   │
│                                                                        │
│ To cancel help now, press the Spacebar.                                │
│                                                                        │
│                                                                        │
│                                                                        │
└────────────────────────────────────────────────────────────────────────┘
```

On-line help

115

the program press **X** and you will be returned to the system prompt.

To get help with the Main Menu just press **J** and this will activate the on-line help facility. This will actually give you assistance with everything that the WordStar program will do, not just the Main Menu. The help available is extremely extensive – perhaps too much so.

Pressing **F** will toggle the directory display on and off.

The basis for the existence of a word processor is the production of documents and WordStar makes this very easy. Before you can load a file you must be in the directory that contains the file. If you have used the Initial Directory Log On facility in WSCHANGE you will find that the directory that you want is the one displayed on the screen. However, if this contains sub-directories you may want a document that is contained in one of these. Changing directory with WordStar is very simple.

L allows you to change the currently displayed drive and/or directory. Pressing this command key will bring up an input menu (see below) that allows you to specify the new destination.

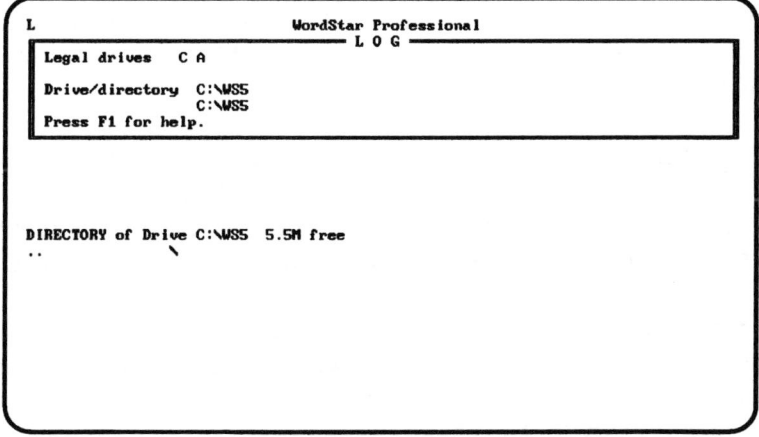

Changing directory

Once the menu appears you have two choices about how you change directory. On the one hand you can enter the new destination directly from the keyboard, while on the other you can use the cursor keys.

■ SECTION 33
Changing directory

Suppose that you were in a directory named DOCUMENT and wanted to move into a sub-directory of that called PRIVATE. On the input screen either you can enter `C:\DOCUMENT\PRIVATE` as a single string or you can move the cursor along the string being displayed and simply add the extra `\PRIVATE` that is necessary. The advantage to the menu is that it displays your current directory as a matter of course, thereby allowing you to make short-cuts when changing directory. Once you have input the new destination, pressing **Enter** will change directory for you.

(Notice that if you input any new character as the first input character in the displayed string, then the entire string will disappear. Thus if you were to press **C** with the cursor under the initial letter 'C' on the menu then the displayed directory string will vanish. You can alter any of the other characters but changing the initial one with your first keypress will obliterate the current string contents.)

The alternative method of changing directory is to use the cursor keys. You will find that if you press **Down** a highlighter will appear in the directory area of the screen. Move this to the sub-directory that you want and then press **Enter**. WordStar will do the rest.

To move back up the directory structure – towards the root directory – you can use the same two options. When the menu appears you can either enter '..' to move up to the parent, or `C:\` to return directly to the root.

On the directory listing you will find that one of the shown directories is '..'; move the cursor to this and then press **Enter** to move back up one level.

Of course, if you know the name of the destination that you want to move to you can always enter it directly. Suppose that you are

■ SECTION 33
Changing directory

in a directory named DOCUMENT, which is a branch off the root, and you want to go to the WordStar directory. Once the menu pops down you just need to enter `C:\` followed by the WordStar directory name (e.g. `C:\WS5` for the WordStar 5 directory) and you will be taken straight there. Doing this using the cursor keys would involve going back up to the root and then down again to the target directory.

Having got to the directory that you want you can now load a document file and here you have three options.

The first is to open a document that you know contains, or will contain, print codes. Press **D** and a menu will pop down (see below) asking you for the filename that you want to load. Either use the cursor keys to move the highlighter to the one you want in the file display or enter the name manually. Pressing **Enter** will then load the file directly into the memory and you will be presented with the editing screen.

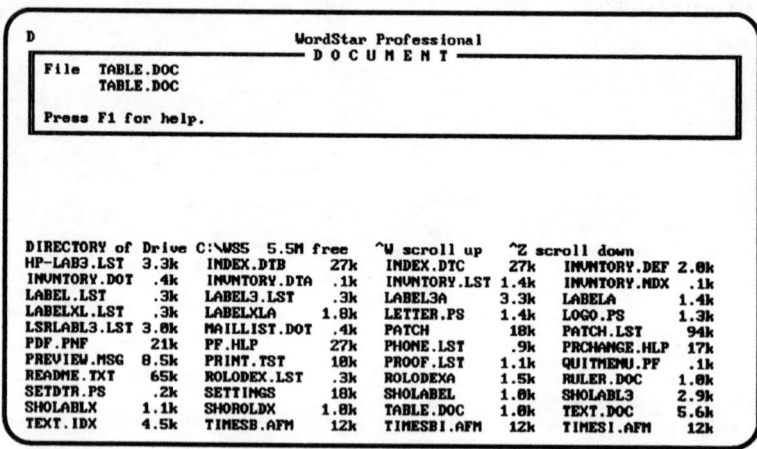

Opening a document

If you input the name of a file that does not exist then WordStar will prompt you with a message saying 'Can't find that file. Create a new one (Y/N)?'. Answer **Y** to initiate the new file and take you directly to the editing screen. Pressing **N** will cancel the operation and allow you to go back and choose again.

■ SECTION 34
Loading a file

The second option is used when you want to create a brand new file instantly. Pressing **S** will take you directly to the editing screen and an unnamed file. This document will only be named when you come to save it.

Lastly, if you want to open a non-document file – that is, one that is pure ASCII like the AUTOEXEC.BAT file – then press **N**. Again you will be prompted to input the name of the file that you want. You can open a standard document file as an ASCII file, work on it and then save it. If you then open it as an ordinary WordStar file the print control codes will still be there – but this is not recommended.

■ SECTION 35
Protecting and renaming files

The MS-DOS command ATTRIB allows you to change the Read-only and Archive attributes of files. WordStar provides you with a facility to do the former, selectively. Pressing **C** will pop down another menu (see below), labelled 'PROTECT', which asks you to input the filename of the document that you want to change. Do this in the same way as described above for entering filenames.

Once the file has been selected WordStar will provide another prompt. Either it will tell you that the file is unprotected or it will inform you that it is already protected; that is, the Read-only bit is on or off. You will then be given the option of changing it by entering **Y** or **N**.

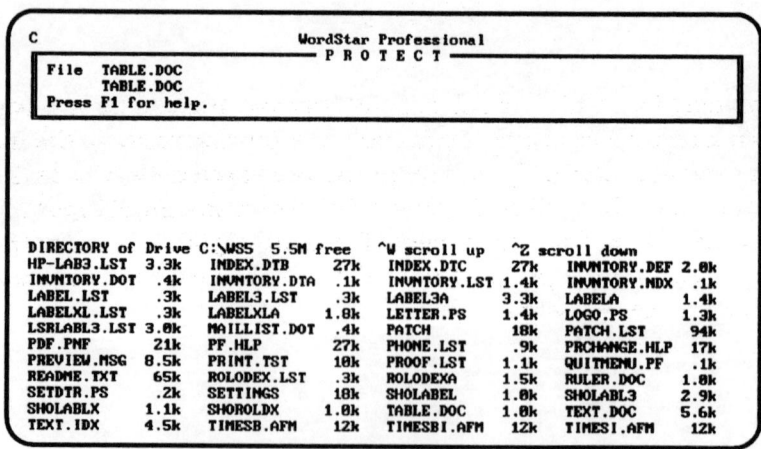

Protecting files

If a file is protected then you will be unable to change it. You can still load it and examine it but you cannot make any alterations to it.

SECTION 35
Protecting and renaming files

```
E                          WordStar Professional
                         ━━━━━ R E N A M E ━━━━━
  Current name    TABLE.DOC
                  TABLE.DOC

  New name        (none)

  Press F1 for help.



DIRECTORY of Drive C:\WS5  5.5M free      ^W scroll up    ^Z scroll down
HP-LAB3.LST 3.3k   INDEX.DTB    27k    INDEX.DTC    27k   INVNTORY.DEF 2.0k
INVNTORY.DOT  .4k  INVNTORY.DTA  .1k   INVNTORY.LST 1.4k  INVNTORY.NDX  .1k
LABEL.LST     .3k  LABEL3.LST    .3k   LABEL3A      3.3k  LABELA       1.4k
LABELXL.LST   .3k  LABELXLA     1.0k   LETTER.PS    1.4k  LOGO.PS      1.3k
LSRLABL3.LST 3.0k  MAILLIST.DOT  .4k   PATCH        18k   PATCH.LST    94k
PDF.PNF      21k   PF.HLP       27k    PHONE.LST     .9k  PRCHANGE.HLP 17k
PREVIEW.MSG 8.5k   PRINT.TST    18k    PROOF.LST    1.1k  QUITMENU.PF   .1k
README.TXT   65k   ROLODEX.LST   .3k   ROLODEXA     1.5k  RULER.DOC    1.0k
SETDTR.PS     .2k  SETTINGS     18k    SHOLABEL     1.0k  SHOLABL3     2.9k
SHOLABLX     1.1k  SHOROLDX     1.0k   TABLE.DOC    1.0k  TEXT.DOC     5.6k
TEXT.IDX     4.5k  TIMESB.AFM   12k    TIMESBI.AFM  12k   TIMESI.AFM   12k
```

Renaming files

Renaming files with WordStar is just as easy. Pressing **E** will pop
down a menu (see above) asking you to input the name of the file
you want to rename. If you have previously saved a file, this is the
default name that will be displayed. Otherwise you must input the
name as before. Once the original file is input you then enter the
new name and the program does the rest. You cannot rename a
file to a name that already exists.

■ SECTION 36
Copying and deleting files

You may produce a document and then want to make some changes to it but still retain the original for comparison. WordStar provides you with a facility to make a copy of any file. You cannot copy it to another directory or drive; the copy must be in the same directory as the original.

Pressing **O** pops down another menu (see below) which asks you to input the original filename and then the name to be given to the copy. Again, as with Rename, you cannot use an existing filename.

```
O                        WordStar Professional
                        ───── C O P Y ─────
   File          TABLE.DOC
                 TABLE.DOC

   Name of copy  (none)



   Press F1 for help.

 DIRECTORY of Drive C:\WS5   5.5M free    ^W scroll up    ^Z scroll down
 HP-LAB3.LST  3.3k   INDEX.DTB    27k    INDEX.DTC   27k   INVNTORY.DEF 2.0k
 INVNTORY.DOT  .4k   INVNTORY.DTA  .1k   INVNTORY.LST 1.4k  INVNTORY.NDX  .1k
 LABEL.LST     .3k   LABEL3.LST    .3k   LABEL3A     3.3k   LABELA       1.4k
 LABELXL.LST   .3k   LABELXLA     1.0k   LETTER.PS   1.4k   LOGO.PS      1.3k
 LSRLABL3.LST 3.0k   MAILLIST.DOT  .4k   PATCH        18k   PATCH.LST     94k
 PDF.PMF       21k   PF.HLP       27k    PHONE.LST    .9k   PRCHANGE.HLP  17k
 PREVIEW.MSG  8.5k   PRINT.TST    10k    PROOF.LST   1.1k   QUITMENU.PF   .1k
 README.TXT    65k   ROLODEX.LST   .3k   ROLODEXA    1.5k   RULER.DOC    1.0k
 SETDTR.PS     .2k   SETTINGS     18k    SHOLABEL    1.0k   SHOLABL3     2.9k
 SHOLABLX     1.1k   SHOROLDX     1.0k   TABLE.DOC   1.0k   TEXT.DOC     5.6k
 TEXT.IDX     4.5k   TIMESB.AFM   12k    TIMESBI.AFM  12k   TIMESI.AFM    12k
```

Copying files

Deleting files from the disk is accomplished by pressing **Y** which pops down another menu (below). You may input any individual file or use the wildcards; for example, to delete all the files with an extension of .BAK, enter ***.BAK**. You will be prompted before the deletion takes place to verify that you do actually want to remove the files. (If you accidentally delete wanted files you can

■ SECTION 36
Copying and deleting files

```
Y                              WordStar Professional
                              ━━━━ D E L E T E ━━━━
  File  (none)
        TABLE.DOC
  Press F1 for help.




  DIRECTORY of Drive C:\WS5  5.5M free    ^W scroll up   ^Z scroll down
  HP-LAB3.LST  3.3k    INDEX.DTB    27k    INDEX.DTC    27k    INVNTORY.DEF 2.0k
  INVNTORY.DOT  .4k    INVNTORY.DTA  .1k   INVNTORY.LST 1.4k   INVNTORY.MDX  .1k
  LABEL.LST     .3k    LABEL3.LST    .3k   LABEL3A      3.3k   LABELA       1.4k
  LABELXL.LST   .3k    LABELXLA     1.0k   LETTER.PS    1.4k   LOGO.PS      1.3k
  LSRLABL3.LST 3.0k    MAILLIST.DOT  .4k   PATCH        18k    PATCH.LST    94k
  PDF.PMF      21k     PF.HLP       27k    PHONE.LST     .9k   PRCHANGE.HLP 17k
  PREVIEW.MSG  8.5k    PRINT.TST    10k    PROOF.LST    1.1k   QUITMENU.PF   .1k
  README.TXT   65k     ROLODEX.LST   .3k   ROLODEXA     1.5k   RULER.DOC    1.0k
  SETDTR.PS     .2k    SETTINGS     10k    SHOLABEL     1.0k   SHOLABL3     2.9k
  SHOLABLX     1.1k    SHOROLDX     1.0k   TABLE.DOC    1.0k   TEXT.DOC     5.6k
  TEXT.IDX     4.5k    TIMESB.AFM   12k    TIMESBI.AFM  12k    TIMESI.AFM   12k
```

Deleting files

always get them back by using a utility like *Norton* or *PC-Tools*, providing you have not saved any other files since the deletion took place.)

125

■ SECTION 37
Using MS-DOS commands

You may find that you need to use one of the MS-DOS commands; for example, to find out if the document you want is in another directory. WordStar has a facility to allow you to do just that. Pressing **R** pops down a menu (below) that asks you to input the command that you want to use. However you can only use the external MS-DOS commands providing that the directory containing them is available on your PATH, as set in the AUTOEXEC.BAT file.

```
R                          WordStar Professional
                         ═══ R U N ═══
┌─────────────────────────────────────────────────────────────┐
│ Enter a DOS command.                                          │
│                                                               │
│ C>COMMAND                                                     │
│ Press F1 for help.                                            │
└─────────────────────────────────────────────────────────────┘
```

Running an MS-DOS command

You can also make WordStar temporarily memory resident by entering COMMAND at this point. The program will vanish into the background and return you to the system prompt. You can then do whatever you wish. To recall the WordStar program just enter EXIT and it will reappear at exactly the point at which you left it. You can also use this ability from within the editing screen by using **Ctrl-K F**.

126

■ SECTION 37
Using MS-DOS commands

Memory usage

Pressing ? will pop up a panel containing the details of what memory WordStar is using. From this you can see that the program is a real RAM hog. It seems that with every new release of WordStar the amount of memory it needs increases. If you use a number of memory-resident programs you may well find that you run into problems when you try running WordStar – if so then I suggest you remove the TSR programs and just run WordStar.

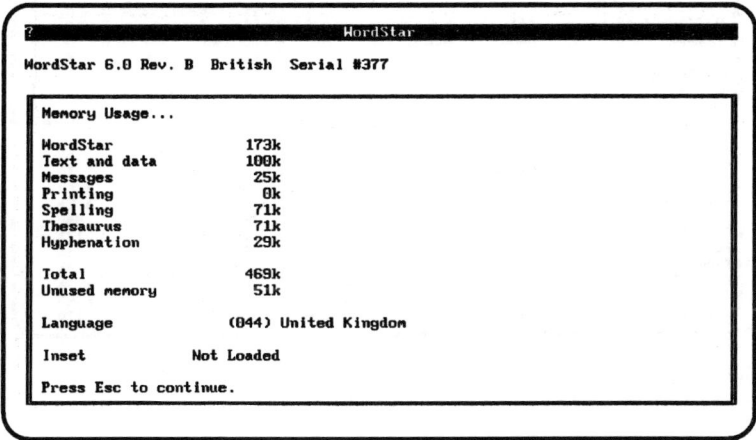

Memory usage

Printing from WordStar is controlled by yet another pop-down menu (see below), activated by pressing **P**. This has a total of nine possible choices. On the first line you enter the name of the file that you want to output, either by entering it from the keyboard or by using the cursor keys. (The name of the last file which you saved will be the default.)

```
P                        WordStar Professional
                         ───── P R I N T ─────
   File  (none)
         TABLE.DOC

   Page numbers    All     A                    Pause between pages  N     N
   All/even/odd pages  All     A                Use form feeds       Y     Y
   Printer name        DRAFT   DRAFT            Nondocument          N     N
                                               Number of copies      1     1
   Redirect output to    (none)

   Press F1 for help.

 DIRECTORY of Drive C:\WS5  5.5M free     ^W scroll up    ^Z scroll down
 HP-LAB3.LST  3.3k   INDEX.DTB     27k   INDEX.DTC    27k   INVNTORY.DEF 2.0k
 INVNTORY.DOT  .4k   INVNTORY.DTA  .1k   INVNTORY.LST 1.4k  INVNTORY.NDX  .1k
 LABEL.LST     .3k   LABEL3.LST    .3k   LABEL3A      3.3k  LABELA       1.4k
 LABELXL.LST   .3k   LABELXLA     1.0k   LETTER.PS    1.4k  LOGO.PS      1.3k
 LSRLABL3.LST 3.0k   MAILLIST.DOT  .4k   PATCH         18k  PATCH.LST     94k
 PDF.PMF       21k   PF.HLP        27k   PHONE.LST     .9k  PRCHANGE.HLP  17k
 PREVIEW.MSG  8.5k   PRINT.TST     18k   PROOF.LST    1.1k  QUITMENU.PF   .1k
 README.TXT    65k   ROLODEX.LST   .3k   ROLODEXA     1.5k  RULER.DOC    1.0k
 SETDTR.PS     .2k   SETTINGS      18k   SHOLABEL     1.0k  SHOLABL3     2.9k
 SHOLABLX     1.1k   SHOROLDX     1.0k   TABLE.DOC    1.0k  TEXT.DOC     5.6k
 TEXT.IDX     4.5k   TIMESB.AFM    12k   TIMESBI.AFM   12k  TIMESI.AFM    12k
```

Printing

The next group of three inputs are used to determine which pages you will print out. 'Page numbers' determines the numbering you will use, while the next choice specifies which of the pages within the document will bear the page numbers – just toggle it to the one you want.

The next line is used to select the printer that you want to use. By default it will be that printer which you have selected from within WSCHANGE but you can change it to whichever one you like. Once the cursor reaches this option another listing will appear bearing the names of all the available output devices. Versions 5, 5.5 and 6 of WordStar come complete with three installed devices; the first is ASCII which allows you to output the printer as pure characters – that is, without control codes – either to another file or to a printer.

The second device is WordStar 4. The file formats used by Word-Star 5 onwards and its earlier cousins are different, but you are unlikely to notice this unless you are using the files within another program. For instance *Timeworks* can import WordStar 4 files but not those produced by Release 5 and later versions.

The third installed device is a draft printer. This is a catchall device driver that will work with most printers but it may not give you exactly the effects that you expected. It is much better to install you own printer properly.

The next group of four choices controls how the document is actually printed. The first, 'Pause between pages', will stop the printing or other output whenever it reaches the end of a page – useful if you are using single cut sheets. 'Use form feeds' controls the throw of the paper.

'Nondocument' will cause the file to be printed out with the embedded printer control commands as text; for example, all dot commands will appear exactly as they do on the editing screen. Next you are asked to input the number of copies of the document that want to print. By default it is usually 1 but you can input any number up to 999.

The final option, 'Redirect output to', allows you to specify a filename to which the file will be sent, usually only used if you are converting a file from one format to another.

SECTION 38
Outputting files

Once you have input all your choices, and providing the printer is switched on (if you are going to use one), the file will be processed.

You can also output files using **M** (Merge print a file) from the Main Menu but we will cover this facility later when we look at MailList.

PART FOUR

Editing documents

■ SECTION 39
The editing screen

Having loaded you document file, using one of the options on the Main Menu, you will now be presented with the main editing screen, (see below). The top line is the Status Line, which gives you the following information:

■ The drive that you are currently logged onto, but not the directory.

■ The name of the current document, including any extension.

■ The number of the page that the cursor is presently on (the one being displayed). On a new document this will normally be 1.

■ The position of the cursor in terms of line and column number, and in inches. The column position is defined in terms of the actual character position – not necessarily the same as that displayed on the ruler line. The column position is dependent on the pitch of the characters that you are really using; thus if you are using 12-pitch the column position might be 78 even though the ruler line only goes up to 65.

■ Which mode you are using – Insert or Overwrite – and whether the paragraph alignment is on or off.

■ Finally, whether the right justification is on or off. If it is off then nothing will appear. If on, then the status line says 'RgtJust' at the extreme right-hand side.

The second line of the screen contains the *ruler line*. This shows the position of the left margin, 'L', and the right margin, 'R', at whatever positions you have set them in WSCHANGE. Between

SECTION 39
The editing screen

```
   C:TEXT          P1  L1  C1  .00"   Insert Align
L----!----!----!----!----!----!----!----!----!----!----!----!----R
                                                                    <
                                                                    <
The answer to each of the following questions will give you a sum
of money in the old pre-decimal currency. When you add them all
up you should have a total of Thirty One Pounds, Sixteen
Shillings, Two and a Half Pence. (Remember that an old pound had
20 Shillings, each containing 12 Pence.)                            <
                                                                    <
      a) An old form of transport.                                 <
      b) Move up and down, in water perhaps.                       <
      c) Mars, Jupiter and Venus are .....                        <
      d) A type of Pig.                                            <
      e) Underwear for a one-legged woman.                        <
      f) A section of a regal head-dress.                         <
      g) An unwell decapod mollusc.                               <
      h) A stone.                                                 <
      i) He turns skin into leather.                              <
      j) A type of singing voice.                                 <
      k) A section of a primate's limb.                           <
                                                                   ^
 -HELP?- >UNDO<< BEG-BLK END-BLK DEL-BLK MOVEBLK COPYBLK -INDEX- REVIEW?1SAVEOUT
1-SPELL-2THESAUR3BOLDTXT4ITALICS5DEL<<<<6DEL>>>>7GO<LEFT8GORIGHT9HIDECHR0BACKUP-
```

Main editing screen

the two letters are shown the tab marks: exclamation marks (!) for
regular tabs, and hash marks (#) for decimal tabs. The spaces
between the tabs – or the margins if no tabs are set – will be filled
with a line of dashes, if you have not changed the character.

The bottom two lines – if you have the help level set at 1, 2 or 3 –
will show the function key labels as you have set them up. They
are there as a reminder of what you have programmed into the
keys.

The main part of the screen is given over to showing the text file
that you have loaded. If this is a new file then it will be blank,
ready to accept whatever you type on the keyboard.

133

■ SECTION 40
Controlling the cursor

Normally the text cursor appears as a thin flashing line when you are in Insert mode, and as a thick flashing line in Overwrite mode. (If if you have changed it in WSCHANGE then this will not be the case.) To switch between the two use the **Ins** toggle key on the numeric keypad or on the cursor keypad. When you move into Overwrite mode the word 'Insert' will vanish off the status line.

The arrow keys will move the cursor in the direction that corresponds with their inscriptions.

■ **Left** moves it one column to the left, or up to the extreme right of the previous line if you are at the beginning of a line of text.

■ **Right** will move it one position right or down to the beginning of the next line of text.

■ **Up** and **Down** move the cursor up and down the lines of text but within the current column.

■ **End** will take the cursor to the last available position on the currently displayed screen of text. If your document extends beyond the currently displayed screen then pressing this key again causes the screen to scroll up as far as is possible.

■ **Home** takes you to column 1 of the first line on the currently displayed screen. Pressing it again has no further effect. **Pg Dn** will scroll the display to the next screen, **Pg Up** has the opposite effect.

■ **Ctrl-End** will take you to the final possible position at the extreme end of the document. **Ctrl-Home** moves the cursor to Line 1, Column 1 – the start of the document.

■ SECTION 40
Controlling the cursor

In addition to using the cursor keys WordStar provides a range of Ctrl-key sequences that allow you to move the cursor quickly through a document. These all consist of two keys used in conjunction with the Ctrl key.

- **Ctrl-Q E** has the same effect as **Home**; that is, it moves you to the top left-hand side of the current screen.

- **Ctrl-Q X** duplicates the effect of **End** and moves you to the bottom right-hand corner of the screen – or as near to it as it can get.

- **Ctrl-Q S** will move the cursor to the beginning of the current line; that is, if you are at the right-hand edge of a line this sequence will move the cursor to the extreme left.

- **Ctrl-Q D** has the opposite effect; that is, it moves the cursor to the extreme right-hand side of a line.

- **Ctrl-Q R** moves the cursor to the beginning of the file – the same effect as **Ctrl-Home**.

- **Ctrl-Q C** takes you directly to the end of the file – the same effect as **Ctrl-End**.

- **Ctrl-Q W** will scroll the entire editing screen display up one line at a time; the cursor remains at the same position, with regard to actual text, but the text itself moves up. To stop the scrolling just press any key.

- **Ctrl-Q Z** has the opposite effect – it scrolls the text down one line at a time. To stop the scrolling press any key.

■ SECTION 40
Controlling the cursor

To activate any of these key sequences, press **Ctrl** and **Q** at the same time and then press the next letter to generate the effect. If you are using the classic menus, pressing the first two keys will pop down a menu that contains a very brief description of some of the possible commands.

■ SECTION 41
Drawing diagrams

Anything that you type on the keyboard, other than the Ctrl-key sequences, will appear on the main editing screen. You can 'build' boxes and diagrams using the **Alt** key combined with the function keys. As the program is shipped, the ten function keys are programmed to display the following characters, when used with the key below.

F1	│	ASCII CODE 179
F2	─	ASCII CODE 196
F3	┌	ASCII CODE 169
F4	┐	ASCII CODE 170
F5	└	ASCII CODE 192
F6	┘	ASCII CODE 217
F7	┬	ASCII CODE 194
F8	┴	ASCII CODE 193
F9	├	ASCII CODE 195
F10	┤	ASCII CODE 180

Box drawing characters

With these characters it is possible to draw simple diagrams: for example, flowcharts or organisational diagrams. However, there are some characters that you might want that are not programmed into the function keys.

To input any character, whether it be alphabetical, numerical or otherwise, you can type it directly from the keyboard, as you do with the normal alphanumeric characters. Alternatively you can hold down the **Alt** key and then enter the ASCII code number of

SECTION 41
Drawing diagrams

the character using the numeric keypad; you cannot use the number keys along the top of the main keyboard. This is very useful, providing you know the ASCII codes of the characters that you want. Normally you would have to look them up in a reference book and then enter the numbers, which can be very tedious.

Fortunately WordStar provides a shortcut. **Ctrl-P 0** will pop down a menu (see below) which contains all the possible extended ASCII characters and codes that you can input; some of the ASCII codes are used as control codes and so cannot be used in a document, hence they are not included in the table. Each character is displayed as it will appear on screen, set in a grid that contains the relevant codes.

Move the cursor to the position that you want the first graphic character to appear and then activate the key sequence. On the

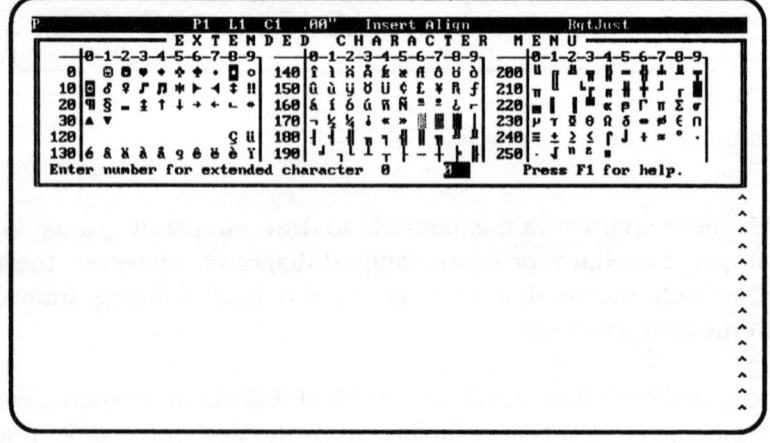

Extended ASCII Character Menu

menu there is a space for you to enter the code number of the character that you want to use. You must enter the code; you cannot use the cursor keys to select a character. Once you have input the code the character will appear at the current cursor position. In this way you can build up extensive illustrations and drawings to enhance your text.

■ SECTION 42
Running the spelling check

Once you have entered text into a document you may want to check the spelling of the whole document. To do so, use the key sequence **Ctrl-Q L**. The program will check the spelling from the current cursor position to the end of the document. While this happens a menu saying 'Checking spelling . . .' will appear across the top of the screen and the text in the editing screen will scroll as the words are checked. (You should note that the checker will present you with error messages for things like abbreviations and postcodes, but this will depend on the setting you have made in WSCHANGE for the smallest word to be checked.)

If there are no spelling errors – and the program will find just about every error that you are ever likely to make – then you will be presented with a prompt telling you how many words have been checked; that is, those that contain a number of letters equal to or greater than the minimum word setting. To remove the prompt press **Esc** and the editing screen will be reactivated. The cursor

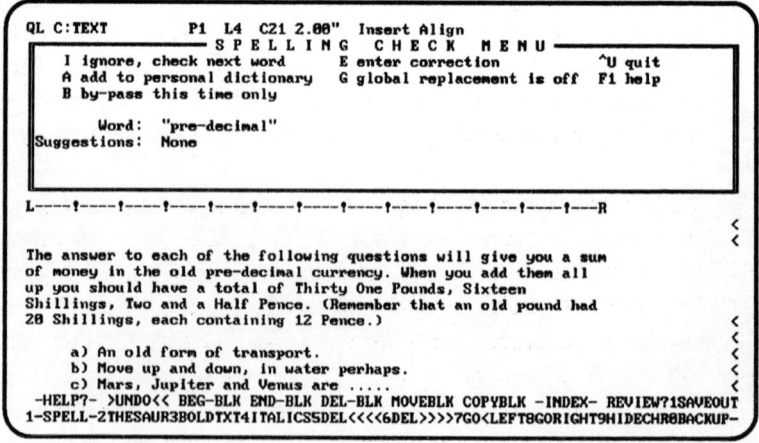

Spelling Check Menu

140

will now be at the end of the document and not where you started the spelling check.

When it finds an error the program will pop down another menu (see above) to inform you of the fact. The menu will contain the word it has encountered that is wrong (or that it assumes is wrong), followed by a number of possible corrections. To enter any of these possibles just press the number relating to the one that you want. If there are more possibles than can be contained on a single screen then the menu will also have a line saying 'M display more suggestions'. In other words, to see the other possible corrections you press the letter 'M'.

The top three lines of the menu contain your options, each activated by a single letter:

■ I tells the program to ignore the spelling of the word; that is, disregard it and carry on checking the rest of the document. During the rest of the spelling check the program will ignore every subsequent occurrence of the word. However if you select this option then the spell-checker will 'trip over' the word every time that you run it because, as far as the program is concerned, the word is wrong and you haven't done anything to correct it.

■ A adds the word, as it appears, to the personal dictionary; that is, it informs the program that the word is spelled correctly and therefore should not be presented as an error. This facility will be used mainly to add non-standard words to the dictionary: for example, specialised terms, place names or scientific names. You can always adjust the personal dictionary later by loading it, from the WordStar sub-directory, as a non-document. The personal dictionary is called PERSONAL.DCT. Be warned; if you load and save

Running the spelling check

it as a standard document then the program will be unable to run the spelling check properly and will give you a message to that effect.

■ **B** is used primarily to tell the program to ignore the spelling of a word for this run of the checker. For instance the word might be a term that you will use very infrequently and thus it is not worth placing it in the personal dictionary. At the same time you still want to check the spelling of the word at every occurrence in the document.

■ **E** allows you to manually enter a correction for the word. Occasionally the spell-checker will find a word – for example, 'dcoumnte' – that it cannot untangle into what it could be. In this case you will not be presented with any suggestions and will have to correct it by hand. Pressing this letter will bring down another menu that allows you to enter the correction. Pressing **Enter** at the end of the word will replace the faulty spelling with the correction and allow the spell-checker to continue.

■ **G** toggles the global replacement on and off. If it is on then every occurrence throughout the document of that incorrectly spelled word, with that spelling, will be replaced when you first enter the correction. If it is off then the words will have to be corrected every time that the spell-checker finds one.

■ **Ctrl-U** will halt the spell-checker in its tracks – and return you to the editing screen. **Esc** has the same effect. Once the checker is finished, either because it has reached the end of the document or because you have interrupted it, you will be told the number of words that have been checked.

■ SECTION 43
Checking individual words

Occasionally we all want to use a word for which we know the pronunciation, more or less, but we are unable to spell it correctly. Rather than just putting it in and then running the spell-checker, WordStar provides a facility that allows you to enter the word phonetically. It will then try and sort out the correct spelling for you.

Enter the word as it sounds, move the cursor to the initial letter and then use the key sequence **Ctrl-Q N**. This brings down a menu (see below) almost identical to the spell-checking one. The major difference is that this time the menu will tell you if the word is spelled correctly, but it will also give you alternative possible words. In addition it will give you a brief definition of the word, thus allowing you to check that the word is actually the one that you want.

Be warned, though, that some of the definitions can be a bit strange; they usually apply to the most probable use of the word,

```
QN C:TEXT        P1  L6  C1  .00"   Insert Align
                    S P E L L I N G   C H E C K   M E N U
    I ignore, check next word      E enter correction        ^U quit
    A add to personal dictionary   G global replacement is off  F1 help
    B by-pass this time only

    Word:  "Shillings" is spelt correctly
Suggestions: 1 Chillings 2 Shellings 3 Shilling 4 Shills  5 Child
             M display more suggestions
Definition: shill: accomplice posing as a customer or gambler etc.

L----!----!----!----!----!----!----!----!----!----!----!---R
                                                                    <
                                                                    <
The answer to each of the following questions will give you a sum
of money in the old pre-decimal currency. When you add them all
up you should have a total of Thirty One Pounds, Sixteen
Shillings, Two and a Half Pence. (Remember that an old pound had
20 Shillings, each containing 12 Pence.)                            <
                                                                    <
    a) An old form of transport.                                    <
    b) Move up and down, in water perhaps.                          <
    c) Mars, Jupiter and Venus are .....                            <
 -HELP?- >UNDO<< BEG-BLK END-BLK DEL-BLK MOVEBLK COPYBLK -INDEX- REVIEW?1SAVEOUT
1-SPELL-2THESAUR3BOLDTXT4ITALICS5DEL<<<6DEL>>>7GO<LEFT8GORIGHT9HIDECHR0BACKUP-
```

Spell-checking individual words

Checking individual words

which is not necessarily the use that you will be making of it. For instance, you might want the word 'match', used in the context of an ignitable piece of word. But the definition you will get says 'being equal'. (Granted that this is a somewhat frivolous example but it does demonstrate the fact that many words in the English language have a wide variety of possible meanings – and WordStar cannot give you them all.)

If the word is spelled incorrectly then the routine will give you a range of possible corrections, just as the main spelling checker does. To select one of these just press the relevant number.

Another way in which you can do the same thing is to use the key sequence **Ctrl-Q O**. This will pop down a menu that allows you to input the spelling of the word you want to use, instead of placing it directly into the document. Pressing **Enter** when you have typed the word will then automatically activate a variation of the individual spelling check menu. This has only three options:

■   **I** ignores the input word and steps back to allow you to enter another word to check.

■   **A** accepts the spelling as you input it and adds the word to the personal dictionary. If you select this option then the routine goes back to allow you to enter another word for checking.

■   **E** is used to enter the word, as you input it, into the text at the current cursor position.

If you want to use one of the suggestions that the routine gives you just press the relevant number and the word will be entered into the text at the current cursor position. To cancel the process use **Ctrl-U** or **Esc** and you will return to the editing screen.

■ SECTION 44
Synonyms

One of the most common examples of bad English is the use of the same word repeatedly in related sentences, a trap that everyone falls into. When you are speaking to someone it does not matter if you use the same word a number of times – in fact it is often done to provide emphasis – but when it is written down it looks careless and sloppy. WordStar provides you with an extensive *thesaurus* which, if used properly, will allow you to escape from this pitfall.

You can also use it to turn a simple, direct sentence into bureaucratic rubbish. For example 'He came in the door' can be turned into:

> A single, unaccompanied particular individual member of the genus homo sapiens entered the domicile chamber through and via the entrance hall doorway, to position himself within the dwelling.

Useful for making up crossword puzzles – but of no use whatsoever for writing clear English.

To find a synonym for any word, move the cursor to the initial letter of that word and then use the key sequence **Ctrl-Q J**. This will pop down a menu (see below), providing the word selected is one of those that is contained in the Thesaurus. If it is not included in the 220,000 words that the thesaurus incorporates then the program will provide you with another menu containing roughly thirty near alphabetical guesses of the word you are looking for. You can then select one of these possibles by using the cursor keys. One major problem with this facility is that some of the guesses with which you are provided are not actually contained in the thesaurus – which can be very frustrating!

SECTION 44
Synonyms

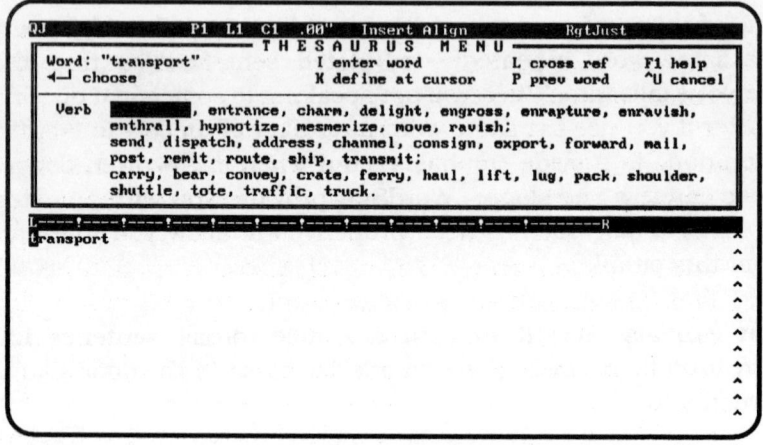

```
QJ              P1  L1  C1  .00"   Insert Align          RgtJust
                       T H E S A U R U S    M E N U
Word: "transport"                I enter word      L cross ref   F1 help
←┘ choose                        X define at cursor P prev word  ^U cancel

 Verb  ███████████ , entrance, charm, delight, engross, enrapture, enravish,
       enthrall, hypnotize, mesmerize, move, ravish;
       send, dispatch, address, channel, consign, export, forward, mail,
       post, remit, route, ship, transmit;
       carry, bear, convey, crate, ferry, haul, lift, lug, pack, shoulder,
       shuttle, tote, traffic, truck.

!----!----!----!----!----!----!----!----!----!----!----------R
transport                                                              ^
                                                                       ^
                                                                       ^
                                                                       ^
                                                                       ^
                                                                       ^
                                                                       ^
                                                                       ^
                                                                       ^
                                                                       ^
```

Thesaurus Menu

The menu is divided into two parts. The top two lines contain the word you have input and possible commands, with the bulk of the display holding the possible synonyms. These are normally presented in groups, which are dependent on the possible context of the word. Thus adjectives are held together, followed by nouns, then adverbs, and so on. If there are more words than can be contained within the menu a downward-pointing arrow will appear in the bottom left-hand corner of the menu, telling you that there are other words below. To select any of the synonyms move the cursor to the one you want and then press **Enter**; the word will then overwrite the original for which you wanted an equivalent.

The possible options within the Thesaurus Menu are:

■   I, which allows you to cancel the current search and input an alternative word for the thesaurus to look for.

Synonyms

■ **K** will give you a very brief definition of the word that is currently highlighted by the cursor. You can also move the cursor up onto the original word to define that.

■ **L** permits you to change the current word for one of those contained within the synonyms. For instance, suppose you had input 'happy' but none of the possible synonyms were quite what you wanted. You could move the cursor to 'joyful' and then press **L** to get synonyms for that because it is a close fit. This cross-reference facility can be extremely useful, as it keeps the thesaurus active.

■ **P** effectively cancels the operation of the previous command. It will automatically return you to the synonyms for the word you were looking at before doing a cross reference.

To cancel the thesaurus you can either press **Ctrl-U** or **Esc**.

■ SECTION 45
Deleting text

WordStar provides you with a number of ways of deleting text and/or characters. As with most word processors, you can use the standard keys: **Del** to remove the character above the cursor; **Backspace** to delete the character to the left of the cursor. However WordStar comes with a whole range of other means and methods:

■ **Ctrl-Q Del** will delete any and all characters to the left of the cursor, to the extreme left-hand edge of the page. Thus to remove an entire line you can move the cursor to the right-hand edge and then press this key sequence to do so.

■ **Ctrl-Q Y** works in the same way but to the right of the cursor. If you accidentally delete a line, using either sequence, it can be restored by using **Ctrl-U** to undo the operation, providing that the line was the last thing deleted.

■ **Ctrl-Q T** allows you to input an individual alphanumeric character and then erase everything up to the first occurrence of that character. One way of using this key sequence is to delete entire sentences. Move the cursor to the beginning of the sentence to be erased and then use **Ctrl-Q T**. The sentence will be deleted. Again, it can be restored using **Ctrl-U**.

■ **Ctrl-G** has the same effect as **Del**; that is, it deletes the character at the cursor.

■ **Ctrl-T** will delete the characters to the right, from the cursor, to the first occurrence of a blank space; that is, it can be used to delete whole words.

SECTION 45
Deleting text

■ **Ctrl-Y** deletes the entire line on which the cursor is currently positioned and moves the cursor to the beginning of the line.

Normally, when you delete text from a document, the program will do its best to realign the remaining words into the proper format. However, this does not always happen correctly and therefore it means that you may have to realign it yourself. Move the cursor to the beginning of the text and then use the key sequence **Ctrl-Q U**. The screen will scroll rapidly as the text is reorganised so that it fits between the margins properly.

■ SECTION 46
Using mathematics

It is not very often that you will need to use mathematical expressions, and their results, within a document, but there are occasions when it is necessary. Normally you would have to use a calculator, work out the equation and then put the result in the appropriate place within the document. However, WordStar comes complete with a built-in calculator (see below) that pops down over your document when you press **Ctrl-Q M**. You can then perform the calculations you need and automatically incorporate them, and/or the result, into the document.

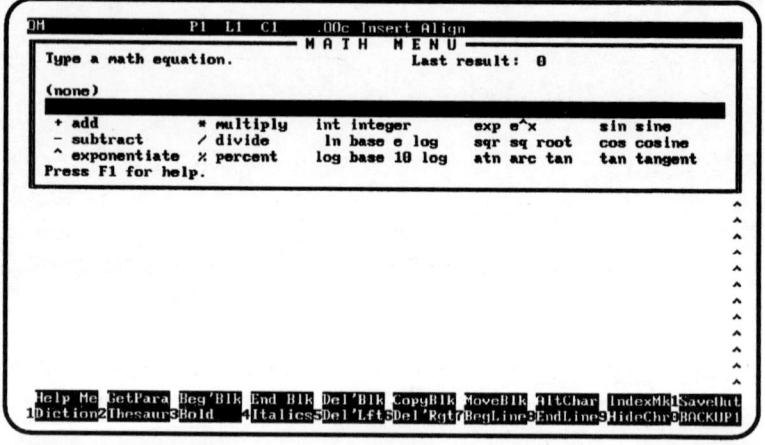

Math Menu

The menu displays the result of the last calculation and has a line for you to enter the calculation that you now want to perform. This line may contain the last formula you used – it can be changed or altered as necessary – but if you change the first figure before anything else then the entire formula will vanish (as with changing directory on the Main Menu).

■ SECTION 46
Using mathematics

On the lines below this are the symbols and brief descriptions of the operands that you can use in the formulae. WordStar uses 14-digit floating point mathematics. Besides the basic arithmetical operands you can use the following:

■ % allows you to find percentages, e.g. 85465*12.5%

■ **int**, short for 'integer', allows you to specify that only the integer part of the result will be displayed. For instance, **int(4.26*1.476)** yields a result of 6; without the operand the result would be 6.28776.

■ **ln** will give you the base *e* logarithm; e.g. **ln(4.26*1.476)** yields 1.83860488646.

■ **log** gives the result in base 10 logarithm; e.g. **log(4.26*1.476)** yields 0.79849595659.

■ **exp** yields an exponential; e.g. **exp(4.26*1.476)** = 537.946977246.

■ **sqr** allows you to find the square root of a number or of the result of a calculation; e.g. **sqr(4.26*1.476)** yields 2.50754062779.

■ **atn** gives you the arc tangent; e.g **atn(4.26)** gives the result 76.7894694891.

■ **sin** provides the sine of a number or calculation; e.g. **sin(4.26)** gives the result 0.0742825420578.

■ **cos** gives the cosine; e.g. **cos(4.26)** = 0.997237235539.

■ **tan** gives the tangent; e.g. **tan(4.26)** = 0.0744883357846.

■ SECTION 46
Using mathematics

Because the calculator provides so many operands, you can develop exceedingly complex formulae and then have them incorporated into a document. For example:

```
int((ln(24+(64*73.826))/((tan(4.23))+(exp(3.33+6.66))))*(2.4e3+9.64e5))
```

To enter a formula into the text use **Esc #**. This will take the formula, as you entered it on the calculator, and copy it into the text. To also include the answer use the key sequence **Esc =**. This will give you the answer as it would appear on any calculator. However, if you want the answer to appear as you would normally write it then use **Esc $** and the result will be shown according to the format you established in WSCHANGE.

WordStar provides a number of ways in which you can page through your text to find any given word or phrase, besides looking for it screen by screen. The quickest and simplest of these options is activated by **Ctrl-Q F**. This pops down a menu (below) which allows you to input the word, or a phrase containing up to 68 characters, that you want to find.

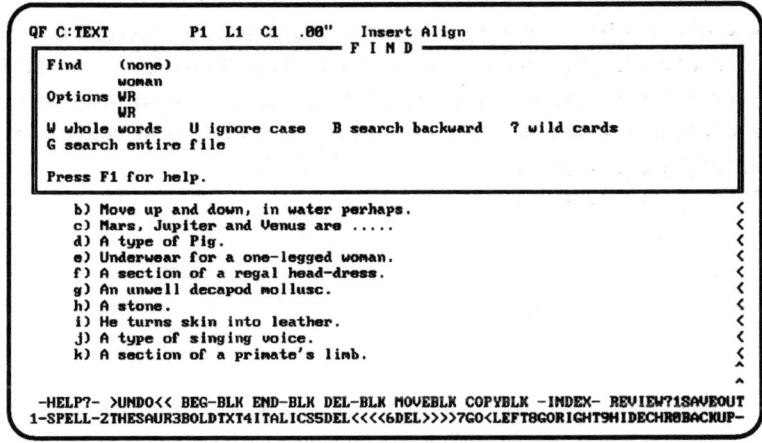

```
QF C:TEXT          P1 L1 C1  .00"   Insert Align
                                 F I N D
 Find    (none)
         woman
 Options WR
         WR
 W whole words   U ignore case   B search backward   ? wild cards
 G search entire file

 Press F1 for help.

     b) Move up and down, in water perhaps.              <
     c) Mars, Jupiter and Venus are .....               <
     d) A type of Pig.                                   <
     e) Underwear for a one-legged woman.               <
     f) A section of a regal head-dress.                <
     g) An unwell decapod mollusc.                      <
     h) A stone.                                         <
     i) He turns skin into leather.                     <
     j) A type of singing voice.                        <
     k) A section of a primate's limb.                  <
                                                         ^
 -HELP?-  >UNDO<< BEG-BLK END-BLK DEL-BLK MOVEBLK COPYBLK -INDEX- REVIEW?1SAVEOUT
 1-SPELL-2THESAUR3BOLDTXT4ITALICS5DEL<<<<6DEL>>>>7GO<LEFT8GORIGHT9HIDECHR0BACKUP-
```

Find Text Menu

Beneath the input line are the special options allowable on this command, with the ones you have preset being displayed by default. The options are as follows:

■   **W** means that the program has to find a perfect match for your input; in other words it will not stop when it finds 'Alpha' if you asked for 'Alphabetical'. The word or phrase must be an identical match.

■ SECTION 47
Finding text

■ **U** cancels the case. For example if you input Alpha then acceptable words which match would be 'alpha', 'ALpha', 'ALPha', 'ALPHa' and 'ALPHA', or any possible combination of upper and lower case letters. This facility is useful if you are looking for a particular word but you cannot remember what case you used to enter it.

■ **B** forces the program to search backwards through the file. Normally the search is carried out from the current cursor position to the end of the file. However if you are already at the end you need not go back to the beginning before starting the search; this option will move you back automatically.

■ **?** allows you, theoretically, to enter wildcards to find words that contain characters that you are unsure of, 'alpha?et' to 'find alphabet'. (However, when I try to use this it never works!)

■ **G** means that the search is to be carried out through the entire file, usually from beginning to end.

You can string these control characters together in any combination that you wish; for example, 'WG' to search for a perfect match throughout the file.

■ SECTION 48
Replacing text

The major advantage to using a word processor is the ease with which you can rearrange and replace the text easily, quickly and without waste. The facility that WordStar uses to replace words or phrases makes this even more effortless than normal. Pressing **Ctrl-Q A** summons a menu (below) very similar to the one used for Find Text, but has some extra options.

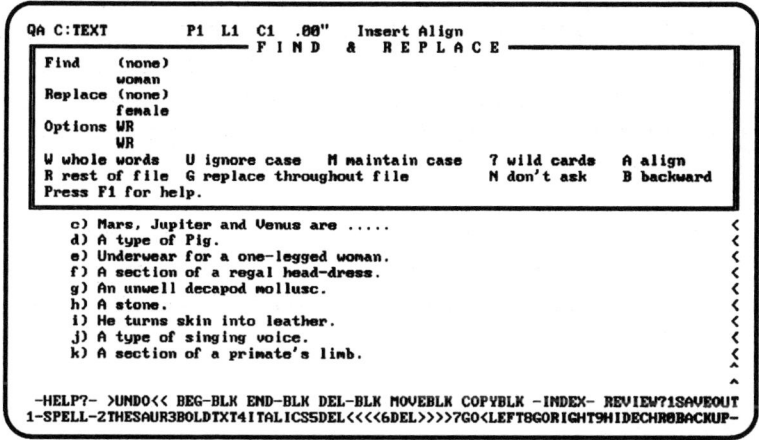

Replacing Text

■ **M** forces the replacement to use the same case as was originally used for the word being replaced; that is, case matches case. The routine will do this by default.

■ **A** ensures that after the replacement is completed the paragraph will be realigned with the margins. Occasionally this will happen anyway but if you are replacing strings of words, rather than individual words, then you should include this option in the command string.

■ SECTION 48
Replacing text

■ **N** is used, primarily, when you are replacing a word or phrase throughout the file. It allows the program to replace every occurrence of the target word or phrase with the new text, without asking you each time if it should do so.

■ SECTION 49
Finding things

WordStar will allow you to move directly to an individual letter or character, either within a given line or inside the entire document. You can do so by going forwards or backwards from the cursor position. **Ctrl-Q G** brings down a menu for you to enter a single character; the cursor will then move forwards from its current position to that character. **Ctrl-Q H** moves it back up through the file to the first occurrence of the character.

Equally, if you have been using a number of different fonts within a document (as I did when writing this book) then you can move directly from one font to the next by using **Ctrl-Q =**. In this case a font is regarded as a different typeface not just a style of lettering: for example, Roman 10 not Bold Draft 12. The cursor will move to the next font marker.

To move from page to page use **Ctrl-Q I**. A menu appears that allows you to enter the page number to which you wish to move. The cursor will move directly to the first line of the target page.

You can also use the find facilities to move directly to a block of text, providing that it has been marked with the block markers. **Ctrl-Q B** will displace the cursor to the beginning of the block. If there is no block marked then you will get an error message. **Ctrl-Q K** takes you to the end-of-block marker. These searches are carried out without taking account of the cursor's current position – all that matters is the block markers and so the cursor may go forwards or backwards through the document.

The final way to move to a specific place within a document is to denote it with a special marker that is set by using **Ctrl-K ?**, where '?' is a numeral from 0 to 9, thus allowing a total of ten possibles. The marker will appear in inverse video on the screen and it has no effect on the actual text. When you want to move to a specific marker you use the key sequence **Ctrl-Q ?**, where '?' is the marker

you want. The cursor will move there directly. If you have not
placed any markers then you will get an error message saying
'Can't move to undefined marker'. Markers are lost when the
document is saved.

■ SECTION 50
Setting the margins and tabs

WordStar is extremely adaptable in the type of formats and methods of setting them that you can use. The default setting for the margins are set using WSCHANGE when you install the program but you are not limited to just using those. The program allows you to format a document in a vast range of possible configurations. By using the key sequence **Ctrl-O L** or **Ctrl-O R** you will bring up a menu (below) which contains details of the existing margins. You can then change these to your new preferences.

The menu contains details of the margins (both sides and top and bottom), the page length, the offset, the current line spacing and the tabs. You can change any of these settings. As soon as you press **Enter** at the end the new parameters will be operable. It is important that you only change the settings with the cursor on a blank line of the editing screen. The new settings are shown through the use of *dot commands*; that is, a full stop followed by

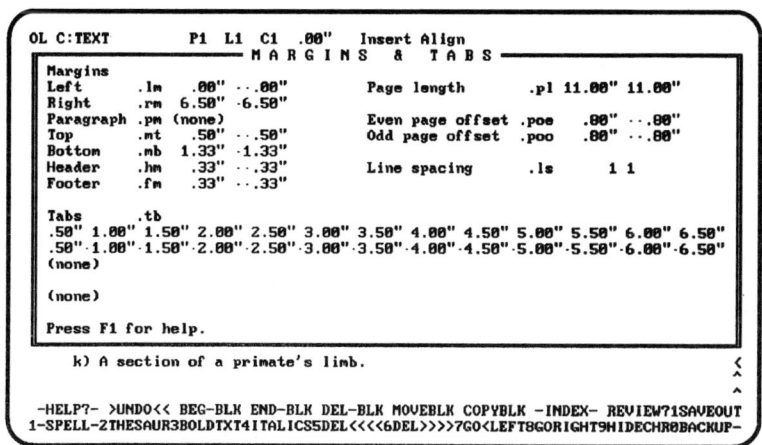

Setting margins

■ SECTION 50
Setting the margins and tabs

a pair of letters and a series of numbers will appear at the extreme left of the screen. These impose the new conditions but they do not actually occupy any lines in the document; they are purely control codes. Though they do appear to be occupying a line you can check that they do not by moving the cursor across them from the line above to the one below. You will find that the line number does not increase.

In the same way you can change the tabs by using **Ctrl-O I**, which brings up the same menu as above.

■ SECTION 51
Using the ruler

The default ruler appears at the top of the screen, immediately below the status line, and is fixed in position. If you are using an EGA or VGA monitor in extended line display – 43 or 50 lines – then the presence of the ruler really makes no difference because you still have more lines than normal. However, if you are using an ordinary CGA monitor the maximum number of lines you can display is 23. If you have the function key labels displayed you are effectively losing four of those lines, which means that your documents appear in very small parts. You can get round this problem by using **Ctrl-O T**, which will turn the ruler line off.

If you should need to have the ruler displayed within the text of the document, you can use **Ctrl-O O** to do so. Make sure you are on a blank line first though. The line will appear as a dot command (**.RR**), followed by the tab settings and the right-hand margin.

You can also call up any of the preset ruler lines – as you created them in WSCHANGE – by using **.rr** *n*, where *n* is in the range 0 to 9 and represents one of the rulers you created. You do not have to leave a space between the command and its value. However the command must be the first, and only, string on the line. This may cause problems if you use full stops within a document and they then become detached from their sentences. A period at the start of a line denotes a dot command and therefore you must be careful about using them.

■ SECTION 52
Indenting paragraphs

In order to make your text appear more presentable you will occasionally want to indent paragraphs or whole blocks of text. There are two basic ways of doing this. The first makes use of the key sequence **Ctrl-O G**. This will automatically indent a paragraph to the first tab marker. The indentation remains in operation until you press **Enter** to end the paragraph. If you want a bigger indent then use the key sequence as many times as necessary. The right-hand margin will not change using this command.

As an alternative to using the key sequence you can use the dot commands directly to set the margins. **.lm** *n* will set the left margin to the position denoted by *n*. This can be either a column number or a measurement in inches. Equally **.rm** *n* will set the right margin. The ruler will change to reflect the new settings and any characters typed thereafter will be indented to match. Their leading spaces will be filled with soft spaces (as illustrated in Section 53). The exact character will depend on what you set in WSCHANGE. To return to the original settings you must use the dot commands again and specify the default values: for example, **.lm0** for the left margin and **.rm65** for the right margin.

Justification

Normal typing (for example, on correspondence) is not justified. That is the right-hand edge is ragged. Books usually are justified, however. With WordStar you can easily do either by setting the justification in WSCHANGE or within a document by using the key sequence **Ctrl-O J**. This again is a toggle so that you may switch it on and off at will. When text is fully justified the spaces between the words are spread out using soft spaces to make the line fit exactly to the margins. You can turn the soft space display on and off by using **Ctrl-O B**.

```
   C:TEXT         P1  L19 C1  .00"   Insert Align          RgtJust
     L----!----!----!----!----!----!----!----!----!----!----!---R
 .oJ                                                              :
                                                                  <
 The answer to each of the following questions will give you a sum
 of  money in the old pre-decimal currency. When you add them  all
 up  you  should  have  a total  of  Thirty  One  Pounds,  Sixteen
 Shillings, Two and a Half Pence. (Remember that an old pound  had
 20 Shillings, each containing 12 Pence.)                          <
 .lm6                                                              :
                                                                  <
 ······a) An old form of transport.                               <
 ······b) Move up and down, in water perhaps.                     <
 ······c) Mars, Jupiter and Venus are .....                       <
 ······d) A type of Pig.                                          <
 ······e) Underwear for a one-legged woman.                       <
 ······f) A section of a regal head-dress.                        <
 ······g) An unwell decapod mollusc.                              <
 ······h) A stone.                                                <
 ······i) He turns skin into leather.                             <
 ······j) A type of singing voice.                                <
 ······k) A section of a primate's limb.                          <
                                                                  ^
 -HELP?- >UNDO<< BEG-BLK END-BLK DEL-BLK MOVEBLK COPYBLK -INDEX- REVIEW?1SAVEOUT
 1-SPELL-2THESAUR3BOLDTXT4ITALICS5DEL<<<<6DEL>>>>7GO<LEFT8GORIGHT9MIDECHR8BACKUP-
```

Soft space display

Normally the cursor will move across a line as you type it and when it reaches the right-hand edge it will automatically move down to the next line, taking with it any word that is too long to fit in the margin. However, you can turn this effect off by using **Ctrl-O W**. Now whenever the cursor reaches the right-hand edge the computer will beep but the text will continue along the same line.

■ SECTION 53
Justification

You can use another dot command to centre lines, usually for headings. **.oc on** will turn the centring process on whilst **.oc off** terminates it. Because the command is a toggle you must specify whether it is on or off. While the centring is in operation all lines will automatically be centred and any gaps will be filled with soft spaces. The left-hand edge of the screen will also bear the tab marker to show that the line is indented. Again the dot commands will not be printed, only their effects.

If the text you are writing is very short you may want it to be centred vertically (that is, appear in the middle of the page). To do so use the key sequence **Ctrl-O V**. The text will be filled with blank lines, from the cursor position to the start of the text.

Changing the line spacing within a document is equally simple. Usually you will be using single-line spacing, as text appears in a book, but you can change the value to anything you wish. For instance this book is being prepared in single line, because it is easier to write it that way, but once it is finished it will be double-line spaced before being printed. To change the spacing you can use either **Ctrl-O S**, which will bring up the menu shown above, or you can use a dot command. **.ls2** will give double-line spacing but the value can be anything between 1 and 9 providing it is a whole number.

Whenever you set a printing effect WordStar will display the effect using characters; for example, bold is shown by ^B, italics by ^Y. These characters do not actually occupy any space within the line but they appear to do so and so the actual text is pushed aside by them. Normally this does not matter but it can be irksome especially when the text is shoved beyond the margins. You can turn the print controls on and off by using the key sequence **Ctrl-O D**. With the characters off the text appears properly (that is, fitting between the margins).

SECTION 54
Seeing what you have done

One 'problem' that WordStar has is that it is not WYSIWYG. This acronym stands for 'What You See Is What You Get' and simply means that the text appears on screen as it will appear when printed. In order to be able to give you a WYSIWYG display the program would have to use the graphics mode rather than the standard text one. This would force the program to use more memory than is probably available because everything you type would have to be converted before being displayed.

However it is extremely advantageous to be able to see exactly what the text will look like. Prior to the release of WordStar 5 it was impossible to do so but this and later versions come complete with a sub-program called Page Preview. This can be used to generate a WYSIWYG display of the document, making the rest of the program memory resident in the mean time. To activate the program use the key sequence **Ctrl-O P**.

The screen will blank and you will then be presented with a white box, on the left-hand side of the screen, full of illegible characters! But at least it gives you an idea of how the text will appear when printed. However, Page Preview does much more than that. Across the top of the screen are four key phrases. To activate any of them just press the initial letter of the one you want.

■   **Go to** allows you to move to any page of the document that you wish. You may move quickly to the Previous, Next, First or Last page of the document. In addition you can go to any specified page. You will be asked to input the number of the page that you want – although the default is always the next one. The pages actually change very rapidly and you can scan through a complete document in a very short time.

■   **View** is used to change the display mode. The normal presentation is the entire page: that is, a proof of a single page reduced in size to fit on the screen, but you can display more than that. Pressing **F** will show you two pages side by side, whereas **M** gives you between four and ten pages at once, depending on the monitor – an EGA display is 8. **T** will display up to 21 pages on an EGA monitor, more on VGA, and is a good way of checking the overall presentation of the document. Using any of these modes you cannot see the actual characters, just blank smudges where the lines of text are.

However, you can examine an individual page, and the text it contains, by using **2** or **4**. The former gives you a view that is roughly 60% of the actual printed page, the full width of the screen and thirty lines deep, enough to see the major effects and read the text. The latter will blow up the page to approximately twice normal size. You can also use the + and - keys to change the magnification. When you are using these options you can quickly change the view of the page by using **A**, which allows you to specify what part of the page you will see; you can also use the standard cursor keys to move rapidly around the page.

■ **Options** is used to flick through the pages swiftly. **A** gives an automatic scan that flicks the pages past one by one, or two by two if you are using the facing page display. **S** allows you to specify a range to be scanned. **G** will provide a grid, only on single pages, marked in lines and columns, so that you can check the alignment of the text.

■ **Return to editing** does just that; it takes you back to the editing screen. However, you can select which page to go back to. **O** will return you to the original page: the one that was on screen when you first activated Page Preview. **C** will take you to the start of the page that is currently being

SECTION 54
Seeing what you have done

displayed by Page Preview. Alternatively, pressing **Esc** will return you to your original position.

■ **F1** provides exceedingly brief help. But then the program is so simple you don't really need any – after all it is only for looking at, not working with.

■SECTION 55
Another window

There are times when it is helpful, or necessary, to be able to work on two documents at the same time: for instance, when copying blocks of text from one to the other. WordStar will allow you to open a second window, which can contain the same document or another one. **Ctrl-O K** will either open a second window or move you back and forth between the two. **Ctrl-O M** allows you to vary the size of either of them; you specify the depth of the window in lines.

Once you have the second window open you can then move text back and forth between the two by marking a block in one, moving the cursor to the other and then using **Ctrl-K A**. The block of text will be deleted from the first window and placed in the second.

Alternatively, if you want to copy the block you use **Ctrl-K G** which allows you to have the same block in both. In either case the original marked block will remain marked. This is the only time that it is possible to have more than one block marked when using WordStar.

To close a window you simply save the text that it contains using **Ctrl-K X**. This will save the text and close the window. If you want to abandon the text use **Ctrl-K Q** to lose the text and close the window.

■ SECTION 56
Adding notes

In addition to creating ordinary text WordStar allows you to create and add footnotes and endnotes. The former are placed at the end of the page, while the latter appear at the end of the document.

To create a footnote use the key sequence **Ctrl-O N**. This will bring down another menu (see below). From here select **F** and a second window will appear at the base of the screen. It is here that you create the footnote. You may manipulate the text in all the ways that you would on the normal editing screen – except that you cannot run the Page Preview for obvious reasons.

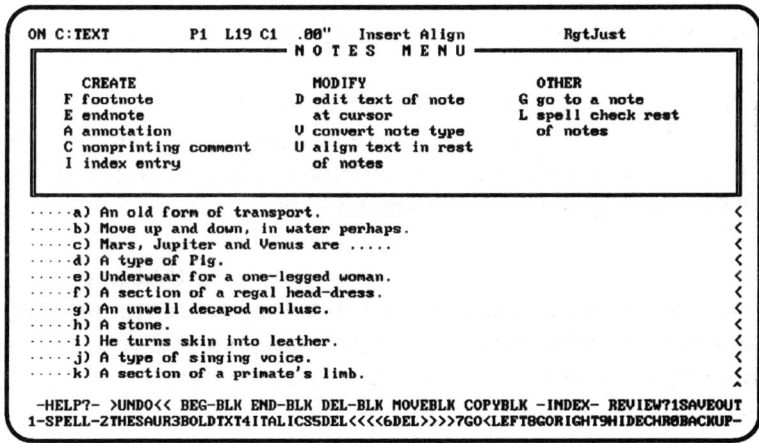

Notes Menu

Once you have finished writing the note use **Ctrl-K S** to cancel the note creation window and return to the editing screen. The note that you have just created will appear in the text in the same way as Bold does or, if you have the printing effects turned off, just as a number.

169

■ SECTION 56
Adding notes

As you add extra notes the numbers will be changed automatically. For example, if you have notes 1 to 7 and you add another note between 3 and 4 then all the notes after the new one will be renumbered in accordance with their position in the text.

To see how your footnotes will appear on the printed page use the Page Preview facility. The number of footnotes you can have is determined by the page size. Each note uses the amount of space that you specified in WSCHANGE and thus a large number of footnotes will use up all the available space. To remove any of the footnotes use the standard deletion keys.

Similarly, you can create annotations using a symbol of you choice – for example, an asterisk – by bringing up the menu (as above) and then pressing **A**. You will be prompted to specify which character you want to use and thereafter the creation of the notes is the same as above. Once you have saved the note the character appears at the cursor position in the main text.

C allows you to create a non-printing comment, that appears in the on-screen text but not on the Page Preview or the printout. Comments appear in the printing-effect format and can be deleted as normal.

You can modify any of the notes and/or comments that you have already created by moving the cursor to the one you want and then using the key sequence **Ctrl-O N D**. The second window will appear, to allow you to change the notes. Terminate it by using **Ctrl-K S** again.

If you find that you have created a footnote but it should have been a comment, or vice versa, there is no need for you to delete it and rewrite it. Pressing **Ctrl-O N V** allows you to change the note type: for example, footnote to endnote, comment to annotation.

■SECTION 56
Adding notes

The numbers used to mark the positions of the notes will be updated automatically again.

■ SECTION 57
Paragraph styles

The new ethos behind WordStar (from Version 5.5 onwards) is that it will allow you to produce documents, pages, even short pamphlets in much the same way as a DTP program. Whether this is needed, let alone whether it is possible using a purely character-based program, is for you to decide. Personally I find that PageMaker is a much better tool for doing such things because you can actually see the changes occurring as you do them without having to fiddle around with alternative displays. Be that as it may, WordStar now comes with some powerful tools that will allow you to format text in a host of different ways.

The one thing that WordStar always lacked was a quick and easy method of making lines of right-justified text; in fact in WordStar 5 it just isn't possible. However, in WordStar 6 it is now very simple indeed. Press **Ctrl-O]** and when you enter any new text the whole line will be right-justified. Unfortunately this only applies to one line at a time; you cannot right justify an entire paragraph – at least, not using this option.

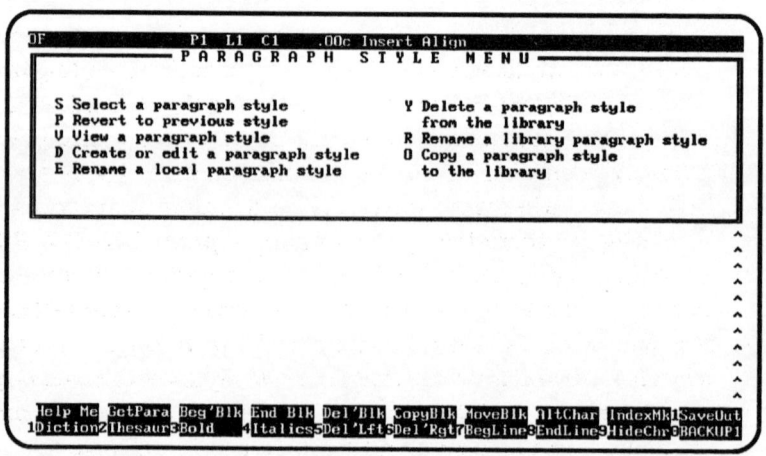

Paragraph Style Menu

■ SECTION 57
Paragraph styles

When you installed WordStar, and again as you ran WSCHANGE, you set the various basic parameters by which the program will operate: the page size, default font, tabs, etc. Each of these can be changed individually using the dot commands, or a number of parameters can be changed at the same time using the page format command **Ctrl-O L** or **Ctrl-O R**. However, to comply with the idea of making WordStar closer to a DTP program, something better is needed and that is where the **paragraph styles** come in. Pressing **Ctrl-O F** will pop up the main Paragraph menu (see above). From here you have a number of options:

■   **S** allows you to select one of the predefined styles, either one that was shipped with the program or one you created yourself.

■   **V** will let you examine, but not change, the settings for any of the paragraph styles.

■   **E** is used to rename a **local** style (see below).

■   **P** is a shortcut to switch between one style and a previous one. For example, you could have a style called Heading and another called Body Text, the latter being the default. At the start of the document you select the Heading style, using **Ctrl-O F S** and the cursor keys, and then enter the heading text. Now, rather than having to go through the process of selecting another style, you can simply press **Ctrl-O F P** to go back to the Body Text style. At any time thereafter, providing you have not used another style, pressing **Ctrl-O F P** will bring back the previous style. In this way you can switch back and forth between the two styles with ease. (Tip: use the macro facility to record this paragraph switch and then you can press **Esc** and a single key to activate it.)

■ SECTION 57
Paragraph styles

All the paragraph styles can be held in a file, called WSSTYLE, in the main WordStar directory. This is the **library**. There are two types of paragraph styles: **local**, which are specific to individual documents, and **library**, which are usable by all documents. Once you create a **local** style it cannot be removed other than by deleting all occurrences of that style within a document, saving the document and then re-opening it. Library styles, on the other hand, can be manipulated much more easily. From the Paragraph Styles menu you have three options that apply to the library.

■   **Y** lets you delete a style from the library. It then becomes a local style in any document that used it prior to its deletion. You can only delete styles one at a time; hence if you want to remove a number of them you have to press **Ctrl-O F Y** for each one.

■   **R** is used to rename individual styles. A paragraph style name can contain up to 24 characters, including blank spaces and those characters which are normally reserved by MS-DOS for its own use. If you rename a style that has been used already within a document then every occurrence of the old name remains in place as a local style.

■   **O** allows you to copy a local style to the library.

But how do you create a style? Answer: using **Ctrl-O F D**. This will pop up the Edit Paragraph Style menu.

Immediately below the menu is a list of the styles already created and stored as part of the library or as local styles. The cursor will be flashing in the Name box. If you press the **Down** key the cursor vanishes and a highlighter bar appears in this list of names. You can then use the cursor keys to select any of the existing styles. This is extremely useful because it means you can make minor

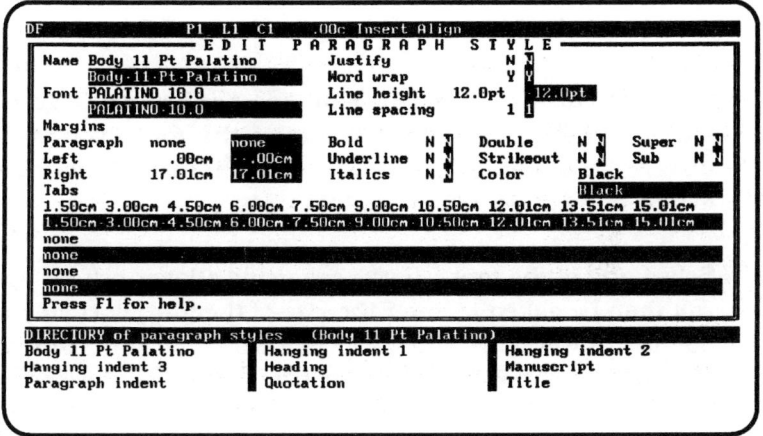

Editing the paragraph style

changes to a style and so create new styles, very easily. For instance, select the style called Heading, change its name to Heading 2 and alter it so that it is not underlined. You can also use the arrow keys to move around within the Edit Styles menu. (At the bottom of the menu it says 'Press F1 for help' but if you have reprogrammed the **F1** function key you must use whatever key now gives you Help. Thus if you are using **Shift-F1** to activate Help then you have to use this and not the **F1** key by itself.)

1 Having opened the menu you can now create a new paragraph style. While the cursor is still on the Name line, type the name Zebidee – or some other name that does not already exist. Providing you have not moved the cursor, whatever you type will automatically delete the previous name and replace it with the new name. Pressing **Enter** will move the cursor down to the next line. If you make a mistake *do not* press **Esc** because that will cancel the entire operation. Instead use the cursor keys and retype the name.

2 Once the cursor reaches the Font line, the list of paragraph styles will be replaced by a list of the fonts you have installed. The paragraph style is based on the printer driver for the current document and its fonts.

3 Select any of the fonts. If you are using a laser printer you will then be asked to enter the size of the font, normally in points. However, if you have changed the Font Unit of Measurement in WSCHANGE then it will be in whatever unit you have set. If you are using a dot matrix printer you will be asked to enter a size in terms of character pitch, i.e. characters per running inch. Pressing **Enter** accepts your choice.

4 The cursor now lies on the Paragraph line. This value does not apply to the paragraph though; rather, it means the first line of the paragraph. In other words, whatever measurement you enter here will be the amount that the first line of the paragraph is indented. You can indent the first line by as much or as little as you want but do not make it less than the measurement you will enter next, for the left margin.

5 **Left Margin** does apply to the whole text in the paragraph. Normally this will be 0; i.e. the paragraph will line up with the default margin of the page. Whatever measurement you enter here is the amount by which the entire paragraph will be shifted to the *right*. The value you enter here must be equal to or greater than the value you entered for the first line indent, above.

6   **Right Margin** is the opposite of the above; it allows you to move the right margin to the *left*.

7   **Tabs** are exactly what it says. By default this part will normally contain the values for those tabs that you have set in WSCHANGE. To delete any of them, move the cursor to one and then press **Del** or **Backspace** . If you start typing with the cursor at the beginning of the line – i.e. as soon as the cursor reaches this line – then all the existing tabs are deleted. If you press **Right** and then **Left**, so that the cursor moves one place to the right and then back to the beginning of the line, whatever you type is inserted before the existing tab settings. Press **Enter** three times to move on to the next field.

8   **Justify** determines how the text will appear. You have a choice of four types: **None**, which will produce a ragged edge at the right-hand margin; **Centre**, which causes the text to be centred between the margins; **Right**, which forces the text to align with the right-hand margin but leaves the beginning of the lines ragged; and **Yes**, which will force both margins to line up by inserting blank areas between the words. (This book is fully justified, for example.) Press the initial letter of the one you want.

9   **Word Wrap** can be either 'Yes' for on or 'No' for off. Again, just press the letter on the keyboard.

10   **Line Height** refers to the amount of space allowed for the characters. Going back to the days of lead characters for a minute, the size of a letter, in points, does not mean how tall the letter will be, as you might expect. The size always referred to the size of the little lead block that held the character. The character never covered the whole face of the block because if it did it would have touched those characters on the lines above and below it. Therefore the character, be it a letter or a number, had a space around it, called **white space**, so that when the letters were put together they would be easy to read without impinging on each other. All laser printers work on the same principle. The problem is that the amount of white space around the characters of a font depends on what the font designer allowed. Thus Times Roman 12-point is apparently much larger than Zapf Chancery 12-point, because the former has much less blank space around the individual characters.

WordStar allows you to set the line height to any size, though you shouldn't make it smaller than the font size you have selected for obvious reasons. You can enter any size you like or you can make the program handle the actual character size, rather than the block size, by entering **Auto** – which actually works the best.

11 **Line Spacing** is just that. The normal setting is 1 – single line spaced – but you can make it any value in the range 1 to 9. The number must be a single digit – you cannot have 1½ spacing as you can on a typewriter.

12 The next set of parameters are the printing effects: bold, italics, superscript etc. Each of these can be either on or off by pressing **Y**(es) or **N**(o).

13 Your final option is to set a colour, which seems odd when you consider that most printers are monochrome. If you are using a dot matrix printer then changing the colour will make no difference. However, if you are using a laser printer, especially a PostScript one, then by changing the colour you will produce grey scales: for example, **blue** gives a dark grey, **yellow** is almost invisible.

14 Once you have selected a colour, or simply pressed **Enter** at that point, a message pops up asking if you want to save the paragraph style to the library. If you do then it can be used in any document you open hereafter, at least until you delete it. Otherwise it becomes a local style and is only applicable to the current document.

The fundamental efficiency of any word processor is based, primarily, on its ability to take advantage of blocks of text and manipulate them in a variety of ways. WordStar possesses a large number of block-manipulation commands, some of which are unique to the program, and they are all accessed via the same menu (see below). Some of the commands available here seem strange at first glance – for instance the save routines – but this is actually the logical place to put them. After all, when you are saving a document to disk you are actually handling a large block of text.

```
K  C:TEXT          P1  L19 C1   .00"    Insert Align              RgtJust
                          ═ B L O C K  &  S A V E  M E N U ═
         SAVE                 BLOCK                FILE                    CURSOR
  D save  T save as    B begin block      C copy    O copy         0-9 set
  S save & resume      K end block        V move    E rename           marker
  X save & exit        H turn disp on     Y delete  J delete
  Q abandon changes    W write to disk    M math    P print            CASE
        WINDOW         ? word count       Z sort    L change drive/dir  " upper
  A copy between       N turn column mode on        R insert a file    ' lower
  G move between       I turn column replace on     F run a DOS command . sentence

 ·····a) An old form of transport.                                         <
 ·····b) Move up and down, in water perhaps.                               <
 ·····c) Mars, Jupiter and Venus are .....                                 <
 ·····d) A type of Pig.                                                     <
 ·····e) Underwear for a one-legged woman.                                 <
 ·····f) A section of a regal head-dress.                                  <
 ·····g) An unwell decapod mollusc.                                        <
 ·····h) A stone.                                                          <
 ·····i) He turns skin into leather.                                       <
 ·····j) A type of singing voice.                                          <
 ·····k) A section of a primate's limb.                                    ^
 -HELP?- >UNDO<< BEG-BLK END-BLK DEL-BLK MOVEBLK COPYBLK -INDEX- REVIEW?1SAVEOUT
 1-SPELL-2THESAUR3BOLDTXT4ITALICS5DEL<<<<6DEL>>>>7GO<LEFT8GORIGHT9HIDECHR0BACKUP-
```

Block and Save Menu

The menu contains six basic groupings of commands:

Save	Write the complete file to disk
Window	Used to move or copy blocks between documents

SECTION 58
Using blocks

Block   Manipulate blocks in various ways

File   Similar to the commands on the **Main Menu**

Cursor   Used to set text markers

Case   To adjust the type case within blocks

■ SECTION 59
Saving text

The commands available here apply to the entire document. They provide you with a number of ways in which you can keep the text that you have created.

■　**D** will save the document, to the same filename as it bore when you opened it, and return you to the Main Menu. If you have used Speed Write to open the file you will be prompted to supply a name for the document before it is saved. The directory that you then find yourself in will be the one that your were logged onto when you opened the file in the first place – unless you changed directory from within a document.

Note that the document will always be saved into the directory that it came from originally. Suppose you were originally in a directory called ALPHA and opened a document there, then changed directory to BETA from within the document – to load a block of text for instance. Now when you save the file it will be stored in the ALPHA directory – not BETA – but when you return to the Main Menu you will find that you are in the BETA directory. You can suddenly find that you have saved a file and it is not there; it is, but in the original directory.

■　**T** allows you to save the current document, regardless of its original name, to another filename. When you select this option your will be prompted to supply a name – the default will show the original name. Just enter the new name and the file will be saved. Again you will be returned to the Main Menu.

■　**S** makes an intermediate copy of the document; that is, it saves it as it stands and then returns to the editing screen to allow you to continue making changes. This is extremely useful and, as all experienced computer users know, it makes a lot of sense to make frequent backup copies of your work. If you have set the program to make backups, using WSCHANGE then the existing disk file will be renamed with the extension of .BAK and the current file will receive the original filename. As you make repeated backups this process continues – the old file becoming the backup and the current one being saved.

- **X** will save the file to the original filename and then terminate the program completely, returning you to the system prompt.

- **Q** discards the file; any and all changes, additions or corrections are abandoned, and you are returned to the Main Menu. Before the file is dumped you will be prompted with a message asking you if you do actually want to abandon the file.

■ SECTION 60
Manipulating blocks

Before you can begin to work with a block it must be marked. To denote the start of a block move the cursor to where it begins and then use the key sequence **Ctrl-K B**. The start-of-block marker (<B>) will appear at the cursor position, in inverse video, and the text will apparently be shunted to the right. Now move the cursor to where you want the end of the block to be and use the key sequence **Ctrl-K K**. The end-of-block marker (<K>) will appear and then vanish as the entire block is turned into inverse video. At this point the text on the line containing the start-of-block marker will move back to its original position. The block can now be manipulated. You can still move to the text with the block and make changes to it – just as you would if it were not marked.

You can turn the block display on and off using **Ctrl-K H**. If it is off then you cannot see the block or the markers – but they are still there. The only way that you can remove the block markers is to move the cursor to the position that they occupy and then apply the same marker again. Thus if you want to delete the start-of-block marker, move the cursor to the marker and then use **Ctrl-K B** again; this will obliterate the original marker. If it is a large block you can just use the key sequence twice at the current cursor position for each marker and the block operation will be cancelled.

To move a block from its original position to elsewhere within the document, move the cursor to where you want the block to be inserted and then use the key sequence **Ctrl-K V**. The block will be deleted from its original position, the surrounding text will flow to fill the gap, and the block will be moved to the cursor position. Again, the text around the cursor will flow to accommodate the block.

However, the reformatting does not always work as well as it might, particularly if the block is using a different format to that

184

■ SECTION 60
Manipulating blocks

used by the text at the new position, and so it may be necessary to manually realign it. Move the cursor to a position above where the block came from and then use the key sequence **Ctrl-Q U**. All the text from the cursor position to the end of the document will be realigned to the margins. If you just want to align the respective paragraphs, move the cursor to the beginning of each and then use **Ctrl-B**. This will realign the individual paragraphs – though **Ctrl-Q U** does it better!

Copying the block to elsewhere in the document is equally simple. Mark the block as above, then move the cursor to where you want the block to be copied to. The key sequence **Ctrl-K C** will then copy the block to the new position. Again, the surrounding text will flow to integrate the block. The original block will remain marked – in inverse video – thus allowing you to make repeated copies if you wish.

To delete a block from the document, mark it as above and then use the sequence **Ctrl-K Y**. The block will vanish into the unerase buffer. If the block is too large for the buffer to hold you will be prompted with a message telling you so and giving you the option of terminating the operation. If the buffer is large enough to hold the block then it can be restored at any time prior to the next deletion by using **Ctrl-U**.

If you are deleting blocks but are unsure about whether you will want them again then the best thing to do is to write them to the disk, where they will be held as normal files. Mark the block and then use the key sequence **Ctrl-K W**. You will be prompted to provide a name for the file block and, once you have supplied this, the block will be saved. You will return to the editing screen. The original block, in inverse video, remains in the document and you can now delete it safely.

■ SECTION 60
Manipulating blocks

To replace the block in the text thereafter use **Ctrl-K R**. Again, you will be prompted to supply the name of the block that you want to load, just as when you loaded the document in the first place. You can either enter the name or use the cursor keys to highlight the one that you want. You can also use this key sequence to combine documents together as the files are all capable of being loaded. However, beware of making the document too long or it will be unable to fit within the available memory. If this happens then part of the document will be stored in a temporary buffer on disk and the program will have to load it in chunks as you call for them. This very effectively slows down the operation of the program!

Finding out how many words you have written is not something that many people will want to do, although for a writer it is essential. WordStar provides a simple routine under the Block Menu that will allow you to count the number of words in a block or in the entire document. To find out the number of words in a block you must first mark it, as above, and then use the key sequence **Ctrl-K ?**. A message panel will appear at the top of the screen telling you the number of words and the number of bytes that the block contains. If you do not mark a block then the routine will give you the word count for the entire document. When it counts the number of words WordStar will use those characters that you have specified in WSCHANGE as parts of words to do the actual counting. This means that the extended graphics characters, for instance, are not counted. But, as a rough estimate of how many words the block or document contains, it beats having to count them manually!

■ SECTION 60
Manipulating blocks

Advanced block actions

All of the previously mentioned block operations are fairly stand-ard to most word processors but WordStar also has some relatively unique ones that have been developed for specialist applications.

Ctrl-K M will add all the numbers that are present within a given block and then give you the answer in a message panel. This can then be incorporated into the text by using **Esc =** or **Esc $**. Thus if you are using WordStar to produce invoices there is no need to use a calculator. Just write the invoice, mark out the block and add them up. This is faster than having to use a calculator – even WordStar's built-in one.

Many people use a word processor for creating files of related data that they ideally want to have in alphabetical order. You can create such a file and then move the individual entries around using the block-move facility. But there is a quick way. **Ctrl-K Z** will sort any block into either ascending or descending order, based on the initial letter of each line. For instance if this paragraph was rearranged in ascending order using this facility then the lines would appear as:

> any block into either ascending or descending order, based on the
> block-move facility. But there is a quick way. **Ctrl-K Z** will sort
> initial letter of each line. For instance if this paragraph was
> Many people use a word processor for creating files of related data
> rearranged in ascending order using this facility then the lines
> such a file and then move the individual entries around using the
> that they ideally want to have in alphabetical order. You can create
> would appear as:

Granted that this is a frivolous example but it does give an idea of the block sort ability.

■ SECTION 60
Manipulating blocks

As you become more proficient in using a word processor – a process that involves using the program rather than treating it as an electronic typewriter with extra abilities – you will find that you want to move blocks of text in columns instead of the normal blocks. Fortunately the creators of WordStar foresaw this and they have provided a simple toggle switch that allows you to do either. Mark out a block of text as normal and then use the key sequence **Ctrl-K N** and watch what happens.

The block is now marked according to the positions of the block markers and the right-hand edge lines up with the end-of-block marker. The block can be moved, copied and generally treated as an ordinary block. However, when you copy it to another position you will find that each line of the block is treated as if it ended with a carriage return and the extra spaces are filled with blank characters. Thus it cannot be realigned using **Ctrl-B** or **Ctrl-Q U**, even if you then turn the column mode off again. One other problem with using columns is that the end-of-block marker must be further to the right than the start-of-block marker – otherwise you will get an error message telling you that the end of block marker is before the start of block marker.

Normally whenever you move or copy a block of text to another position the existing text will be pushed aside to make room for it, even if you are in Overwrite mode. In order to have the text of the block overwrite the text in the target area you have to switch the column replace on using **Ctrl-K I**. Now whenever a block is copied or moved the text at the target position will be destroyed as the block is copied into it. Note that you cannot get this text back – it is not placed in the unerase buffer.

WordStar has a couple of other tricks it can perform with blocks, relating to changing the case of the letters they contain. If you mark a block and then use the key sequence **Ctrl-K "** the entire

SECTION 60
Manipulating blocks

block will be turned into upper case (capitals). Using **Ctrl-K '** does the opposite and turns the whole block into lower case. To turn the block back into standard sentences – the first letters of the sentence being capitals and the remainder being lower case – use **Ctrl-K.** . Note though that if you have 'i.e.' in the sentence then the 'i' will be raised to a capital, as will the first letter occurring after the full stop following the 'e'. This is because the letter 'i' by itself usually denotes the first person singular and if it is followed by a period then it must be by itself – hence WordStar makes it upper case. Equally, any letter occurring at the beginning of a word, immediately after a full stop, is treated the same way.

You can set non-block markers within the text using this menu: for example, because you want to go back to a particular point later using this menu. In total you can have a maximum of ten markers, denoted by the numerals 0 to 9, and they are placed by using the key sequence **Ctrl-K _n_**, where _n_ is the number of the marker. These markers are only present while you are working on the document; they are not saved with the rest of the file. So you cannot set them, save the file and then reload the file and expect to find the markers.

Equally, block markers themselves are lost when you save a file. If you have marked a block and then you write the document to disk, when you come to reopen it you will find that the block markers are not present – though the text they contained will be.

If you want to leave markers within the text you are better off using **Ctrl-O N** and leaving Annotations or Non-printing Comments in the text because they will be saved with it.

■ SECTION 61
File operations

In addition to running the various file commands from the Main Menu you can also access and use them from within a document – useful because it means that you don't have to stop working on the text each time you want to manipulate a file. The options available to you are:

■ **Ctrl-K O** allows you to make duplicates of files by copying any file in the directory to another one. You can specify a different directory for the copy.

■ **Ctrl-K E** will let you rename any file. Activating the command brings down a menu which will bear the name of the current file as the default but you can actually rename any file in the directory.

■ **Ctrl-K J** permits you to delete files from the current directory. This can be extremely useful if you find that your disk is reaching saturation point and there is no room for the file you are currently working on to be saved. You can use the MS-DOS wildcards to delete groups of files if you wish.

■ **Ctrl-K P** allows you to print any of the files in the directory, including the backup copy of the currently open file. When you access the command you will be asked if you want to just print a file or merge print one. Thereafter the process is the same as using the print option of the Main Menu.

■ **Ctrl-K L** enables you to change directory: for example, to load a document from a different directory so that you can incorporate it within the current file. Use the menu in the same way as you would when changing directory from the Main Menu.

■ SECTION 61
File operations

■   **Ctrl-K F** allows you to run an MS-DOS command, providing it is available on the PATH, and WordStar will become temporarily memory resident while you do so. You can make the program totally memory resident by entering **COMMAND** at this point as this will create an operating system shell. To restore WordStar you must then enter **EXIT** when you are ready. However, be cautious about using this because you will find that you have lost over 300 Kb of the available memory and so many programs will no longer operate. Also, beware of using programs that use overlays as you might cause a system crash.

In fact you can use any program or command that is available on the PATH by using this command string, not just MS-DOS commands.

■ SECTION 62
Making macros

WordStar will allow you to create a total of 36 macros – these are effectively shortcuts to producing various effects – in addition to those that are built-in. Each macro can contain up to 64 characters which may be text, ASCII characters, WordStar commands or key sequences.

To activate the macros press **Esc** within a document and a menu will pop down (see below). This shows the available commands and, below this, the macros already created. The built-in macros are:

■ = which will display the result of the last calculation that was carried out, either by the calculator or through using **Ctrl-K M**. The number will appear in the same format as it would on any electronic calculator.

■ $ gives the same result but in the format that you selected using WSCHANGE e.g. the thousands are separated by commas.

■ # will display the equation that was last used on the calculator, allowing you to enter it into the text of the document.

■ '@' enters today's date, again in the format you created using WSCHANGE.

■ ! enters the current time as held by the computer's memory.

To use any of these macros just press **Esc** and the symbol of the one that you want. The result will appear at the current cursor position on the editing screen.

Making macros

```
 C:TEXT          P1  L19 C1   .00"   Insert Align          RgtJust
                        SHORTHAND  MENU
 ? display and/or change definitions              F1 help

 = result from last ^QM or ^KM math              @ today's date
 $ formatted result from last ^QM or ^KM math    ! current time
 # last ^QM math equation

 1 Wordstar            2 Super Contact        5 SuperCalc
 9 Home and Align      A PC-Outline           C [Ctrl
 D document            E E-mail               K key sequence
 M Main Menu           N <number>             P See Part 5, Section
 Q Which word see      S Sincerely            T Transpose Word
 U Partition Line      W Word Count




 -HELP?- >UNDO<< BEG-BLK END-BLK DEL-BLK MOVEBLK COPYBLK -INDEX- REVIEW?1SAVEOUT
 1-SPELL-2THESAUR3BOLDTXT4ITALICS5DEL<<<<6DEL>>>>7GO<LEFT8GORIGHT9HIDECHR0BACKUP-
```

Macro Access Menu

Apart from those outlined above you can create your own shorthand by pressing **?**. This will bring down another menu and expand the definitions of the existing macros to show what they contain. To build the macro, decide which letter or number you will use – no distinction is made between upper and lower case letters – and press it. This will automatically activate the creation screen (below) onto which you enter first the key phrase and then the sequence of keys for the macro itself.

You can include any of the command sequence keystrokes that you want – for example, **^K ?** to perform a word count, **^M** to perform a carriage return – providing you remember that you must precede each one with **Ctrl-P**. Thus to input a carriage return you use the sequence **Ctrl-P M** and this will appear on the macro as **^M**.

What you use as macros is entirely up to you; they are specific to the individual user. As a guide it is well worth creating macros for

193

```
   C:TEXT          P1  L19 C1   .00"   Insert Align              RgtJust
                              ─ S H O R T H A N D ─
   Shorthand    S
   Description Sincerely
               Sincerely
   Definition  Yours sincerely,^M^M^M^M^M  Alan Balfe^M^M
               Yours·sincerely,^M^M^M^M^M··Alan·Balfe^M^M
   Press F1 for help.

 MENU & KEY DEFINITIONS    Bytes available: 48    ^W scroll up    ^Z scroll down
   1   Wordstar
       Wordstar
   2   Super Contact
       SUPER CONTACT
   5   SuperCalc
       SuperCalc 5
   9   Home and Align
       ^Q^R^Q^U
   A   PC-Outline
       PC-Outline
   C   [Ctrl
       [Ctrl

  -HELP?- >UNDO<< BEG-BLK END-BLK DEL-BLK MOVEBLK COPYBLK -INDEX- REVIEW?1SAVEOUT
  1-SPELL-2THESAUR3BOLDTXT4ITALICS5DEL<<<<6DEL>>>>7GO<LEFT8GORIGHT9HIDECHR8BACKUP-
```

Macro Creation Menu

repeatedly-used long sequences of key strokes. For instance, you could place your address in one, or two if necessary; or you could have a macro that will take the cursor to the top of the document and then realign it (^Q^R^Q^U). In fact you can build quite extensive sequences of commands and text into the macros and they are well worth experimenting with.

Type the string that you want and then press **Enter** at the end of the second field. You will be prompted with a message saying 'Store macro changes on disk (Y/N)'. Pressing **N** cancels your creation while **Y** will write the macro to the disk.

To delete a macro, first load it using **Esc ?** followed by the relevant character and then delete everything it contains. When the fields are empty press **Enter**. You will get a message and by answering **Y** the macro will be deleted.

SECTION 62
Making macros

If you find that you no longer have room for the macros you want to store – you are told how many bytes there are available on the creation menu – then you will have to increase the memory allocation using WSCHANGE.

PART FIVE

Printing effects

■ SECTION 63
Selecting a printer

When you installed the WordStar program in the first place, using WSCHANGE, you will have installed one or more printers and then selected one of these to be the default: the one that will be used most of the time and thus the one that is pre-selected whenever you create a document.

However, you do not have to use the default for every document. For instance, you may have a dot matrix which you will be using for your general documents but also have a laser which will be used for specialised letters and publicity material. Rather than having to run the installation program again and change the default WordStar will allow you to choose a printer from within the editing screen. This printer will then be the one for which the document is configured, so that if you decide to use another printer for it, after it has been composed, you will have to change the one assigned to it.

To select a printer directly from the editing screen use the key sequence **Ctrl-P ?**. This will pop down a menu allowing you to change the default. Either type in the name of one of the printers which are displayed below the input line or use the cursor keys to select one of them. Once you press **Enter** the printer you have chosen will be assigned to that document – as will its fonts and typefaces.

An important point to note is that the laser printers define their typefaces in terms of points – the height of the characters – whereas the other printers all differentiate the typefaces according to the pitch – the width of the characters.

You may select any printer which has been installed in WSCHANGE or PRCHANGE but, for obvious reasons, you can only have one printer assigned to one document. Therefore if you are combining two documents, using **Ctrl-K R**, the printer that was assigned to the first file loaded will also be applied automatically to the second file – within that new document. The original files will still bear their own assigned printers.

■ SECTION 64
Changing fonts

Most printers will come with a range of possible fonts, though the default drivers supplied with the WordStar program come complete with only one font. You will have selected one font to be the default and one to be the alternative for your printer in WSCHANGE but you can change this font within a document very easily. **Ctrl-P =** will pop down a menu (see below) from which you can select any of the available fonts, either by typing in the name of the one you want or by using the cursor keys to move the highlighter. The new font will become active at the current cursor position on the editing screen and is effectively a toggle. Providing you have the print controls turned on – you can check by using **Ctrl-O D** – you will be able to see where the new font begins.

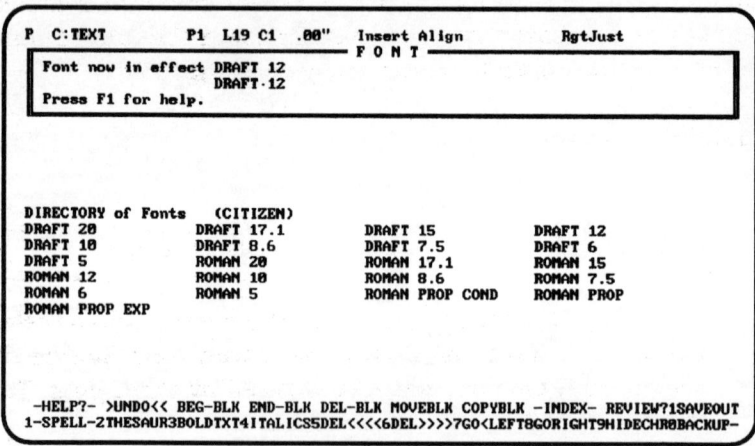

Selecting fonts on a Citizen HQP-40

Any text that you enter after selecting a new font will automatically be aligned to accommodate the new size. You can see the effect using the Page Preview, **Ctrl-O P**. You may change font as often as you like within a line or a complete document. To return to the default font you can either use **Ctrl-P =** and reselect the one you want, or you can use **Ctrl-P N**; the default will be shown in the text as **<NORMAL>**. To switch to the alternative use **Ctrl-P A** and the switch will be shown as **<ALTERNATIVE>**. At any time you can find out what font you are currently using by pressing **Ctrl-P =**, as the menu will show the current font by default.

If your printer is capable of printing in colour you can use the **Ctrl-P -** command to change the current colour that will be used. By default it is always black on white.

PostScript printers

Selecting fonts for a PostScript printer is very much the same but there is one big difference – you have to input the size yourself. How you do this depends on the way you change font.

Changing typeface

1 Press **Ctrl-P =** to bring up the Font Select menu.

2 Either type the font name or use the cursor keys to select the one you want and then press **Enter**. Note that on the screen each typeface name is followed by three dots. This tells you that it is a PostScript font.

3 Another box appears asking you to input the size, normally in points. To accept the default, which will be the size of the font you were previously using, just press **Enter**. To change the size simply enter the number of points. (You can use decimal numbers but on the whole you will be much better off using only whole numbers: e.g. 10-point instead of 10.2 point.)

4 Both menus vanish and you are returned to the page of the current document; the new font name and size appears in the text.

Changing size only

1 Open the font menu using **Ctrl-P =**.

2 Move the cursor, using the **Left** key, to the displayed size.

3 Press **Del** as many times as necessary to remove the current size.

4 Enter the new size and you will be back at the document with the new size showing in the text.

PostScript and WordStar

There is a major problem regarding the use of PostScript with WordStar. It has to do with the fact that WordStar is character-based. Normally the problem does not occur, if you are using nothing but text in standard paragraphs, but once you begin to use tabs you may encounter difficulties. What is on screen is nothing like what will appear on the printed page. You can go to a lot of trouble getting a layout looking good, on screen, but then when you print it out the text is all over the place and definitely does not look anything like the screen or even Page Preview.

The reason appears to be what can best be described as a hardware/software difference. The PostScript drivers in WordStar make a number of assumptions about the printer they are intended for. For example, it is assumed that if you install an Apple

LaserWriter then that is what you are using, even if you are using a printer that is merely an emulation of that printer. When WordStar sends the document to the printer it sends it on the basis of finding micro-justification, kerning, fonts, etc. that match the actual printer driver you have installed. But, because an emulation is never perfect, the printer may actually be using slightly different justification, kerning and fonts and this produces the error. (It's rather like driving someone else's car; very often you find that the indicators are in a different place. They are still there but not where you expect them to be.)

Another problem has to do with the Extended ASCII characters. WordStar will allow you to put these into any document, regardless of the printer you are using, even though that particular printer may be using a different set: for example, the Epson set instead of the IBM one. PostScript printers in particular are very finicky about any Extended ASCII characters and you may well

```
P                    P1  L1  C1    .00c  Insert Align
                              ┌──── F O N T ─────
 Font now in effect PALATINO 10.0
                    │PALATINO-10.0             │
 Press F1 for help.

DIRECTORY of Fonts   (STAR-PS)
AVANT GARDE ...   BOOKMAN ...      COURIER ...      HELV NARROW ...
HELVETICA ...     N CNTRY SCHL ... PALATINO ...     SYMBOL ...
TIMES ...         ZPF CHANCERY ... ZPF DINGBATS ...
```

The font directory

■ SECTION 64
Changing fonts

find that in place of the character you expected all you get is a question mark, at best.

A variation of the problem occurs with both Zapf Dingbats and Zapf Chancery. The Page Preview does not show these properly – in the case of the former it doesn't show them at all! The result is that what is on screen, either as text or in the Page Preview, is not what will be printed. You have been warned. WordStar, the company, are aware of these problems and they are looking into them.

■ SECTION 65
Printing effects

WordStar is capable of producing text with the usual word processor effects and all of these, which are toggles, are accessed by using **Ctrl-P** followed by one of the following letters. The appearance of the effects in the text will depend on the settings that you made in WSCHANGE.

■ **B** will start or stop the bold printing. The switch is a toggle and so you would use **Ctrl-P B** to begin the effect and then the same key sequence again to turn the effect off. You can embolden any typeface or font; however, it is a bit pointless if you have set Roman type or Letter Quality printing to then make it bold because it will wear the printer ribbon out.

■ **D** is double strike and produces an effect similar to bold above.

■ **S** turns on the underline mode. Whether the spaces are underlined or not will depend on the setting you made in WSCHANGE. You can also use this effect to produce a double line by entering a string of hyphens and then underlining them.

■ **T** activates the superscript. Any text entered after this switch will be printed above the standard lines and is usually used to produce the effect for mathematical expressions, e.g. $2*10^3$. If you are going to be using superscript then it improves the clarity of the printing if you also change the character that will be raised into a smaller font or you are likely to find that the character(s) will impinge on those on the line above.

■ **V** activates the subscript. Any characters entered thereafter will be printed below the standard line, e.g. H_2NO_4. Again it makes sense to reduce the size of the typeface being used when the subscript is in operation.

■ **X** toggles the strikeout. Any characters typed thereafter will be overprinted with the strikeout character that you set when you installed the program in the first place.

■ **Y** sets italics, i.e. slanting type.

In addition to these effects WordStar can produce a myriad of effects by using the dot commands.

■SECTION 66
Dot commands

The dot commands are a series of two-character commands, preceded by a period and followed by an operand where applicable. They must be the only thing on a given line but they do not actually take up any space on the printed page. Thus if you insert one directly after a paragraph and then begin the next paragraph on the following line it will appear on the screen that the two paragraphs are separated but when they are printed they will run one into the other. When using the dot commands it makes sense to check how the document will be printed by using the Page Preview facility to check it.

Some of the dot commands will duplicate the facilities available from the standard **Ctrl** key commands; which you use is entirely dependent on your personal choice. You can get brief on-line help about the commands by using the key sequence **Ctrl-J ..** This will present you with a series of message panels that detail the various commands and give a general outline of their effects. The big advantage to using the dot commands is the speed with which you can reformat a document or generate special effects. The commands are:

.aw   A toggle which has the same effect as **Ctrl-O W**; that is it turns the word wrap and auto-aligning on or off. To turn it on, place **.aw on** on a blank line. The period must be the first character for the command to operate. **.aw off** will turn the effect off again. Thus by using this command you can have parts of a document aligned and others not.

.bn *x*   This is used if you are using a printer which has multiple sheet feeders – for example, a laser – attached and you want to use one – other than the default. Specify a number (*x*) after the command for any one of the four possibles. For instance you might be using different coloured papers in each bin.

.bp A toggle switch used with daisywheel printers to turn the bidirectional printing on and off. Simply add the appropriate status to the command.

.cb x Specifies a column break when you are using column mode; see Part 8.

.cc x Will force a new column to begin if there are less than the specified number of lines available. The number is attached to the command, e.g. **.cc 3**.

.co x Used to create a number of columns. The value added to the command forces the printout to appear in that number of columns.

.co x,z Causes the number of columns specified by x to be printed side by side, z number of spaces apart. You can also specify z in terms of inches or decimals thereof.

.cp x Will start a new page if less than the specified number of lines remain on the current page. For instance if you are near the end of a page but want the new paragraph to begin on the next page, you can specify that the page must start there if there are insufficient lines for it to appear in its entirety on the current page.

.cs

When the printing is being done this command will clear the screen for embedded messages – the ones created by **.dm** (q.v.) – to appear instead of the standard printing information.

.cv 1>2

If you want to change the appearance of the notes within the text on the printout then you use this command. It forces the program to output the note of type *1*, e.g. a footnote, as a note of type *2*, e.g. an endnote.

.cw x

Allows you to change the width of the characters by specifying a value that is *x*/120 of an inch. By default the value is 12, thereby allowing 10 characters per inch – 10 pitch – unless you have specified other than this in the WSCHANGE program when you installed WordStar.

.dm <note>

The embedded message contained in <note> will appear on the screen while the document is being printed: for example, a reminder to change the paper. Usually used in conjunction with **.cs** (above) to clear the screen and **Ctrl-P C** to pause the printing.

.e# <number>

Provides a symbol, specified as the ASCII code <number> in the command, to be used by endnotes rather than the default. This can be any of the alphanumeric characters that you wish.

.fi <filename>

Allows you to insert a file, either from the current directory or from anywhere on the hard disk (if you include the full PATH) into a document for printing. The command can be used to chain files together and so have them printed one after another – which saves them having to be welded into a single, huge file.

.fn <note> Prints the contents of *<note>* on the footnote line specified by *n*. This is not necessarily a footnote *per se*, but rather a comment that you insert for some reason. *n* may be any number in the range 1 – 3, allowing you a total of three possible comments. There must not be a space between the f and the number.

```
    C:TEXT          P1  L1  C1          Insert Align          RgtJust
L----!----!----!----!----!----!----!----!----!----!----!----!---R
.oj                                                                      .
.op                                                                      .
.rm 60                                                                   .
.po                                                                      .
.oc on                                                                   .
.....................THE MONEY PUZZLE                                     <
.oc off                                                                  <
                                                                         <
The ·answer ·to each of the following questions will give you a ·sum ·of
money ·in ·the old pre-decimal currency. When you add them ·all ·up ·you
should ·have ·a total of Thirty One Pounds, Sixteen Shillings, Two and ·a
Half ·Pence. ·(Remember ·that ·an ·old ·pound ·had ·20 ·Shillings, ·each
containing 12 Pence.)                                                    <
.lm6                                                                     <
                                                                         <
·····a) An old form of transport.                                       <
·····b) Move up and down, in water perhaps.                             <
·····c) Mars, Jupiter and Venus are .....                              <
·····d) A type of Pig.                                                  <
·····e) Underwear for a one-legged woman.                              <
·····f) A section of a regal head-dress.                               <
 -HELP?- >UNDO<< BEG-BLK END-BLK DEL-BLK MOVEBLK COPYBLK -INDEX- REVIEW71SAVEOUT
1-SPELL-2THESAUR3BOLDTXT4ITALICS5DEL<<<<6DEL>>>>7GO<LEFT8GORIGHT9HIDECHR0BACKUP-
```

Example of dot commands

.fm <number> Forces the footnotes to be printed *<number>* of lines below the true text of the document. By default the value is 2 lines, or 0.33". You may specify *<number>* either as a number of lines or in inches.

.f*<number>* e   The footnote line specified by *<number>* will only appear on pages with even numbers.

.f*<number>* o   The footnote line specified by *<number>* will only appear on pages with odd numbers.

.f# *<number>*   Provides a key symbol for footnotes that is used within the text of a document in place of the default, similar to .e# *<number>* above.

.h*<number>* e   Header line specified by *<number>* will only appear on pages with even numbers.

.h*<number>* o   Header line specified by *<number>* will only appear on pages with odd numbers.

.h*<number>* *<note>*

Print the contents of *<note>* on the header line specified by *<number>* which may be any number in the range 1 – 3, allowing you a total of three possible comments. There must not be a space between the **h** and the number.

.hm *<number>*   Prints the header notes *<number>* of lines above the standard text. By default this value is 2 lines, or 0.33". Again the value may be stipulated in lines or inches.

.ig *<note>*   Show the contents of *<note>* as a non-printing comment when the printout is being produced.

.ix <*note*>   When a document is being indexed the comment that is specified in <*note*> will be used as the index entry. You are allowed a maximum of fifty characters in this string. This is usually used in conjunction with **Ctrl-P K** (see Section 67) as an adjunct to the actual index entry.

.kr   Allows you to turn automatic kerning on or off.

.la <*number*>   WordStar comes complete with an English Language dictionary but because the program is meant to be international you can also use foreign dictionaries. Use this dot command to tell WordStar which dictionary to use.

.lh <*value*>   This allows you to define the height of the lines in terms of $\frac{1}{48}$ths of an inch. By default the setting is 8, thereby allowing six lines per inch, but you may change this by inputting any whole number at <*value*>.

.lm <*number*>   Allows you to change the left margin from the default to anything you wish. <*number*> should be specified in either columns or inches. By default the left-hand margin is column 1. Using a dot command is much faster, and easier, than using the key sequence **Ctrl-O L** and it means that you do not have to interrupt the word flow. If you change the margins you should return them to their default values at the end of the document. This command is illustrated above.

.lq <*parameter*>

A three-way toggle that changes the printer

output type. The three parameters that you can specify are ON, OFF or DIS. This last is short for 'discretionary' and is used to produce letter quality printing if your printer is capable of doing so but you are unsure.

.ls <number>   Changes the line spacing. It is quicker and easier than using **Ctrl-O S** but has exactly the same effect. You may input any whole number between 1 and 9 at <number>. The default setting is set using WSCHANGE and will normally be 1. Using line spacing of 2 or more will cause some funny effects when you input typeface effects – for example, bold – so you are better off creating the document using single-line spacing, then changing to another value when you are finished.

.l# 0   Turns the line numbering off. Normally you would have turned this off in WSCHANGE but you can also do so within a document using this dot command.

.l# d<number> Turns on the continuous line numbering; the <number> is the line spacing to be used.

.l# d/p 1   Makes the line numbers single line spaced.

.l# d/p 1/2 <value>
Tells the program to put the line numbers <value> columns to the left of what is normally column 1.

.l# d/p 2   Makes the line numbers double line spaced.

■ SECTION 66
Dot commands

.l# p<*value*> Makes WordStar restart the line numbering on every new page. <*value*> is the line spacing that is to be used.

.mb <*value*> Defines the size of the bottom margin, possibly because you want to use extensive footnotes. You may specify <*value*> as either lines or inches. By default the bottom margin is 8 lines, or 1.33 inches.

.mt <*value*> Specifies the top margin by entering a whole number at <*value*>. Again this can be in lines or inches. By default the setting is 3 lines, or 0.5", but this can be changed in WSCHANGE or with this command.

.oc A toggle switch, either on or off, that forces all the lines typed thereafter to be centred within the currently-set margins (see the illustration above).

.oj Toggles the full right justification on or off. Using the command by itself – without specifying on or off – will set the justification but to cancel it you must use the command as **.oj off** (see above).

.op Normally every page will have the page number printed at the bottom, unless you turned it off when you installed the program. However you can turn the page numbers off from within a document by using this command. It has no parameters.

Dot commands

.pa

Sets a page break. Instead of you having to enter lots of blank lines to reach the next page, if you enter this command you will automatically get a new page. You cannot use this command on the first line of a new page.

.pc *<column>*

The page number is usually printed in the centre of the last line of the paper. However, you can specify that it is printed at whatever column you wish by entering the column number at *<column>*.

.pe

Forces the program to print the endnotes, which would normally appear at the end of the document, on the lines immediately after this command.

.pg

If you have changed the page numbers for some reason, you can reset them to the default using this command.

.pl *<size>*

Specifies the page length in terms of lines or inches. By default the setting is 66 lines, or 11 inches, though you may have changed this in WSCHANGE when you installed WordStar.

.pn *<number>*

Changes the page number to *<number>*, instead of the default. For instance, when producing the manuscript for this book I invariably write each section separately, to reduce the size of the disk files. Therefore each one is numbered consecutively using this command, so that when they are printed they follow in order.

■ SECTION 66
Dot commands

.po \<*column*\>   You may change the offset of the actual printed page by entering a value here (see above). The default is 8 columns, or whatever you set when you installed the program. You can also cause different pages to be offset by different amounts by using the command as **.po e \<*column*\>** or **.po o \<*column*\>** where 'e' and 'o' refer to the even and odd numbered pages.

.pr or=l   Switches the orientation of the printing so that it appears in landscape mode, i.e. the length of the paper becomes the width.

.pr or=p   Turn the printing into portrait mode – the normal default setting.

.ps   A toggle switch that controls the proportional spacing, either on or off.

.rm \<*column*\>   Sets the right margin to the value expressed in \<*column*\>. Much quicker than using **Ctrl-O R** but generating the same effect. Again this value may be columns or inches. The usual default is 65 columns, or 6.5 inches, though again you may have set this to something else using WSCHANGE.

.rp \<*number*\>   Rather than using the Print Control menu to print a document a number of times you can use this dot command. The \<*number*\> you enter will be the number of copies of the document that are printed.

.rr *\<number>*   A shortcut to allow you to use a prepared ruler line assigned the value of *\<number>*. Within WSCHANGE you can create up to nine separate ruler lines.

.sr *\<value>*   Allows you to change the default setting for the sub/superscript roll value. The normal default is $3/48$ of an inch.

.tb *\<values>*   Changes the tabs. You can use normal tabs, by simply entering a number, or decimal tabs, by preceding each number with a hash mark, e.g. **.tb 10 20 #30**. Each setting must be separated by a space. Alternatively you can set them in inches, e.g. **.tb 2" 3"**.

.tc *\<note>*   Used when you intend producing a table of contents – see Part Six – where the contents of *\<note>* is the table entry.

.uj *\<setting>*   A toggle switch that allows you to set the micro-justification. The settings can be ON, OFF or DIS.

.ul   A toggle that controls whether the underlining will apply to blank spaces between words or not. Enter ON or OFF as you wish.

.x *\<letter>*   Allows you to redefine the custom print characters **e**, **q**, **r** and **w**.

.xl   Redefines the form feed character.

.xx   Redefines the strikeout character.

■ SECTION 67
Creating an index

In order to create an index of a document you have a number of options. On the one hand you can index every single word. In this case you will get a very large index that you can then load into WordStar and change to suit your taste. If you select this option then you will be presented with a list (see below) of all the words that the document contains, followed, in each case, by the page number(s) on which that word occurs. However it is not very often that you will want to adopt this approach; more likely you will want to produce a selective index.

```
   C:TEXT.IDX      P1  L1  C1  .00"   Insert Align
L----!----!----!----!----!----!----!----!----!----!----!---R
·····Add, 1                                                    <
·····Answer, 1                                                 <
                                                              <
·····Containing, 1                                            <
·····Currency, 1                                              <
                                                              <
·····Decapod, 1                                               <
                                                              <
·····Following, 1                                             <
·····Form, 1                                                  <
                                                              <
·····Give, 1                                                  <
                                                              <
·····Half, 1                                                  <
·····Head-dress, 1                                            <
                                                              <
·····Jupiter, 1                                               <
                                                              <
·····Leather, 1                                               <
·····Limb, 1                                                  <
                                                              <
-HELP?- >UNDO<< BEG-BLK END-BLK DEL-BLK MOVEBLK COPYBLK -INDEX- REVIEW?1SAVEOUT
1-SPELL-2THESAUR3BOLDTXT4ITALICS5DEL<<<<6DEL>>>>7GO<LEFT8GORIGHT9HIDECHR0BACKUP-
```

Index sample

To generate a selective index involves two or three steps, depending on the kind of index you want to produce. First, you must go through the text of the document and decide which of the words and/or phrases you wish to use for the index entries. Each of these then has to be marked by using **Ctrl-K I** at both ends of the word or phrase. An index marker is just like the bold print marker; it applies to everything that occurs between a given pair. Thus if you were to set only the one marker the program would assume that the entire document was a single index entry!

The second step is optional but it allows you to add descriptive text to each of the indexed words, using a dot command. **.ix** *<text>* allows you to use up to a maximum of fifty characters; any additional characters will be ignored. Within the index string you may add cross references by the use of commas. For instance:

```
.ix Chapter 1, Part 8
```

will produce an index entry like this:

```
Chapter 1
  Part 8, 108
```

If you want the page numbers to appear in boldface then add a plus sign before the text of the entry. For example:

```
.ix + Chapter 1, Part 8
```

To omit the page number entirely from the index entry use a minus sign. For example:

```
.ix - Loading files, see Ctrl-K R
```

will create the index entry but not give a page number.

An alternative way to add index notes is to use the key sequence **Ctrl-O N I**. Again this allows you to add up to fifty characters for the index entry and the note you create will be embedded in the text. This may be better than using the dot command because you can place it exactly where you wish, whereas the dot command has to be on a blank line in the document.

■ SECTION 67
Creating an index

Having marked the words you want included, and added any remarks or notes you wish, save the document using **Ctrl-K D** to get back to the Main Menu. Once there, select **I** and a menu will pop down (see below). This provides the parameters by which the index is created.

The first line allows you to enter the file that you want indexed; by default this will be the last file you saved. Either accept the default or enter another filename using the keyboard or the cursor keys. The next option allows you to specify whether you wish to generate a global or a selective index. By selecting **Y** you will generate an index of every word in the file. Entering **N**, on the other hand, will produce a selective index only of those words you have specified and their related comments. Next you may enter a range of pages to be indexed; normally you will want to index the entire document so enter **A** here. Finally you may specify which pages within the range selected will be indexed: odd, even or all of them.

```
 I                         WordStar Professional
                          ────── I N D E X ──────
     File   TEXT
            TEXT

     Index every word   Y    Y
     Page numbers      All   A
     All/even/odd      All   A

     Press F1 for help.


 DIRECTORY of Drive C:\A1\HEINEMAN  5.4M free
 FIGURES          \     LETTERS          \     ..              \     APENDIX1.LS2 8.0k
 APENDIX2.LS2 19k      APENDIX4.LS2 1.4k      BOX           .5k     COPYRITE       .9k
 PICTURES    2.5k      TEXT         1.1k      TEXT.IDX      .9k     WORDS-TO.NOW 1.8k
 #1-DUN.LS2   24k      #2-DUN.LS2    92k      #3-DUN.LS2    19k     #4-DUN.LS2    79k
 #5-DUN.LS2   34k      #6-DUN.LS2    31k      #7-DUN.LS2    16k     #8-DUN.LS2    52k
 #9           .3k
```

Indexing menu

220

■SECTION 67
Creating an index

Again **A** is probably the one you want. Once you have set the parameters, pressing **Enter** will begin the index generation.

Once the process is complete you will find a new file in the directory with the extension **.IDX**: this is the index. You can now load it straight into WordStar to examine it or make changes.

SECTION 68
Creating a Table of Contents

Creating a Table of Contents is very similar to indexing a document, with the exception that you can only use dot commands. To input an entry for inclusion in the table you use the command **.tc** *<note>* #, where *<note>* contains the entry as you want it to appear, including any punctuation. You can include any form of indentation that you wish because normally the text for the entry will begin at the position shown by the < above. Thus to indent the text you could use:

```
.tc    Entry
```

in which case the entry will be indented by five columns. When inputting the text for the entry you can include any printing effects – such as boldface or a different font – but the entire entry must be on one line. There is no limit on the number of characters that you can include in the entry. (To check this I made this entire paragraph a Table of Contents entry.)

The hash mark at the end of the entry defines where the page number will appear when you generate the Table of Contents. It does not have to be at the end. When you create the table it will be replaced by the page number. If, at a later stage, you add additional text to the document, or renumber it, you will have to run the Table of Contents generation again, as described below, to reassign the numbers correctly. If you want to include a hash mark within the entry you must precede it with a backslash, i.e. '\#'. The backslash is ignored but the hash will be printed as is, not as the page number.

Having entered all the text that you wish in the document, save it using **Ctrl-K D** to return to the Main Menu. Now select **T** to generate the actual table. You will be presented with a menu similar to that used for creating an index. Having made your selection, pressing **Enter** will cause the Table of Contents to be

222

SECTION 68
Creating a Table of Contents

created. Once the process is complete you will find a new file in the directory with an extension of .TOC. You will probably have to load this and format it, especially if you have used long entries. In fact you can treat the file as a standard document and manipulate it as you wish.

There may be occasions when you want to produce multiple Tables of Contents: for example, one to give details of illustrations, one to give headings and another to give particular points. WordStar will allow you to create up to nine extra tables, besides the normal one, by using the command as .tc? <note> where the question mark is replaced by a number in the range 1 – 9. When you then generate the actual table you will find that the files for these extra lists will have the final 'C' of the normal suffix replaced with the digit that you have used: .TO1, .TO2, etc.

■ SECTION 69
Additional printing effects

So far we have discussed the fairly standard printing effects that can be obtained from WordStar, however the program is also capable of producing more specialised effects. They are all accessed from the **Ctrl-P** menu, by following the command with the relevant letter.

■ **C** causes the printer to pause when it reaches this command. It would normally be used to allow you to change the stationery being used: for example, individual envelopes or labels.

■ **F** prints a phantom space but this will depend on the character that your printer uses as ASCII code 32. In reality this applies only to daisywheel printers. The code will not need to be used for dot matrix or laser printers.

■ **G** is similar to **F** above; it produces a special character on daisywheel printers – normally a backspace – but this will depend on the printer. The code will not need to be used for dot matrix or laser printers.

■ **H** causes one character to overprint another; for example, to create a foreign accented character like ê. In essence the printer will take the second character and print it over the top of the character immediately preceding the command letter. You can only superimpose one character on another. Any additional characters on the line are all moved left by one space to fill the line properly.

■ **I** moves the cursor eight columns to the right: in effect, an adjunct to the normal tabs.

■ **O** prints a binding space. This will be used where it is important to keep two words together – e.g. Silver Nitrate –

which might otherwise be printed on separate lines. In order to keep them together use this command in place of the standard space created by the spacebar.

■   . moves the cursor to the next tab stop and fills the intervening spaces with full stops.

■   * is a graphics tag which is used in conjunction with a program called *Inset*. This was supplied with *WordStar 2000* and all releases of WordStar 5.5 or greater. If you have a copy of WordStar with an earlier release number than this then you will be unable to use the facility. *Inset* is a special screen capture program that generates files with the suffix .PIX that can then be included into a standard WordStar document.

In addition to these, WordStar will allow you to create up to four customised print controls using the letters **Q, W, E** and **R**. These can be used to define effects that are specific to your printer, such as double-height characters. Then, whenever you want the effect to apply to the text in a document, you use the key sequence **Ctrl-P Q** (or whichever letter you have defined). The definitions are entered in WSCHANGE.

■ SECTION 70
Columns

WordStar will allow you to produce a printed output in the form of columns, rather than as standard text. You could generate such an output by changing the left and right margins but this would only allow you one column per page. However, WordStar can actually produce true newspaper-type columns and produce as many columns per page as you wish.

To create newspaper-style columns enter **.co** <*number*> on a blank line. The <*number*> tells the program how many columns you want to use. You can also specify how far apart the columns will be by using **.co** <*number*>,<*number*> where the first number refers to the number of columns and the second is the displacement factor. For example, **.co 3,2** will produce three columns separated by two spaces.

Each column will be as wide as the currently set ruler line and also uses the tabulations that are in operation. Therefore you will have to change the right-hand margin as well, using **.rm** <*number*>, otherwise you will get no effect. Once you input the column command the left-hand side of the screen will be highlighted with the column symbol, ASCII code 240. WordStar cannot show the columns on screen as they will appear on paper; to view what you have done you will have to use the Page Preview facility, **Ctrl-O P**, or else wait until you print the document.

As you fill the page, the length does not normally change unless you adjust it. The text will appear to fit within the margins you have set and as it reaches the end WordStar will automatically insert a column break, so that the next page – actually column – will be placed correctly. The column break will appear on screen as a twin line, the normal page break being a single line, and the left hand margin will contain twin column marks. Once you have filled the last defined column on the page WordStar will then begin a new page.

■SECTION 70
Columns

Once the columns are set the program will handle them automatically; for instance, entering additional text cause them to flow to their correct positions. The column and page breaks will adjust to fit the additional text.

If you wish to start a new column before the end of the page use the dot command **.cb**, which forces a column break. This will not be changed as you enter new text. To cancel the column production enter the command **.co** on a new page and reset the margins and tabs to what they were originally. When you are using column mode any footnotes that the text contains will automatically become endnotes.

Using the column mode takes a bit of practice but once you have mastered the commands it can give you an added format for your documents. Getting the settings for the spacing between the columns is probably the hardest element; this depends largely on the number of columns you wish to use. However, don't forget to change the margins or you will find that you don't have any columns at all. To generate true newspaper-style columns you should also turn the right justification on.

PART SIX

MailList

■ SECTION 71
What is it?

MailList is one of the two sub-programs that WordStar Professional Versions 5 onwards come complete with; the other is TelMerge which is covered in Part 7. Essentially the program is a pre-formatted database that can be used to store names and addresses or inventory items. Either of these, or parts of them, can then be included in other documents using the linking characters.

To run the MailList program select **A** from the Main Menu and then **M** to activate the program. If you are logged onto the main WordStar directory then the program will load immediately. However, if you are logged onto another directory you will get a message saying 'Can't find WSLIST.DTA on current drive'. The file WSLIST.DTA is the default database file that the program uses whenever it is selected; it must exist in the current directory. However, if it is not present then the program will create the file automatically and then the Main Menu of MailList will appear.

```
FORM:C:WSLIST          M A I L L I S T   M E N U          C:WSLIST.DTA
 ┌──────────────────────────────────────────────────────┬───────────┐
 │  Choose a data file      Locate records by number     │  F1  Help │
 │  Add new records         Sort records                 │    Quit   │
 │  View and edit records   Use another form             │           │
 └──────────────────────────────────────────────────────┴───────────┘
               Press a highlighted letter.
```

MailList Main Menu

Even if you have other files which have been created by the MailList program you must have WSLIST.DTA in the directory for the program to load!

Just as with the WordStar Main Menu you select the option you want by pressing the appropriate letter. In theory the program will provide on-line help; however, you can only get this if you are in the directory that contains the help overlays – usually the Word-Star directory.

■   'Choose a data file' allows you to select a file other than WSLIST.DTA either by entering the name or using the cursor keys, in the same way as you would load a document into WordStar itself. If you enter a non-existent filename then the program will create a new file with that name – you will not be prompted before this creation takes place.

■   'Add new records' is used to do just that. It increases the size of the database once a file has been loaded.

■   'View or Edit records' will permit you to scan through the existing records and make changes to them if you wish, but you cannot add extra records using this option.

■   'Locate records by number': you can find a particular record if you know the number of it in the first place; if you don't then there is no point in selecting this option.

■   'Sort records' rearranges the order in which the records are presented.

■   'Use another form' allows you to discard the standard address form and load a new one – providing it exists.

■ SECTION 71
What is it?

MailList is not the most user-friendly program you will ever come across but if you allow for its foibles then it can be extremely useful and even powerful.

■ SECTION 72
Adding records

A database is a file that contains a number of records; for instance, a card index is a database. Each record is a single entry form that contains a number of fields, which in turn contain the characters. Thus a database can include anything from one record containing a single field (though it would be a bit unusual) to thousands of records containing hundreds of fields, such as the national census returns.

In the case of MailList you may include as many records as your disk space will allow but each one will contain 24 user fields, whether they are filled in or not, plus a number of system fields. The address record is intended primarily for business users, as you can see from the layout of the form.

```
FORM:C:WSLIST        A D D   N E W   R E C O R D S        C:WSLIST.DTA

 ┌──────────────────────────────────────────────────────┬──────────┐
 │ ^Copy from previous record    ^Write/save record in file │ F1   Help │
 │                                                        │          │
 │                                                        │  Escape  │
 └──────────────────────────────────────────────────────┴──────────┘
                    Type data and press ─┘.


        Record Number: 00000

First, Initial, Last: _____ _ _ _____      Mr/Ms: _____
               Title: _____
             Company: _____
      Address Line 1: _____
      Address Line 2: _____
  Town, Cty, Post Code: _____ _____ _____
             Country: _____
           Telephone: _____  Date:00/00/00   type date as dd/mm/yy

      User Fields—  Remarks—
   1: _____  _____
   2: _____  _____
   3: _____  _____
```

Adding records

At the left-hand side of the top line it tells you which form you are using: in this case WSLIST, the address form. On the right is the name of the actual file you are using: for example, WSLIST.DTA.

Adding records

Immediately below this is a panel containing two control codes; ^C will allow you to copy the details from a previous record into this record, while ^W writes the changes to the disk file. To terminate the data entry press **Esc**.

The bulk of the screen is used to contain the record form itself and is divided into three main sections, plus the record number.

Enter the record number. If this is the first record in the database, the program will automatically number any additional records. The next six fields are to do with a person's identity. The first contains the person's Forename and allows you up to eleven characters; the next two are the middle Initials; and the fourth is for the Surname, allowing a maximum of fourteen characters. (The fact that there are two middle initials shows that MailList is an Anglicised version of an American program.) The next field is for the Salutation, twelve characters, and then finally the Title of the person concerned, using a maximum of thirty characters.

The next field, entitled Company, allows you to enter up to forty characters, as do the two address lines. The following two fields, Town and County, will accept a maximum of fifteen characters, while Post Code can only accept eight – this should be sufficient for most places within the U.K. The Country field will allow thirty characters, ample for most countries in the world. Telephone accepts up to sixteen, more than ample for most U.K. telephone numbers but you may have problems if you want to include International Dialling codes. The Date is entered in the standard U.K. date format.

The final six fields, divided into two groups of three that accept twelve and 59 characters each, are intended to be used for general notes about the person concerned. One minor quibble about the way they are presented is that you move through the short fields first and then start at the top of the large fields. One feels that you should have been able to go across the page rather than down and then up again.

When you have entered onto a record all the details that you wish, pressing **Ctrl-W** will write it to the database and automatically bring up the next record ready to accept your input.

A point to note about entering records is that you should not include commas at the end of the fields because when you come to mailmerge a document with the database entries later you will separate the fields yourself. If you include commas here you can easily end up with a mistake on the form letter.

To move to the next field simply press **Enter** or use the **Right** arrow key. However, to go back to a previous field you cannot just use the cursor keys. MailList uses special control keys to move through the fields.

■ **Ctrl-A** moves you to the beginning of the current field or, if you are there already, it will move you up to the previous field.

■ **Ctrl-D** shifts the cursor right one character, or you can use the **Right** arrow key in this case.

■ **Ctrl-F** moves you to the next field.

■ **Ctrl-L** or **End** will move the cursor to the beginning of the final field on the record.

■ **Ctrl-S** moves you one character to the left, or you can use the **Left** cursor key.

SECTION 72
Adding records

■ **Ctrl-T** or **Home** will move you to the start of the first field on the record.

■ SECTION 73
Sorting records

Records are usually held in the database in the order in which they were entered originally but when you come to View or mailmerge them this might not be the most appropriate. Therefore the MailList will allow you to sort the records in any order that you desire by using one or more of the fields as the sorting key. Once they are sorted the records remain in that order until you sort them again, and any new records will be appended to the end of the file. You cannot use this facility if the database does not contain records.

```
SORT ORDER RECORDNO      S O R T   R E C O R D S        C:WSLIST.DTA
  ┌─────────────────────────────────────────────────────────────┬──────────┐
  │ ^Erase order         ^Use this order                         │ F1   Help│
  │ ^Key field           Ascend/Descend                          │          │
  │ ^Save sort order     ^Choose/Create sort order               │  Escape  │
  └─────────────────────────────────────────────────────────────┴──────────┘
                   Press a highlighted letter or number.

         Record Number: 1111A  *****************************

 First, Initial, Last: ************ *** **************  Mr/Ms: ************
                Title: ****************************

              Company: *******************************************
       Address Line 1: *******************************************
       Address Line 2: *******************************************
 Town, Cty, Post Code: ****************** ************** ********
              Country: *****************************
            Telephone: ***************** Date:********    type date as dd/mm/yy

       User Fields—  Remarks—
    1: **************    *******************************************************
    2: **************    *******************************************************
    3: **************    *******************************************************
       system fields: [*][***********][************][************] YY/MM/DD[*******]
```

Sorting records

Select **S** from the Main Menu and you will be presented with a screen as shown above. The default sort order uses the record numbers that were automatically assigned to the records as you entered them. Records will always retain the number they were assigned – hence the ability to find a record by number. If you want to sort the records on a different basis you must create a new sort order first. Press **Ctrl-C** and a list of the available sort

■ SECTION 73
Sorting records

orders will appear. The first time you run the program there only will be one order available – **RECORDNO**, the default. However you can enter a name for the new order, using up to eight characters, as you would for naming a file. Pressing **Enter** will then take you back to the sorting screen, the only difference being that every field will contains asterisks.

The sort order you select can be embedded; that is to say that you can sort on a *primary field* and then have the order dependent on subsequent fields. All told you may use up to nine separate fields for this operation. Move the cursor to the primary field – the main one that you want to use for the sort – using **Ctrl-A** or **Ctrl-F**. When you reach the field press **Ctrl-K** and the asterisks will be replaced by a string of 1's; the last character will be an 'A'. The letter denotes that the sort order will be ascending – i.e. ABC123 – but if you would prefer the order to be reversed – i.e. ZYX987 – then press **D** for descending.

Having selected the primary field you may now move on to select the dependent fields. The program will allow you to use a maximum of nine fields for a sort order – though you don't have to use them all. Once you have finished selecting fields, pressing **Ctrl-S** will save the sort order to the filename that you input. When that is complete, pressing **Ctrl-U** will sort the database. If you decide that you don't actually want to use the order you have created you must press **Ctrl-E** to erase the sort order – before you have saved it – and then start again.

MailList comes complete with two pre-designed forms for you to use. The first is the address form shown in Section 72, while the second is an inventory form (see below). You may use either of these to build a database. The inventory form is intended to be used as the basis for a simple stock control exercise – though it is not comprehensive enough to be used solely for this purpose.

```
FORM:C:INVNTORY        A D D   N E W   R E C O R D S        C:INVNTORY.DTA
 ┌────────────────────────────────────────────────────────┬──────────────┐
 │  ^Copy from previous record    ^Write/save record in file│ F1   Help   │
 │                                                          │     Escape   │
 └────────────────────────────────────────────────────────┴──────────────┘
                        Type data and press ─┘.

    Record Number: 00000                        Date: 00/00/00  dd/mm/yy
    Item: _____     Code: _____ Status: _____
 Description: _____
              _____
              _____

        Account: _____  _____  _____
       Quantity: _____  _____  _____
          Price: _____  _____  _____
 User Fields─                      Remarks─
          1: _____     _____
          2: _____     _____
          3: _____     _____
```

Inventory form

To use the form, select MailList from the WordStar Main Menu and, once the menu appears, press **U**. You will be asked to select a form definition file from those available in the current directory. Because MailList uses the address form by default it is capable of creating the form definition, ADDRESS.DEF, that it needs. Therefore this file does not have to be in the directory you are logged onto. But in order to use the inventory form you must have the definition for it in the current directory. If, as I usually do, you are logged onto a directory other than the WordStar directory the definition will not be available and so you will be unable to load it. This is a major problem with the MailList program! In order to load the new form you must exit MailList back to the WordStar Main Menu, then log onto the WordStar directory before re-activating MailList and loading the definition file. Alternatively you must use the MS-DOS COPY command to copy the definition file, called INVNTORY.DEF, to the directory in which you want to work.

Once you have copied the definition you can then activate MailList again and load the Inventory file by using **Ctrl-U**. Select the new form and then you will be asked to input a filename for the new database; again, if the filename you input does not exist it will be created automatically for you.

As with the address form, each record in the inventory has a unique number. The form is divided into five parts. The first three fields – Item, Code and Status – can all contain up to fifteen characters and follow one after the other. The next field, Description, occupies three lines and can hold a maximum of 189 characters. The following group of fields is concerned with the Account, Quantity and Price and you have three groups of three. Each of the individual fields here can hold up to fifteen characters. When you put something into the Account field and move to the Quantity you will find that you are at the end of the field; the same thing happens with Price. This is because the Quantity and Price fields are right justified and as you enter characters they appear to the left of the cursor. The final group of fields are the User fields which are identical to those on the address form.

To move through the form you use the same key combinations as on the address form. Once you have at least one record you can then create a sort order in the same way as with the other form.

■ SECTION 75
Combining MailList with WordStar

The advantage of MailList, ignoring its foibles and quirks, is that you can use it in conjunction with WordStar to create form letters – quickly, easily and without having to mess around with importing additional files. However, the initial process of creating the layout for a form letter is such that it is well worth creating a special file, which can be saved as a block, and then loading this every time that you create a new form letter.

A form letter must contain the details of the data file that you will be using and you must specify every single field it contains – otherwise it won't work! So to create the basic block file do the following:

1 Open a standard document file on WordStar using Speed Write.

2 On the first line enter **.df** *<filename>*. The dot command tells WordStar the name of the database file that you will be using and it must be included. You can include the full path of the database if it is in another directory. For example:

.df C:\WS\address.dta

3 Use the dot command **.rv** to name each field in the data file, using as many lines as necessary. The first field must be an 'x', which represents the Date field, and thereafter you must include every single field, in the order that they occur, even if you will not be using all of them in the letter. If you do not include the 'x' then the results will not be what you expected.

```
    C:FORMMAIL      P1   L12  C59  4.83"   Insert Align
L----?----?----?----?----?----?----?----?----?----?----?----?---R
.op
.ls1
.df wslist.dta
.rv x,number,full-name,first,mi,last,Mr-Mrs,Title,Company,Addr 1
.rv Addr 2,Town,Cty,Post Code,Country,Telephone,Date
.rv User1,Remark1,User2,Remark2,User3,Remark3

&full-name&,
&Addr 1&,
&Addr 2&,
&Town&,
&Cty& &Post Code&

Dear &Mr-Mrs& &last&,

As you may know we at AlphaCorp have established a reputation for producing
high-quality, durable PC's. Now &first&, we would like to bring our new range
of 80286 and 80386 based AT-compatibles to your attention.

 -HELP?- >UNDO<< BEG-BLK END-BLK DEL-BLK MOVEBLK COPYBLK -INDEX- REVIEW?1SAVEOUT
1-SPELL-2THESAUR3BOLDTXT4ITALICS5DEL<<<<6DEL>>>>7GO<LEFT8GORIGHT9HIDECHR0BACKUP-
```

Form letter parameters

If you want to omit the page numbers from the letter you should also include the dot command **.op**. The example below uses the address form.

Once this is completed move the cursor to the top of the document and use **Ctrl-K B** to set the start-of-block marker. Move to the end of the text, preferably onto a blank line, and use **Ctrl-K K** to set the end-of-block marker. Finally, use the key sequence **Ctrl-K W** to write the block to your disk using a filename of your choice that should reflect what this is. Then use the key sequence **Ctrl-K Q** to abandon the document.

Having created the parameters file you can now design the actual form letter. Open a document file, using either **D** or **S**, and then load the block you have saved into it using **Ctrl-K R**. You can now create the heading for your letter. Each field that you want to include must be enclosed in ampersands (&) but they can be joined any way that you wish. See the illustration above for an example.

Once the heading is complete, simply enter the text of the letter. Don't forget to end it with the **.pa** dot command so that each letter is printed on a new sheet of paper. If you omit this command the next letter will start where the first one ends! Once the letter is completed return to the Main Menu.

■ SECTION 76
Mailmerge conditional statements

In order to print out a form letter you must use **M** ('Merge print a file') from the Main Menu. This will bring up a menu identical to the one used by the normal print command, only this one is capable of reading and combining two files into one document.

Mailmerge will work with files other than those produced by MailList, and also contains a semi-programming language that allows ultra-fine control. However, to use these facilities you must use additional dot commands in the definition file. The commands are:

.av <*note*>   Halts the printout whilst it displays the text contained in <*note*> and asks you to input a string. For instance **.av NUMBER** will pause the printing and display **NUMBER?** on the screen. Once you have input the answer the string that you entered will be used at every occurrence of &NUMBER& in the document being printed until you change it again. In essence this allows you to totally customise your form letters but it means that you must be on hand during the printing to supply the necessary information.

.df <filename> Uses data from named file for merge printing.

.ei   Indicates the end of a conditional print statement. This is used in conjunction with **.if** (see below). Abbreviation for 'End If'.

.el   Short for Else. Used in conjunction with **.if** (see below) to perform conditional responses.

.go bottom   Halts the printing and skips to the bottom of the document.

.go top   Halts the printing and returns to the beginning of the document to start again.

.if *<condition>*

This is the basis of the conditional printing statements and works in much the same way as the IF statement in BASIC. This command has a host of operands that affect how it operates. These are:

=   Is identical to; i.e. has the same meaning. For example:

> `.if &name& = Smith`

will cause a true statement if the variable &name&, either from the file or from an input, is Smith; thus printing will continue. Generally speaking an **.if** statement will be followed by an **.el** statement so that the two combined can produce different effects.

<   Checks that the first string comes before the second string, alphabetically, and then returns either a true or false statement depending on the result of the test. For instance:

> `.if &name& < Smith`

will return a true statement if the &name& is Smedley, but a false statement if the &name& is Smithson.

245

> Checks that the first string is alphabetically superior to the second string, then returns either true or false depending on the result. For example:

    `.if &name& > Smith`

is true if &name& is Smithson but it is false if &name& is Smedley.

<= If the second string is inferior or identical to the second string then the statement is true. For example:

    `.if &name& <= Smith`

is true if the &name& is Smedley but false if the &name& is Smithson.

>= When the second string is superior or identical to the first string then the statement is true. For example:

    `.if &name& >= Smith`

is true for Smithson but false for Smedley.

<> Examines the two strings and returns a true statement if they are dissimilar. For example:

    `.if &name& <> Smith`

is true for all &name& strings other then Smith.

To check the strings numerically then each operand must be preceded by a hash mark (#), as in:

`.if &number& #= 12`

An important point to bear in mind when using these operands is the way that they work. WordStar ignores any leading spaces for alphabetical comparisons and also ignores any letters for numerical ones. Thus 'Alan Balfe' is identical to '   Alan Balfe' (ignoring the spaces) and '123' is a perfect match for 'A1BC2DE3' because the letters are ignored.

.ma *<variable>* = *<equation>*

Allows you to perform a calculation, written in the same way as you would input it on a calculator, and then store the result in a variable that will be used in the printout. However you can also use the names of fields within the document in the calculation.

For example:

`.ma total = &price& * 1.15`

will take the value expressed in the field &price& and multiply by 1.15, to produce a VAT–inclusive amount, and then store the result in **total**. Thereafter, whenever the program has to print this variable name it will perform the calculation, giving each page a different amount if necessary.

.pf
This is a toggle switch that is used to align the numerical amounts in the variables. The toggle can be ON, OFF or DIScretionary. You simply specify which one you want.

.rv <*variables*>
The list of variables' names – fields – that will be used within the document. You must specify every single field even if you are only going to be using some of them.

.rv*
Allows you to read and use comma delimited files – for example, those produced by dBASE – and then only some of the fields. You may, for instance, be using a database that contains 24 fields but only want to use the fourth. Using this command you can do so but you must include the first three fields as well. For example:

.rv* <*field1*>,<*field2*>,<*field3*>, <*field4*>
WordStar reads the fields from the first to the last specified; if you do not include the interim ones then you will not get the correct results.

You may use data files from *dBASE*, *Lotus 1-2-3*, *Quattro*, *MailList*, *Symphony*, or you can create you own comma delimited files to use.

SECTION 76
Mailmerge conditional statements

.rv* $x   Reads in a column, or row, from a spreadsheet file that has been produced as a comma delimited file.

.rv* $x,$y   Reads in a spreadsheet cell, specified by x,y, from a comma delimited file.

.sv *<variable>*, *<text>*

This allows you to change the contents of the *<variable>*, or field, so that it will always be what is expressed in *<text>*. This is useful if you have only two or three fields within a document and you do not want to create a new database record for the names. You can thus produce a single form letter that contains the variables. By changing these at the start of each document you can automatically produce the form letter as you wish. An example might be a specific report or a Contract of Employment.

■ SECTION 77
Additional merge print commands

WordStar will also allow you to use other field names other than those contained in the record with which you are merging, but only when you are Merge Printing. These are the system fields:

&#   This will force the program to insert the current page number of the document at this point. You can combine this with the conditional statements to produce different results, as the page number enclosed in ampersands like this is a usable variable.

&_   Prints the current line number.

&@   Causes the insertion of the current date as set on the computer. The date format will be identical to that set in WSCHANGE, which you can see if you use **Esc @**.

&!   Inserts the current time, in the format you set when you installed the program using WSCHANGE.

Conditional merge printing example

What follows is an example of a merge-printing document, using some of the preceding commands. Of necessity any document you produce will be different but this should give you a guide.

```
.op
.ls1
.df wslist.dta
.rv x,number,full-name,first,mi,last,Mr-Mrs,Title,Company,Addr 1
.rv Addr 2, Addr 3,Town,Cty,Post Code,Country,Telephone,Date
.rv User1,Remark1,User2,Remark2,User3,Remark3
.sv Company1 = Delta Electrical Products

.oc on
                        CONTRACT OF EMPLOYMENT
.oc off

Memorandum of Agreement between &first& &mi& &last& and &company1&
covering the terms and conditions of employment made this day, &@&,
.............

1) TEXT.............

.if &Mr-Mrs& <> Mr

The employee shall be entitled to Six Months maternity leave at full
pay, in the event of her becoming pregnant whilst in the employ of
&company1&. Such leave shall run from two calendar months prior to
the expected date of birth of her baby and continue for four months
thereafter. In the event of the birth being delayed then any
additional leave shall be granted at the rate of three quarters of
her full pay for a maximum period of one calendar month.

.el

The employee shall be entitled to Three months Paternity leave at
full pay beginning one week prior to the expected birth date and
continue thereafter. In the event of the birth being delayed an
extension to this period, at the rate of three quarters of his full
pay, shall be allowed to a maximum of One Calendar Month.

.ei
```

The first line turns off the page number printing, while the next sets the line spacing to 1. The following four lines detail the MailList file to be used and the fields it contains, in the order that they occur. Immediately thereafter is the command that sets up a specific variable, in this case using the company name 'Delta Electrical Products', that is not part of the MailList file but which will be wanted throughout the document. For the sake of neatness the heading wants to be centred on the page which is what the **.oc** commands do.

The conditional statement, **.if &Mr-Mrs <> Mr**, will operate depending on the contents of that field. If the contract is for a male, and the MailList field has been correctly completed, then the first clause will not be printed. In its place the second one will be output. On the other hand if the employee is female – that is, the MailList field uses something other than 'Mr' – then the first clause will be printed but the second one will not. The final **.ei** command terminates the conditional printing.

PART SEVEN

TelMerge

■ SECTION 79
The electronic office

The dream of the total electronic office is as old as computers themselves; the idea that people could work wherever they wished and then transmit the results of their labours to a central point, for onward processing, is endemic to the world of computers – and has been for years. In the early days of computing, when the machines were giant brontosaurus-like boxes that, like the dinosaurs, needed special environments to exist and work properly, the dream seemed to be far in the future. However, with the development of the transistor and then the silicon chip, and the resultant decrease in size, coupled with an increase in power and capabilities, the dream has gradually become more and more attainable.

The electronic office is dependent on three basic factors. Firstly, computers are needed that have sufficient power and storage to allow people to work effectively with the relevant data. In the same vein the machines must be cheap enough and versatile enough to warrant the necessary investment. Equally, they must be small enough, and possibly transportable, to fit comfortably into the average home. Today's modern PCs and ATs meet all these requirements – though it must be said that there are problems caused by the memory limitations of the machines. However, disregarding that, it is now possible to get all the power (and much more) of the mainframes of even ten years ago into a plastic case no larger than a couple of shoe boxes. You can even carry them around and work with them on the train or in the middle of nowhere.

The second requirement for the dream to become reality is a decent communications network that will allow the transmission of data, quickly, efficiently and faultlessly, from the user's computer to the central point – and preferably at a low cost. In the U.K., until very recently, British Telecom had a monopoly on the telephone network, ignoring the special local conditions that prevail at Hull, and the service tended to vary according to how far you were from the capital. Thus if you lived in the Home Counties you could use the 'phone lines without any real problems, but if you lived in the Outer Hebrides the quality of the lines available caused insurmountable problems with data transmission. However, over the past five years BT has gradually been improving the cabling system and installing System X. (The availability of this system depends on where you live; for instance my local exchange in Mountsorrel won't be upgraded totally until around 1993 but Bath has had System X for a couple of years already!) In addition we now have the Mercury network which drastically undercuts BT in terms of price and already uses a digital network. Thus there is now the second element of the equation for the electronic office.

The final element is an interface between the user's computer and the telephone network. After all it's a bit pointless having the first two elements if they cannot be connected together. This interface consists of a modem and the necessary software to link the two main elements. Modems are getting to be smaller and more dynamic. Once they were just as ponderous as computers but these days you can get a highly efficient modem, with many more capabilities, that fits on a single half card and occupies a single slot in the computer. Equally, the software required to drive it and provide a user-friendly interface has been improving in leaps and bounds, and the range of possible software is huge – from shareware products to commercial programs. At the same time there is a recent tendency to include communications software with word processors. This is exactly what WordStar International have done with *TelMerge*. You can now run WordStar and automatically transmit documents and data using this program.

In fact there is probably another element that must be taken into account – the willingness, confidence and discipline of people to work at home. There is not much point in having all the technology if the people concerned are unable, for whatever reason, to use it! Working at home requires a rigid discipline, much more so than working in a specific office, and if you cannot develop the right approach then you are wasting your time. Coupled to this is the accommodating approach of the company concerned. If they are unwilling to allow you to work at home then having all the technology in the world is not going to make a blind bit of difference.

However, the dream lives on, part of the collective unconsciousness defined by Jung perhaps, and gradually it comes closer and closer to reality. Who knows but in another ten years' time it may well be a fact and we'll all wonder what people ever did beforehand.

■ SECTION 80
TelMerge – what is it?

Electronic Mail – E-mail for short – is the name given to the transmission of documents across the telephone network. In the U.K. it includes access to such networks as Prestel, Micronet and Telecom Gold, amongst others. Each of these is a large database of information, held on a mainframe, onto which people can log and so exchange information, news and ideas. The services also provide hard information as part of their commitment to the ideal. For instance, you can use Telecom Gold to run checks on a number of companies because their end-of-year accounts are available for examination. However, the real benefit of E-mail is that it allows the transmission of textual documents rather than just words; thus you can send contracts, bills of sale, etc. from one person to another. (To transmit illustrations you need to use a fax which is related but separate to E-mail.)

TelMerge is the user interface between the telephone network and the computer: that is, the method by which you can link the two.

```
                          TelMerge
                C O M M U N I C A T I O N S    M E N U
       ─────────────────────────────────────────────────────────
       IBM IBM Users Group              TCT The Crystal Tower

       BTG British Telecom Gold         MCI MCI Mail

       EYP Electronic Yellow Pages      ONE One to One Email Service

       BPS British Packet Switch        DIR Direct Connect Mode

       ANS Answer mode                  NEW Add New service here
       ─────────────────────────────────────────────────────────
       Enter your selection:



  F1 Help  2      3      4      5Other  6      7      8 Go online   10 Exit
```

TelMerge Main Menu

■ SECTION 80
TelMerge – what is it?

As the program is menu-driven (see below), it provides this link in the simplest and easiest to use way possible. In order to use the program you must have a Hayes-compatible modem – either a 300 or a 1200 – connected to the serial port of the computer. If you do not have a serial port fitted then you can use an add-in modem on a card, which fits in one of the available slots inside the computer. In addition you need a telephone that is fitted with the new British Telecom plug.

The program is usually run from the WordStar Main Menu, by pressing **A** then **T**. The program files must be located in the WordStar directory. It can also be run as a stand-alone program. Change into the WordStar directory, using **CD** followed by the directory name at the system prompt; then enter **TELMERGE** and the Main Menu will appear.

■ SECTION 81
Setting the program parameters

TelMerge comes complete with a number of services already programmed into it so that it is ready to run: for example, Telecom Gold. However before you use it you should check that the numbers are correct for your area. To do so you should activate WordStar and then log onto the WordStar directory. Load the file called TELMERGE.SYS using the non-document mode. This is the file that controls the way in which the program works, just as CONFIG.SYS controls the way in which your computer works.

You can page through the file, using the standard cursor keys. By following the on-screen instructions, you can change the parameters by which TelMerge operates, from altering the default settings to changing the pre-programmed telephone numbers.

To change the system set-up move through the file until you reach the part labelled 'System Section'. By default the program is set to work with a Hayes Smartmodem operating at 1200 baud. However, you can change the setting to a Hayes 2400, Direct, Answer or Acoustic – these are your only choices. The original setting will work with any Hayes-compatible modem and so you should try that first.

The second line allows you to specify which serial port you are using. By default this is COM1 but you can change it to COM2 if you wish, and if you have two serial ports fitted to your computer.

BAUD is the rate of data transmission. Most standard modems operate at 1200 but you may have to change this depending on the modem you are using. The available choices are 110, 300, 1200, 2400, 4800 or 9600.

PRINT deals with how your computer handles the files that it receives from another source. By default the setting is NO so that printing of the files does not occur. However you can turn this

■ SECTION 81
Setting the program parameters

setting to YES, in which case any files received while you are using the program will be sent directly to you default printer. COM2 or LPT2 will send the same files to a different printer, providing one is connected. Alternatively you can specify a filename, in which case the incoming files will be stored directly on your disk.

The remaining settings are a matter of personal choice and you should set them according to your own preference.

■ SECTION 82
Changing the menu

The menu, as it comes on the master disks, contains eight pre-programmed numbers and two additional features. The way it appears depends on the section of the TELMERGE.SYS file – labelled, appropriately enough, 'Menu Section'. The 'Say' commands down the left-hand side specify the lines that will be displayed as the menu. To add a new line enter 'Say' followed by what you want to appear on that line. You can use any of the entire ASCII character set – except the control codes – to design the menu. However, you have only one display parameter, '|', which toggles the highlighter appearance when the program is run.

At the end of the menu definition there are three lines which define what happens next. The first, 'Hold ?3', allows you to input a string of three characters to select which service you want to log onto. The next line clears the screen and the final line tells the program to dial the service you have input.

Whenever you add a new service you must include its details in the 'Service Section' of this file. TelMerge will dial the service you have requested and is also capable of automatically transmitting the necessary User ID and password to log onto it – providing you tell it what these codes are!

Once you have finished the customisation, save the file and return to the WordStar Main Menu. Make sure that the modem is connected, and plugged into the phone line, then select **A** and **T** to activate the TelMerge program.

■ SECTION 83
Adding services

Once the front-end menu appears on the screen you select which service you want by inputting the three-character code for it. TelMerge will then dial the relevant number and, if you have set the User ID and password, log you directly onto the service.

As an alternative to changing the TELMERGE.SYS file you can add additional services directly at the Main Menu. Select **F5** and you will be given a list of all the files that have an extension of .TEL in the current directory. If these are normally stored in the WordStar sub-directory you should log onto this one first. Otherwise, you may find that you have service files all over your hard disk; ideally, you want them in a sub-directory of their own.

Select the file that you want to change or, if you are adding a new file, simply enter a name for it. The name must conform to the standard MS-DOS filename criteria. If the filename does not exist then the program will create it spontaneously and add the extension .TEL. You will then be asked to input the telephone number of the new service. The number should be entered as a single string; don't include any spaces or separating characters. For instance the normally written number may be (089) 326-9876; when input to TelMerge it must be written as '0893269876'.

You will then be asked to input a Service Name. This is a string of three characters, which may include extended ASCII characters if you wish. It will be used to activate the service call automatically. After that you input the User ID and the Password. Next, enter the Baud rate that you will use to dial and respond to the service. This is usually 1200 but it can be any of the available range of rates.

Once you have finished inputting the details, the number will be dialled instantly, so be sure that the modem and phone are connected before you set up an individual file.

■SECTION 83
Adding services

If you are likely to be using this new service on a regular basis then you should include it in the TELMERGE.SYS file so that it is instantly available from the Main Menu.

■ SECTION 84
Using the program

The advantage to using TelMerge in conjunction with WordStar is that you can use the latter to create documents first and then send them directly with the former. Normally, if you are using an E-mail program, you can only send the document as you compose it – and thus pay for the time you are logged onto the system – though there are some notable exceptions to this rule. However, using E-mail with TelMerge means that you can compose the document, then send it in a short burst, and so save money.

There are a number of ways in which you can use E-mail and TelMerge will allow you to do all three:

■　　Use the service as an electronic postage system. This means that you can compose a letter and then transmit it to someone else who uses the same system and deposit the letter in their 'mailbox'. This is the way Prestel works.

■　　Use the system as a Telex. Providing that the recipient has a telex machine you can send your document to the target, where it will be printed out.

■　　Log onto services to obtain information. This is the way that some parts of Micronet work: for example, there are a number of pages of information that are available to anyone who logs onto the system.

Thus to send a document to another person all you need do is write the document using WordStar and save it to disk. Activate TelMerge and dial the recipient's number; once you are logged on to them, transmit the text file. It's as simple as that.

The WordStar manual covers using TelMerge in depth and also provides a number of (American) 'phone numbers of various services that you might like to try – providing your 'phone bill will stand it.

PART EIGHT

PC-Outline

■ SECTION 85
What is it?

PC-Outline, from Brown Bag Software, is normally sold as shareware but the version that comes with WordStar is not. Shareware is a concept that is almost unique to the computer software industry. Basically it means that you can obtain disks containing the programs you might want for little more than the cost of the actual disks. You can then try out the program at your leisure. If you like the program and it fulfils your needs you pay the Registration Fee and get a full manual, technical support, and other goodies. On the other hand, if you don't like the program or it doesn't do what you want it to, then you just scrap it and pay no-one anything.

However, the version that comes bundled with WordStar is not shareware; you have purchased it as part of the WordStar Professional package, and it is slightly different to the shareware version. So what is it?

Essentially it is an ideas organiser; it allows you to get ideas from your head onto the computer screen quickly and easily. You can then rearrange then, move them around, add or delete detail, hide elements of what you have done, print the file, re-sort it, and manipulate it in any way that you please.

The program is menu-driven and so it has a fast learning curve; that is, you can quickly produce the results that you want as you explore its capabilities. Files can be output as standard outline files, as pure ASCII or in WordStar format. Once you start using the program you may well begin to wonder what you ever did without it!

■ SECTION 86
Installing the program

Installing PC-Outline is accomplished in the following steps:

1 Boot up your computer so that the system prompt appears on screen.

2 Make sure that you are in the root directory, by entering CD\, and then enter **MD \PCO** to create a sub-directory to hold the files. Next enter **CD\PCO** to move into the directory you have just created.

3 Place the PC-Outline disk in Drive A, close the latch and then enter **COPY A:\PCO*.* C:\PCO** to copy the main files into the directory you have created.

4 Enter **COPY A:*.PCO C:\PCO** to copy the sample outlines to the directory.

5 Now copy the KEYSET program by entering **COPY A:\KEYSET.COM C:\PCO**. You may also need a program called GOODCLK; to copy it enter **COPY A:\GOODCLK.COM C:\PCO**.

6 Remove the PC-Outline master disk and store it with the other WordStar disks. The installation is complete.

■ SECTION 87
Loading the program

PC-Outline can run in two different ways: either stand-alone or as memory resident. To do the former, make sure that you are in the right directory and then enter **PCO**. The program will load and you will be presented with the opening screen (see below).

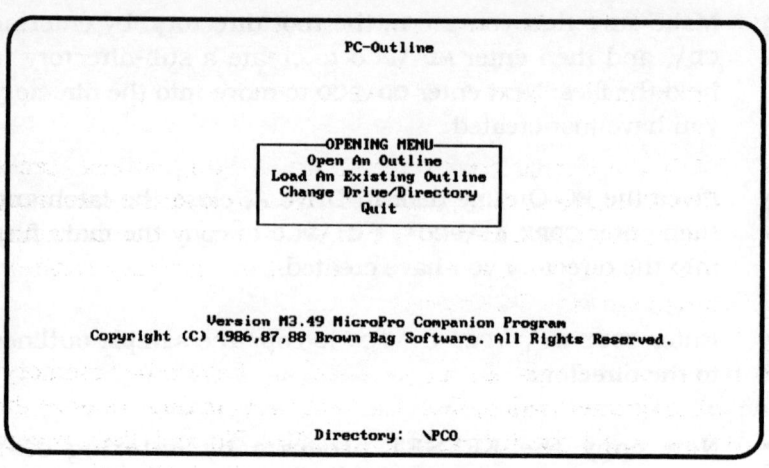

PC-Outline opening screen

To run the program as memory resident – that is, permanently loaded and occupying a chunk of the computer's memory – enter **PCO/R**. This will load the program, display a short message and then return you to the system prompt. If you intend running PC-Outline in memory-resident mode it must be loaded before any other such program; in particular, it must be loaded before WordStar. Ideally, if you want to run it this way then you should add a line saying **PCO/R** to your AUTOEXEC.BAT file. To activate the program just press the backslash (\), and the opening screen will appear.

270

■ SECTION 87
Loading the program

You can change the hotkey that activates PC-Outline by running the program called KEYSET. Just follow the on-screen instructions.

If you find that you need the memory that PC-Outline is using you can remove it from the memory as follows:

1 From the system prompt load PC-Outline.

2 With the cursor positioned on the editing screen, press **Ctrl-Backspace** three times in succession and the memory will be freed. However you can only use this option providing that you have not loaded any other memory-resident programs after PC-Outline.

If you cannot use this option, because you have other memory-resident programs loaded, then the best thing to do is remove the PC-Outline line from the AUTOEXEC.BAT file and then reboot your computer from scratch. Don't just use **Ctrl-Alt-Del**; switch the machine off, wait for the disk to stop spinning and then turn it on again.

■ SECTION 88
Loading an outline

From the opening screen, you have four possible options. In reverse order they are as follows:

■ **Quit** allows you to terminate the program, i.e. return to the system prompt, without going any further.

■ **Change Drive/Directory**. By default PC-Outline, as supplied with WordStar, will always automatically log onto the **\PCO** directory – even if you have installed it in a different directory. This option allows you to change the default and so load outlines from elsewhere on your disk.

To use the option move the cursor down, using the arrow keys, or just press **C**. You will be presented with another menu that allows you to specify the name of the directory or drive that you want. For safety you should include the drive letter and the directory every time that you use the option: for example, **\OUTLINES**.

■ **Load An Existing Outline** does exactly that. You may load any of the existing outlines from the current directory. The Outlines all have the extension **.PCO**. If you have changed this then the files cannot be loaded.

When you select the option you will be presented with another menu, containing a two-column list of the existing outlines. To select the one you want just move the cursor to it press **Enter** and the outline will load. If you have more outlines than can be displayed in this box then moving to the last outline mentioned will automatically bring up another list.

■ **Open An Outline** allows you to create a new outline. Activating the command will bring down a menu that asks you to input a name for it. Just enter the name – using up

to eight characters but excluding any extension – and the
file will be created.

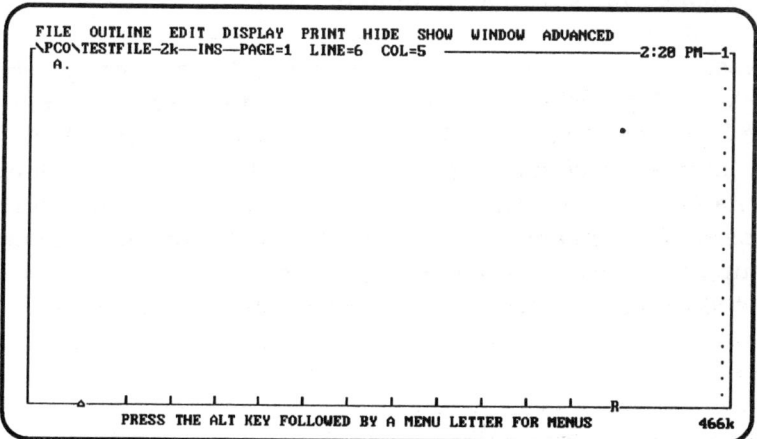

PC-Outline editing screen

Once you have opened an outline, either by creating a new one or
loading an existing one, you will be presented with the PC-Outline
editing screen, as shown above.

You create entries just as you would with a word processor; that
is, whatever you type will be displayed on screen. However PC-
Outline is more adaptable than most word processors, in that you
can layer your entries. When a new outline is first loaded you will
find that there is a label 'A)' at the top left-hand corner; this is the
first parent entry. Whatever you type will be placed here.

However, you can create additional entries by pressing **Ctrl-Enter**
which will generate another main entry. This will always be at the
same level as the current one. For instance, on the new outline

screen, pressing this key combination will create another entry labelled 'B)' on a blank line below the first one. The entry will be highlighted until you input something into it, and while it is highlighted you can move it around.

Pressing **Up** will move the entry to above the first entry, while pressing **Right** will move it laterally so that it become a 'child' of the first entry. This is how PC-Outline works. There is no limit on the number of children, grandchildren, etc. that any entry can contain – other than the total memory available for them. Entries consist of parents and children; normally, the former are shown in upper case while the latter are lower case, but you can change this to your preferences as explained in Section 92.

■ SECTION 89
The File Menu

Across the top of the editing screen are a series of menu headings. To evoke any of them you can use either of two methods. First, pressing **F10** will automatically bring down the File Menu and you can then move to the others using the cursor keys. Alternatively you can press **Alt** and the initial letter of the menu that you want; for example, **Alt-F** brings down the File Menu (see below). Once the menu appears you can select any of the options it contains using the cursor keys or the initial letter. To cancel any of the operations before they take effect, press **Esc**, which will cancel the current operation and/or take you back one level. The commands available on the file menu are:

■ **Save Current Outline (^S)** writes the contents of the currently-displayed outline to your hard disk. You can have as many as nine outlines open at once. You can make PC-Outline do this automatically (see Section 97). An equivalent to using this command from the menu is to press **Ctrl-S**, which does exactly the same thing.

■ **Load Existing Outline** allows you to open another, existing outline and discard the current one in the process. If you have made changes to the current outline you will be prompted with a message saying 'Lose Changes'. This is just a reminder to inform you that the changes you have made have not been saved. If you want to discard them press **N** otherwise, **Y** will cancel the loading operation, thus giving you a chance to save the outline.

■ **Start New Outline** will replace the current outline with a new one, for which you have to specify a name. Again, if the on-screen outline has been changed you will be prompted if it has not been saved.

■ **Rename Current Outline** permits you to rename the outline in use. The name displayed in the top left-hand corner of the screen will be changed to the new name. Note that the last saved edition of the current outline will still exist on your disk – only the outline on screen is renamed.

■ **Change Drive or Directory** switches to a different disk location, generally to save the current outline there, rather than in the default directory. Again, the original outline will also exist in the default directory.

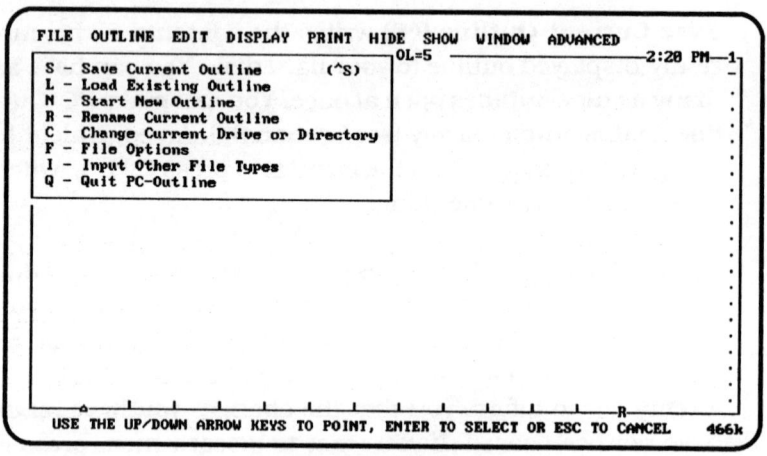

PC-Outline File Menu

■ **File Options** brings down another menu, which contains the following sub-options:

– **Pick A Sub-Directory** allows you to move to a sub-directory of the current directory. If there are none such then the option is spontaneously cancelled.

- **Set Parent Directory** theoretically makes the current sub-directory into a parent directory – but it doesn't do so on my machine!

- **Create New Sub-Directory** allows you to create a new directory within the current one. The new directory must be a child of the one that you are logged onto; you cannot use this option to make a sub-directory elsewhere on your disk.

- **Erase An Outline** brings down the original outline selection box and allows you to choose one of the existing outlines to delete.

- **Quit This Menu** removes this sub-menu from the screen and takes you back to the File Menu. Pressing **Esc** has exactly the same effect.

■ **Input Other File Types** allows the importation of files in a format other than that used by PC-Outline. Using this option will cause any file read in to be placed into a single outline division. The file you input will be inserted at the current cursor position on the editing screen. Again this option brings down a sub-menu containing the following:

- **A – Read in an ASCII file** accepts pure ASCII (what WordStar calls non-document files). You can also use this option to read in a comma delimited file but you will have to spend some time aligning it to the margins!

- **W – Read in a WordStar 4 file** allows the insertion of a document file created by Release 4 of WordStar Professional.

- **C – Read in a WordStar 5 file** accepts files from the current version of WordStar; this is a different format to that used by previous releases of the program.

- **S – Read in a Structured file** allows the insertion of files produced by some other outline programs; that is, ones that already contain an outline structure.

- **2 – Read in a WordStar 2000 file** accepts files produced by WordStar 5's cousin program. PC-Outline is also bundled with this program.

- **Q – Quit this menu** takes you back to the File Menu.

■ **Quit PC-Outline** terminates the program and returns you to the system prompt or, if the PC-Outline is memory resident, it will take you back to the program you were using before you invoked PC-Outline.

The second menu that you can access is labelled 'Outline' (see below) and basically it controls the appearance of the entries in the current document.

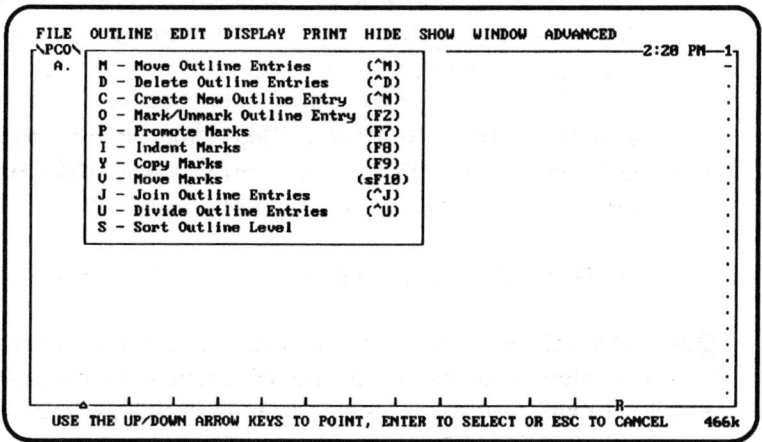

```
 FILE  OUTLINE  EDIT  DISPLAY  PRINT  HIDE  SHOW  WINDOW  ADVANCED
 \PCO\                                                        2:28 PM—1
 A.    M - Move Outline Entries        (^M)
       D - Delete Outline Entries      (^D)
       C - Create New Outline Entry    (^N)
       O - Mark/Unmark Outline Entry   (F2)
       P - Promote Marks               (F7)
       I - Indent Marks                (F8)
       Y - Copy Marks                  (F9)
       U - Move Marks                  (sF10)
       J - Join Outline Entries        (^J)
       U - Divide Outline Entries      (^U)
       S - Sort Outline Level
```

```
 USE THE UP/DOWN ARROW KEYS TO POINT, ENTER TO SELECT OR ESC TO CANCEL   466k
```

PC-Outline Outline Menu

■ **Move Outline Entries** is used to 'pick up' the single entry on which the cursor is positioned, along with its children, and move it to another location – either horizontally or vertically. Thus you can turn a child into a parent entry or vice versa, or pick the whole thing up and move it elsewhere. When you move an entry the labels of the surrounding entries are changed to match the new position of the one you move. You can produce the same effect directly from the keyboard by pressing **Ctrl-M**.

■ **Delete Outline Entry** erases the entry on which the cursor is positioned. If it contains children then they are erased at the same time. Use **Ctrl-D** to delete entries without having to use the menu.

■ **Create New Outline Entry** has the same effect as using **Ctrl-Enter**; that is, it produces a new entry, immediately below but on the same level as the current entry.

■ **Mark/Unmark Outline Entry** designates entries ready for additional treatment. An entry that is marked is highlighted, along with any children it contains. Pressing **F2** has the same effect. Using the same combination twice will unmark the entry.

■ **Promote Marks** moves all those entries which have been previously marked one place to the left: that is, up one level, so that children become parents. The numbering will be adjusted to accommodate this. **F7** is the hotkey to be used if you do not want to use the menu. Note that you can only promote an entry providing that it is not the parent of an unmarked entry.

■ **Indent Marks** has the opposite effect to Promote Marks. It moves all the marked entries one place right: that is, parents become children. You can only do this providing there are higher-placed parent entries. **F8** has the same effect.

■ **Copy Marks** duplicates the marked entries elsewhere but you cannot copy an entry onto itself. **F9** does the same thing.

■ **Move Marks** is a variation on Copy Marks. This will physically move the marked entry from its present position to a new one. **Shift-F10** or **Ctrl-M** have the same effect direct from the keyboard.

- **Join Outline Entries** allows you to append a child, or another parent, directly to the first parent. In other words you can make a number of entries and then join them into a single entry by using this command. **Ctrl-J** is the shortcut. Position the cursor at the end of the entry to which you want to join a subsequent entry and invoke the command to join the entries.

- **Divide Outline Entries** has the opposite effect and allows you to split an entry into two. Move the cursor to the position where you want the entry to be split and then invoke the command by using the menu or **Ctrl-U**.

- **Sort Outline Level** allows you to sort the entries in the entire outline according to your preference. Invoking the sort will bring down another menu that allows you to specify the order of the sort (Ascending or Descending), the type of sort (Pure ASCII or Dictionary) and a field to sort on.

SECTION 91
The Edit Menu

This menu is concerned primarily with the text within entries, either in strings or blocks.

■ **Insert Deleted Text** is the equivalent to the WordStar **Ctrl-U**; that is, it restores the last deleted block of text. You can use the keyboard shortcut **Alt-U**.

■ **Find String** will allow you to search through an outline entry, or a series of them, for a string of characters. Activating the command, either through the menu or by using **Ctrl-F**, will bring down another menu containing the following:

– **Search String?** allows you to enter exactly what you are looking for. You can also use the MS-DOS wildcard '?' to replace any given character – but don't use it at the beginning of a string or the search will take forever (because it will match everything!)

– **Force Case to be the Same?** Answering 'Yes' means that the string that it is searching for must match identically to your input. Otherwise, if you answer 'No', the program will find the first occurrence of the string regardless of its case.

– **Search Scope?** defines which entries will be searched. 'Only On Entries' means that the search will only look at those entries which are currently displayed. 'All Entries' will force the search of every entry, even hidden children.

■ **Find and Replace** searches for the first input string and replaces it with the second input string – just as in WordStar itself. **Ctrl-R** is the shortcut.

282

SECTION 91
The Edit Menu

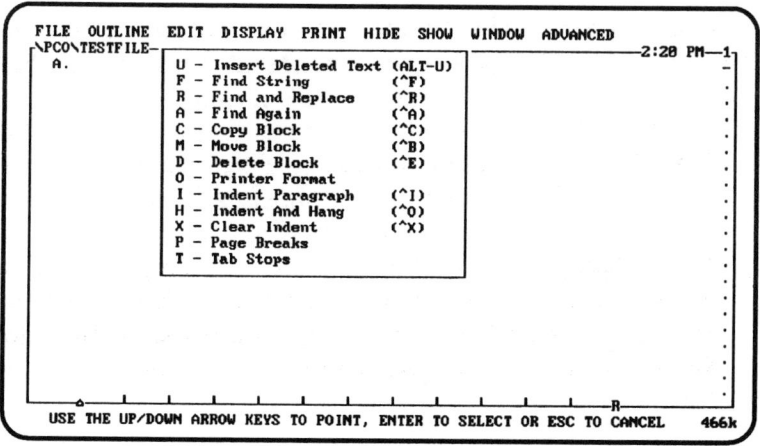

PC-Outline Edit Menu

■ **Find Again** is similar to Find and Replace, above, but it looks for the next occurrence of the string. The characters being searched for are identical to those used in the first search – you cannot change them. **Ctrl-A** provides the keyboard activation.

■ **Copy Block** allows you to mark and then copy blocks of text. Move the cursor to where you want the block to begin and then invoke the command, through the menu or using **Ctrl-C**. You will be prompted to outline the block and then position the cursor where you want the block copied to. You cannot copy a block to itself.

■ **Move Block** is similar to above but allows you to physically move the blocks from one place to another. In this case the hotkey combination is **Ctrl-B**.

283

■ **Delete Block** allows you to mark out a block, in the same way as for copying one, and then delete it from the outline. It can later be restored using **Alt-U** if necessary.

■ **Printer Format** allows you to enter printing effects. There is a wide range of these and they operate in much the same way as they do in WordStar. The codes are:

Ctrl-F1	Starts underlining
Ctrl-F2	Turns it off
Ctrl-F3	Starts the boldface
Ctrl-F4	Stops it
Shift-F5	Causes double strike to commence
Shift-F6	Stops it
Ctrl-F5	Begins italics
Ctrl-F6	Ends it
Shift-F7	Turns superscript on
Shift-F8	Turns it off
Ctrl-F7	Starts subscript
Ctrl-F8	Terminates it

■ **Indent Paragraph** moves the left-hand margin to the next tab stop. The entire paragraph will be indented, not just the top line of it. Use **Ctrl-I** in place of the menu if you wish.

■ **Indent and Hang** or **Ctrl-O** indents the second and subsequent lines of a paragraph but not the first line.

■ **Clear Indent** allows you remove the indent of a paragraph, but not if it is hung; that is, the margin will be moved back to the first column. The keyboard command is **Ctrl-X**.

■ **Page Breaks** inserts an end-of-page marker. You may set a hard page break – one that is rigid – or you can set a conditional one – one that will only occur if the specified number of lines would run off the page anyway.

■ **Tab Stops** allows you to position or remove the default tab stops.

This menu has to do with the way in which the outline entries are presented on screen, their overall appearance and style.

- **Current Paragraph Style** will bring down a subsidiary menu that allows you to make the following changes:

  - **Paragraph Alignment** – how the paragraphs are presented:

    - **Left Aligned** keeps the leading letter of every line in the same column; the right-hand edge will be ragged. This convention will override any Indent setting that you may make with the Edit Menu.

    - **Justified** makes the first and last letters of lines even. Additional spaces are added where necessary to do this.

    - **Centred** shoves the lines into the middle of their lines, extra spaces are added at the beginning and end to do so.

    - **Right Aligned** allows the right-hand edge of the lines to be all in the same column, the left-hand edge will be ragged.

  - **First Line Alignment** is used to set the left margin for the first line of the paragraph.

  - **Left Margin** allows you to set the left margin for each paragraph. This is always contingent on the start of the outline entry; the indentation of the entry plus this setting gives the actual margin. However if you

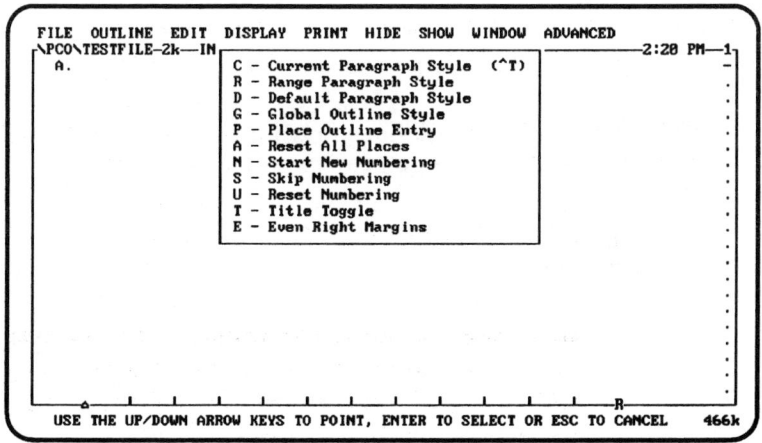

PC-Outline Display Menu

make the margin less than the indentation then the
margin setting will overrule the latter.

– **Right Margin** sets the right margin. As with the left
   margin this is conditional on the outline entries.

– **Make Default Setting** forces the default setting for
   the outline to match the current settings that you
   have made.

■ **Range Paragraph Style** works in the same way as Current
Paragraph Style but only applies the settings to a designated
range.

■ **Default Paragraph Style** allows you to make the current
settings the default for all future entries.

■ **Global Outline Style** brings down another menu that allows you to make global changes.

■ **Indent Outline Level** defines how far across the page new outline entries will appear. The default setting is 3 but you can make it anything in the range 0 to 20.

■ **Spaces for Numbering** specifies how much room the program will allow for the outline entry numbers. By default it is 4; if you make it less than this then the numbers may be chopped and unreadable.

■ **First Entry Number** allows you to specify the first entry value. The reason for this is that any outline cannot exceed 64 Kb and you may want to link two or more of them together; for example, for printing.

■ **Numbering Type**. PC-Outline allows you to use *sequential numbering*, i.e. 1, 2, 3, or A, B, C. If you use this option then the numbering style, set next, will operate so that you can have different characters for different levels.

Procedural numbering is based on numbers only and it will override any style you select. Entries will instead be labelled as 1.0 for the first level, 1.0.1 for the second, and so on.

■ **Numbering Style** allows you to select Upper Case, Lower Case, Numbers, Roman Numbers, Bullets or None for up to the first eight levels; beyond this the settings will be repeated. Immediately after that you can also select the punctuation character for these, using any standard keyboard character.

- **Place Outline Entry** allows you to move the entry left and right using the cursor keys. Pressing **Enter** fixes its position.

- **Reset All Places** cancels any placings and returns all outline entries to their default positions.

- **Start New Numbering** is used to change the default numbering for the current entry at that level.

- **Skip Numbering** allows an entry to be placed but not assigned a positional number. If, later, you want the entry to be numbered, use the next option.

- **Reset Numbering** cancels any settings made with Start New Numbering or Skip Numbering by returning all entries to their default settings.

- **Title Toggle** switches the numbering for the first level on and off. To prepare quick documents using PC-Outline – for example, letters – start a new outline and toggle the entry. You can then use the program as a word processor, albeit with limited functions.

- **Even Right Margins** allows you to select a block of text that will have the margins aligned.

■ SECTION 93
The Print Menu

This menu is used for outputting the outline, or part of it, to various devices.

■　　**Go Start Printing** is used to output the outline, usually after you have set the parameters with the other options in the menu. Used directly it will simply output the outline to the connected printer in its entirety.

■　　**Select Range** allows you to mark a block of text, including multiple outline levels, that will be output.

■　　**Set Device for Output** brings down a sub-menu that allows you to select where the file will be sent:

－　　　**Send to Printer** is the default, which dumps the file to the connected printer. PC-Outline, as supplied with WordStar, only supports three printers: a Daisywheel, an IBM and a Standard. The last of these will work with the majority of dot matrix printers.

－　　　**Send to File** dumps the outline to a disk file with the extension .PRN and bearing the same name as the outline.

－　　　**Send to ASCII** creates a disk file that contains no printer or outline information. Every line in the file will end with a hard carriage return. If you select this option you will also have to supply a filename when you select Start Printing.

－　　　**Send to WordStar 4** converts the outline to the format used by WordStar Professional Release 4.

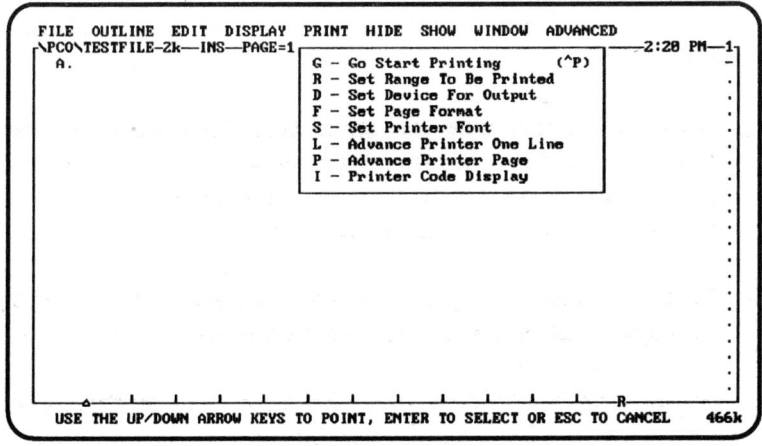

```
FILE  OUTLINE  EDIT  DISPLAY  PRINT  HIDE  SHOW  WINDOW  ADVANCED
\PCO\TESTFILE-2k—INS—PAGE=1                                    ————2:28 PM—1
 A.                          ┌─────────────────────────────────┐          —
                             │ G - Go Start Printing     (^P)   │          .
                             │ R - Set Range To Be Printed      │          .
                             │ D - Set Device For Output        │          .
                             │ F - Set Page Format              │          .
                             │ S - Set Printer Font             │          .
                             │ L - Advance Printer One Line     │          .
                             │ P - Advance Printer Page         │          .
                             │ I - Printer Code Display         │          .
                             └─────────────────────────────────┘          .
                                                                          .
                                                                          .
                                                                          .
                                                                          .
                                                                          .
                                                                          .
                                                                          .
    ▲___│___│___│___│___│___│___│___│___│___R___│___│___
 USE THE UP/DOWN ARROW KEYS TO POINT, ENTER TO SELECT OR ESC TO CANCEL   466k
```

PC-Outline Printer Menu

- **Send to WordStar 5** converts and saves the outline in WordStar Professional Release 5 format.

- **Send to Structured File** saves the file in a format that can be used by other outlining programs.

- **Send to WordStar 2000** converts the outline to this format.

■ **Set Page Format** again brings down a sub-menu that allows you to define how the page will appear when printed.

■ **Set Printer Font** sends a code to your printer so that the entire file being output will be printed in this typeface. Any embedded codes set using Printer Format will likewise be treated the same. For instance if you have used bold in an outline and then set the printer font to italics then when the

291

SECTION 93
The Print Menu

printer encounters the former command you will get bold italics.

■ **Advance Printer One line** sends a line feed directly to the printer.

■ **Advance Printer Page** sends a form feed to the printer.

■ **Printer Code Display** toggles the display of the printer codes on the screen, in much the same way that **Ctrl-O D** does in WordStar itself.

SECTION 94
Hiding and showing entries

The two menus labelled 'Hide' and 'Show' control the visibility of the outline entries. The first contains five options:

■ **Current Entries Children** causes any child entries below that on which the cursor is positioned to vanish, but only on the current entry. You can also use the **plus** key on the numeric keypad to toggle this action; that is, pressing it once hides the children, pressing it again brings them back.

■ **All Children at Level** hides every child that is below the current level throughout the outline.

■ **Current Entries Text** hides the text on the second and subsequent lines within the current entry on which the cursor is positioned.

■ **All Text at Level** leaves only the first line of text on every level of every entry at the same level throughout the outline.

■ **All Text in Outline** hides all the text at every level in the outline.

The Show Menu reverses the activities of the previous menu.

■ **Current Entries Children** brings back the children of the entry on which the cursor is lying.

■ **All Children at Level** shows all the children in every entry that occur below the level of the cursor.

■ **Current Entry's Text** restores the hidden text on the current entry only.

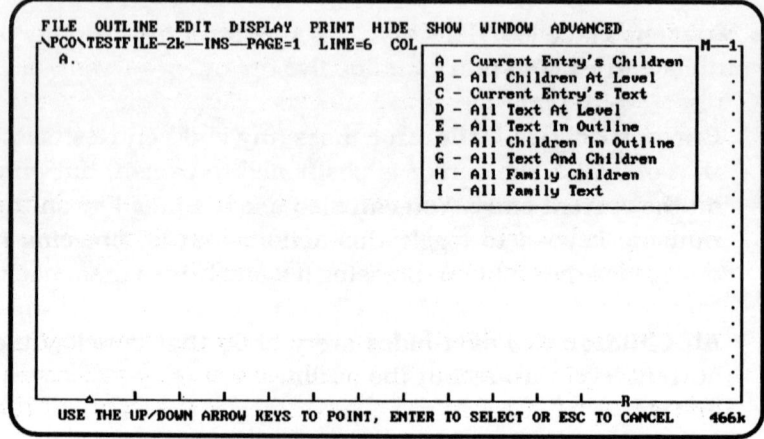

PC-Outline Show Menu

■ **All Text at Level** restores the text of all entries at the same level as the cursor is positioned – but not the children.

■ **All Text in Outline** restores all hidden text throughout the outline.

■ **All Children in Outline** allows you to see every child entry within the outline; the text of the displayed entries will be moved to allow this.

■ **All Text and Children** effectively cancels every hidden option that you might have operated.

■ **All Family Children** displays all the children, and their children, of the current entry.

■ **All Family Text** restores any hidden text for the current family of entries.

■ SECTION 95
The Window Menu

PC-Outline will allow you to have more than one outline – up to nine in fact – loaded into the memory at one time. You can also move them around and have them interact. This menu controls this ability.

■ **Load Outline New Window** allows you to open another existing outline and place it into the next available window. The first or previous outlines are retained.

■ **New Outline New Window** is used to create a new outline in a subsequent window. You will have to supply a filename, just as if you opened a new outline at the start of the program.

■ **Close Window** terminates the currently displayed outline. If changes have been made to it you will be prompted with a messages saying 'Lose Changes', which gives you the option of cancelling the operation, saving the outline and then closing the window.

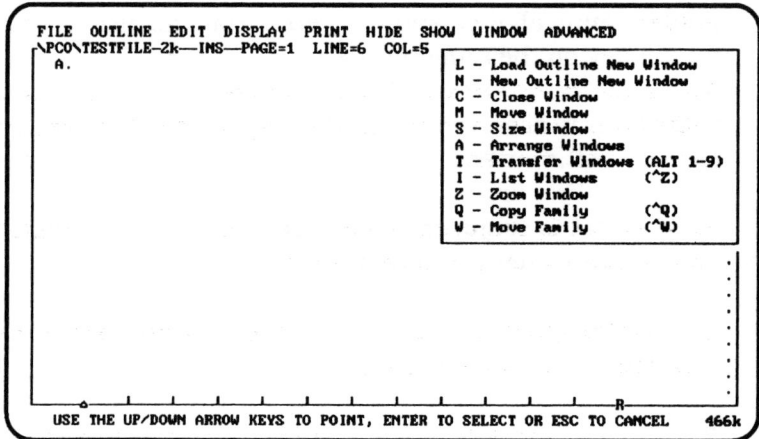

PC-Outline Window Menu

■ **Move Window** allows you to move outline windows around; however they cannot be full-screen sized.

■ **Size Window** is used to change the size of the current window. The minimum size allowed for any window is seven lines by four columns. Use the cursor keys to change the size.

■ **Arrange Windows** returns windows to their original positions and size.

■ **Transfer Windows** is used to move between the open windows. You can also use the **Alt** key and a numeral to do the same thing: for example, **Alt-3** will take you directly to the third window.

■ **List Windows** gives you a menu showing the currently open windows, their names and sizes.

■ **Zoom Windows** changes the size of the current window to the minimum allowed and vice versa. You can also use the **minus** key on the numeric keypad to get the same effect.

■ **Copy Family** allows you to copy an entire family to another position in the outline. You can also copy it from one outline to another by marking the entry you want to copy and then pressing **Alt** in conjunction with the number of the window you want the family copied to.

■ **Move Family** is similar to the above but transposes the entire family to another position.

■ SECTION 96
The Advanced Menu

This menu controls a variety of settings:

■ **Config Settings** brings down another menu (see below) that controls how the outline is configured.

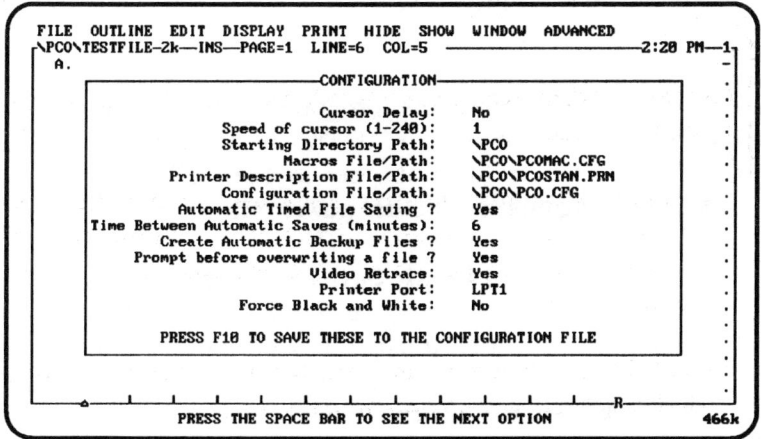

```
FILE  OUTLINE  EDIT  DISPLAY  PRINT  HIDE  SHOW  WINDOW  ADVANCED
┌─\PCO\TESTFILE-2k──INS──PAGE=1  LINE=6  COL=5 ─────────────2:28 PM─1┐
 A.                                                                  ─
  │─────────────────────CONFIGURATION─────────────────────│         .
  │                Cursor Delay:        No                 │         .
  │         Speed of cursor (1-240):    1                  │         .
  │         Starting Directory Path:    \PCO               │         .
  │               Macros File/Path:     \PCO\PCOMAC.CFG    │         .
  │     Printer Description File/Path:  \PCO\PCOSTAN.PRN   │         .
  │         Configuration File/Path:    \PCO\PCO.CFG       │         .
  │      Automatic Timed File Saving ?  Yes                │         .
  │ Time Between Automatic Saves (minutes): 6              │         .
  │        Create Automatic Backup Files ?  Yes            │         .
  │     Prompt before overwriting a file ?  Yes            │         .
  │               Video Retrace:        Yes                │         .
  │               Printer Port:         LPT1               │         .
  │           Force Black and White:    No                 │         .
  │                                                        │         .
  │   PRESS F10 TO SAVE THESE TO THE CONFIGURATION FILE    │         .
  │                                                        │         .
  └────────────────────────────────────────────────────────         .
  └─┴──┴──┴──┴──┴──┴──┴──┴──┴──┴──┴──┴──R─────────┘
           PRESS THE SPACE BAR TO SEE THE NEXT OPTION        466k
```

PC-Outline Config Settings

■ **Cursor Delay** allows you to change the delay of the cursor.

■ **Speed of Cursor** affects how fast the cursor move; 1 is the fastest speed while 240 is a snails pace.

■ **Starting Directory Path** sets the directory that PC-Outline will initially log onto. Any path entered here must conform to the MS-DOS rules and include the drive and directory path.

■ **Macros/File Path** tells PC-Outline where to find the macro file, normally in the \PCO directory.

- **Printer Description File** sets the path for the program to find the printer information and the default printer you will be using.

- **Configuration Path/File** tells the program where to find the file labelled PCO.CFG that contains the default configuration details.

- **Timed Saves** allows the program to save your current outline automatically, if YES. This means that the outline will be saved at intervals, set in the next option, as a safeguard against accidental power failure.

- **Time Between Automatic Saves** is the interval used by the previous option. Set the figure, in minutes, to whatever you wish; a setting in the range of 5 to 10 minutes is ideal.

- **Create Automatic Backup** causes the existing disk file to be given the suffix .BAK whenever the current outline is saved. In this way you have two copies of the file. However, you can turn this facility on and off according to your preference.

- **Prompt Before Overwriting** is a toggle that provides you with a message before a save operation is done. Setting the toggle to NO means that you do not get the prompt.

- **Video Retrace** will speed up the screen display on some monitors. Experiment by turning it ON or OFF to see if it makes any difference to your set-up.

- **Printer Port** tells the program which port your printer is connected to.

■ SECTION 96
The Advanced Menu

■ **Force Black and White** turns everything into mono. Normally PC-Outline uses a blue screen and sets various colour attributes. However, if you have a mono monitor this may become illegible. Changing this setting will improve matters.

Whenever you make changes to the configuration settings you should save them by pressing **F10** and then press **Esc** to return to the editing screen. The new settings are stored in the PCO.CFG file.

■ **Key Definition** allows you to create keyboard macros. You select which combination of keystrokes you want to redefine – for example, **Alt-W** – when asked and then enter the keystrokes which you want it to contain: for example, **WordStar**. When you have finished, press **Ctrl-Break** to terminate the input. Then, by selecting **Save** from the next menu you can store the macro permanently.

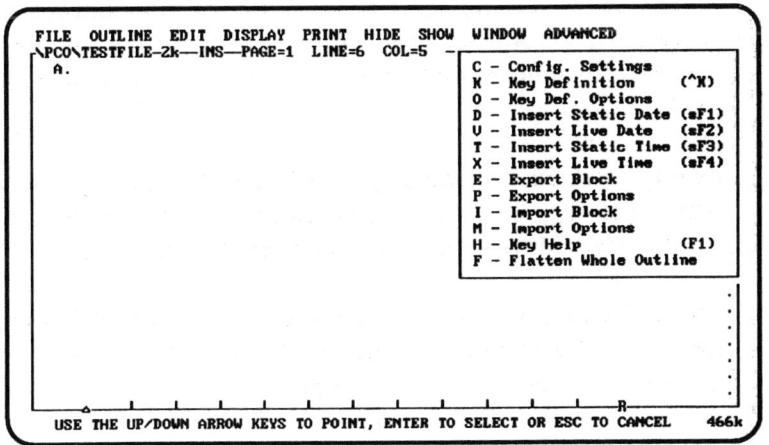

PC-Outline Advanced Menu

■ **Key Definition Options** brings down a sub-menu that contains four possible options.

   – **Clear a Definition** cancels the macro definition.

   – **Save all Definitions** is used to store any macros that you have created. Until they are saved, the macros are only available on the current outline and will be lost when you terminate the program.

   – **Inhibit Key Definitions** is a security device to prevent the macros being changed.

   – **Restart Key Definitions** cancels the above option.

■ **Insert Static Date** reads the date set on your computer and inserts it at the current cursor position.

■ **Insert Live Date** inserts the date as currently held by the computer. Thus whenever you reload the outline the date will be the same as that on the computer.

■ **Insert Static Time** reads the time on the computer and inserts it at the current cursor position.

■ **Insert Live Time** inserts the time as currently held by the computer. Every time that you load the outline thereafter the time will be automatically changed to the current system time.

■ **Export Block** is only available if PC-Outline is memory resident. It allows you to export a block of text to another program.

- **Export Options** sets the defaults for how the exportation of text will occur. If these are set incorrectly then the exporting of text will be wrong.

- **Import Block** is the reverse of Export above. Again, PC-Outline must be in memory-resident mode.

- **Import Options** sets the defaults for importation.

- **Key Help** overlays a screen with some of the preset key definitions. Pressing **F1** will do the same thing. The help screen is, actually, not that helpful because it contains the definitions only for the keys – it does not provide on-line help.

- **Flatten Whole Outline** moves everything up to the top level; that is, it promotes all children, grandchildren, etc. to make them part of the first entry.

■ SECTION 97
Using the program

The big advantage to PC-Outline is that it allows you to create structured files. For instance, you could store names and addresses in an outline. On the first level you would have the person's name; as a child you could have their 'phone number, and as a grandchild their full address. Alternatively, you could hold company names, addresses and 'phone numbers on the first level and then have your contacts within the companies as children of that level. The possibilities are almost endless.

Using PC-Outline as an address book is probably one of the simplest uses you can make of it and, because the program can sort the entries into whatever order you like, it is easy to use.

PC-Outline almost begs to be experimented with, and the more you use it the more you come to realise its capabilities. Even though it doesn't have a spelling checker or thesaurus it can, sometimes, be better to use than WordStar – especially if you are only writing single-page documents. However, for real word processing it doesn't even come in the same class as WordStar – but then it was never meant to. Comparing the two is rather like trying to compare a thoroughbred race horse with a heavy working horse. Granted they are the same species but their differences are so radical that they might as well not be.

■ SECTION 98
PC-Outline control key summary

Use **Alt** key plus initial letter of menus to activate them. Or use the following key combinations to produce effects:

+	Toggle to hide children
-	Zoom toggle
End	Move to end of screen, again to go to end of file
F1	Help screen showing hotkeys
F2	Mark entries toggle
F5	Promote entry
F6	Indent current entry
F7	Promote previously marked entries
F8	Indent marked entries
F9	Copy marked entries to new position
F10	Activate File Menu
Home	Move to top of screen, again to go to top of file
Pg Dn	Move screen down 20 lines
Pg Up	Scroll screen up 20 lines
Alt-F1	Toggle printer display codes
Alt-F2	Clear any and all marks
Ctrl-A	Find string again
Ctrl-B	Move block
Ctrl-C	Copy block
Ctrl-D	Delete family
Ctrl-E	Delete block
Ctrl-End	Move directly to end of the outline
Ctrl-Enter	Begin new outline entry
Ctrl-F	Find string
Ctrl-F1	Begin underlining
Ctrl-F2	Stop underlining
Ctrl-F3	Begin bold printing effect

PC-Outline control key summary

Ctrl-F4	Stop bold printing effect
Ctrl-F5	Begin italics printing effect
Ctrl-F6	End italics printing effect
Ctrl-F7	Begin superscript
Ctrl-F8	End superscript
Ctrl-F10	Insert non-break space
Ctrl-G	Insert/overwrite toggle
Ctrl-H	Hide current entry's children
Ctrl-Home	Move directly to top of outline
Ctrl-I	Indent paragraph
Ctrl-J	Join neighbouring entries into each other
Ctrl-K	Define keyboard macros
Ctrl-L	Hide all children at level
Ctrl-Left	Move cursor to start of next word
Ctrl-M	Move outline entries
Ctrl-N	New entry
Ctrl-O	Hanging indent
Ctrl-P	Print
Ctrl-Pg Up	Move to parent of current entry
Ctrl-Q	Copy family of entries
Ctrl-R	Find and replace
Ctrl-Right	Move to beginning of previous word
Ctrl-S	Save current outline
Ctrl-T	Set paragraph style
Ctrl-U	Divide entry into separate entries
Ctrl-W	Move family
Ctrl-X	Cancel paragraph indent
Ctrl-Y	Delete current line
Ctrl-Z	List windows

■ SECTION 98
PC-Outline control key summary

Shift-Del	Delete to end of line
Shift-Down	Move cursor to next entry on same level
Shift-End	Move directly to end of the outline
Shift-F1	Insert static date
Shift-F2	Insert live date
Shift-F3	Insert static time
Shift-F4	Insert live time
Shift-F5	Begin double strike print effect
Shift-F6	End double strike print effect
Shift-F10	Move marked entries
Shift-Home	Move directly to beginning of outline
Shift-Left	Delete word to left of cursor
Shift-Pg Dn	Move cursor to end of paragraph
Shift-Pg Up	Move cursor to top of paragraph
Shift-Right	Delete word to right of cursor
Shift-Up	Move cursor to previous entry on same level

PART 9

ProFinder

■ SECTION 99
Installing the program

ProFinder is a disk and file management program, rather like *Xtree* from Executive Systems. As such it is a utility; it does not relate directly to the WordStar program but it is another example of WordStar International's commitment to their customers. If you have only a floppy disk-based machine then the program will be of only limited use to you; on the other hand ProFinder really comes into its own on a hard disk.

When you copied the master disks onto your hard disk, the ProFinder files could have been copied, along with the other WordStar files. ProFinder consists of three files – PF.EXE, PF.HLP and PFINST.EXE – the first two are the actual program while the last is the installation routine. Because you will want to be able to access the program at all times you should either make the WordStar directory part of your MS-DOS PATH, or copy these files into your utility sub-directory. If the program is not available on the path then you will have to use command lines to activate it – which rather defeats the object of the exercise.

Once the files have been copied to whatever directory you are using you should run PFINST. This will allow you to customise the program to your preferences; for example, to set the display. However, you can run the program without installing it and just use the shipped defaults.

The installation is fully menu-driven. When activated you will be asked to input the directory that holds the ProFinder files. By default this is the WordStar directory so, if you have placed the files elsewhere, you must tell the program of the new location. Having input this information you will then be presented with the menu shown below.

■   **Video** allows you to configure the program for your monitor. It contains three options:

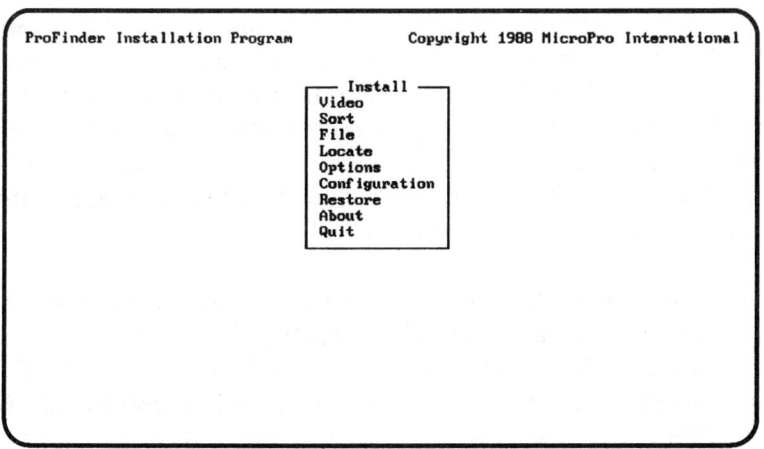

```
ProFinder Installation Program          Copyright 1988 MicroPro International

                              ─── Install ───
                              Video
                              Sort
                              File
                              Locate
                              Options
                              Configuration
                              Restore
                              About
                              Quit
```

ProFinder Installation Main Menu

Monitor   Assigns the type of monitor you have fitted, either a monochrome or an active colour one. ProFinder uses the standard 23-line display pattern whichever you use, unless you use the hotkey to flip back and forth between WordStar and ProFinder. In this case, if you have used the EGA 43-line or the VGA 50-line display then that is what ProFinder uses – but it only displays 23 lines!

Speed   Used to set the screen updating rate. Fast will work on most fully compatible monitors whereas Slow uses the ROM BIOS calls. This makes it slow but will reduce the amount of snow.

Colour Allows you to define the various pigments that will be used for the different elements of the display. As they are online, you can see what the result will be.

■ **Sort** sets the order in which the files will be displayed; you select the criteria and the order.

■ **File** defines how the program treats files: for example, by confirming when a file is overwritten.

■ **Locate** defines the conventions by which the files will be found.

■ **Options** is used to set what will be displayed, for example files only.

■ **Configuration** allows you to specify the fine detail of the program.

■ **Restore** will cancel any and all changes that you have made and return the program to the shipped defaults.

■ **About** pops up a menu giving the copyright details of the program.

■ **Quit** terminates the installation and allows you to save your changes or abandon them.

SECTION 100
Using the program

Having made your changes in PFINST, or not as the case may be, you can now run the program by entering **PF**. This will activate the program and display the contents of the current directory: that is, the one that you are currently logged onto.

```
C:\WS5\*.*
              UPDIR  3-04-89 12:42a
$INDEX    OVR    3712  9-23-88  5:00a
$TOC      OVR    1408  9-23-88  5:00a
01120036  CRT   14704  5-09-89  7:09p
01120048  CRT   17008  5-12-89  6:01p
01120060  CRT   18016  5-04-89  8:11p
01120072  CRT   19296  5-05-89 11:42a
02120060  CRT   18432  5-04-89  8:11p
03120048  CRT   16832  5-12-89  6:01p
03120060  CRT   18032  5-04-89  8:12p
04120060  CRT   18304  5-05-89 12:32p
05120060  CRT   17408  5-09-89 10:10p
05120072  CRT   18816  5-09-89 10:10p
05120084  CRT   20208  5-04-89  8:11p
05120120  CRT   24160  5-04-89  8:11p
05120144  CRT   26496  5-18-89  3:11p
07120060  CRT   17632  5-11-89 11:39a
07120120  CRT   24448  5-18-89  3:10p
07120144  CRT   26960  5-18-89  3:11p
43        EXE  155008  5-19-89  4:00p
ASCII     PDF     956  9-23-88  5:00a
BORDER    PS      309  9-16-88 10:40a
BOX       512          9-23-88  5:00a
F1Help  F2LocateF3Tag   F4Files F5View  F6OptionF7Sort  F8Exit  F9Run   10Menu
```

ProFinder main screen

The contents of the directory will be displayed in the order that you selected them, presented in a single column down the left-hand side of the screen. The right-hand side is used to display your comments about the files. When you first run the program there are no comments and so the area is blank. To add a comment to a file, use the cursor keys to move to the file, then press **Right**. A highlight appears in the blank area on the right-hand side of the screen. You can now add whatever comment you wish, using up to 39 characters. To add comments to the other files, just move the highlight down. Pressing **Enter** will move the cursor back to the files list. The comments remain in place as long as the file does, unless you delete them or change them. They are actually

■ SECTION 100
Using the program

stored in a file called TITLES.PF, which is created in the directory that holds the files (one file in each directory).

Along the bottom of the screen are the function key labels, many of which activate pop-up menus.

- ■ **F1** activates the on-line help. This is context-sensitive and so provides brief assistance with all of the possible options that the program provides.

- ■ **F2 (Locate)** is used to do a speed search for either files or text within a file. A menu will appear that allows you to specify the search type. You may enter a maximum of three strings of text to search for, using 20 characters each. Once you have done so, select Begin Search and the program does the rest. The search can be performed in the background, thus allowing you to carry on working with the other files at the same time.

- ■ **F3 (Tag)** marks files for use with the next option. The key activates a toggle so you can untag files by pressing it twice.

- ■ **F4 (Files)** pops up a menu that deals with file handling (see Section 101).

- ■ **F5 (View)** allows you to view files, in ASCII, WordStar or Lotus 1-2-3 format (See Section 102).

- ■ **F6 (Option)** is used to set the options by which the files are displayed, for example the mask used to present them. You can use this in place of running PFINST or to change the settings you made in the installation.

- ■ **F7 (Sort)** controls the order in which the files are shown.

■ **F8 (Exit)** terminates the program and places you back at the system prompt, in the directory that you are currently logged onto. Thus if you were originally in one directory but changed it while running the program you would now be in the second directory. Pressing **Esc** will also terminate the program but return you to the directory you were originally in when you started the program.

■ **F9 (Run)** makes ProFinder temporarily memory resident while you run another program. Move the cursor to the program you want and select this option. When the program terminates you will be returned to ProFinder. A word of caution: watch the memory you have available or you may find that the program will not run in its entirety. You cannot use the option if you are using the flip routine.

■ **F10 (Menu)** allows you to build a menu of programs to run. There is a default menu that you can use (see Section 103).

```
C:\WS5\*.*
              UPDIR  3-04-89 12:42a
$INDEX   OVR     3712  9-23-88  5:00a
$TOC     OVR     1408  9-23-─────── Files ───────
01120036 CRT    14704  5-09-    No files have
01120040 CRT    17008  5-12-     been tagged
01120060 CRT    18016  5-04-   ──────────────────
01120072 CRT    19296  5-05-   Copy
02120060 CRT    18432  5-04-   Move
03120048 CRT    16832  5-12-   Delete
03120060 CRT    18032  5-04-   Time/date stamp
04120060 CRT    18304  5-05-   Print file list
05120060 CRT    17408  5-09-   Write filenames
05120072 CRT    18816  5-09-   Go to DOS
05120084 CRT    20208  5-04-   Select tagged files
05120120 CRT    24160  5-04-   List all files
05120144 CRT    26496  5-18-   File tag by wild card
07120060 CRT    17632  5-11-   Retag
07120120 CRT    24448  5-18-   Untag all
07120144 CRT    26960  5-18-   ──────────────────
43       EXE   155000  5-19-89  4:00p
ASCII    PDF      956  9-23-88  5:00a
BORDER   PS       309  9-16-88 10:40a
BOX              512  9-23-88  5:00a
F1Help  F2      F3      F4      F5      F6      F7      F8      F9      10
```

ProFinder Files Menu

ProFinder is predominantly file-based; that is, it is not really geared up to allowing you to manipulate directories, and when it comes to handling the files it is in many ways better than *Xtree*.

Selecting **F4 (Files)** from the main menu pops up another menu that allows you to work with the files. The menu will work with files that have been tagged using **F3**, or you can input the files as you go along. If you have tagged files then the total number and the space that they occupy will be displayed at the top of the menu.

■   **Copy** allows you to make duplicates of any of the files, either into the current directory or to another sub-directory on your disk. In essence, it is the same as the MS-DOS COPY command; it's just easier to use because you can tag the files. Activating the command without any files being tagged allows you to specify a filename, or group of files using the wildcards, in the current directory. You then input the target directory and filename. Omitting a filename will copy the files to the same name in the target directory. The option provides you with:

- The facility to notify you of any overwriting that it does

- The option of including any titles you have appended

- The facility to verify that the file has been copied correctly

- The ability to skip files that already exist in both directories

■ **Move** is similar to copy but it allows you to copy files to the target directory and then delete them from the source directory in one operation. It provides the same options as Copy above.

■ **Delete** erases files from the directory. You can either tag the files or input the names. Pressing **Enter** to confirm the operation will remove the files – without giving you any confirmation of the individual erasures.

■ **Time/date stamp** allows you to change the date and time of the files. (This is probably the easiest date/time stamp I have ever used!) Simply tag the files you want to change, then select this option. A second dialogue box appears showing the current date and time; you can change either, using the cursor keys and then inputting the new values. Pressing **Enter** then applies the new stamp to all the tagged files.

■ **Print file list** simply sends a full list of all the files to your printer. Any files that have been tagged will be underlined on the printout. If the printer is not connected you will get an error message telling you so.

■ **Write filenames** allows you to make a disk file that contains the names of the files in the directory, similar to the previous option.

■ **Go to DOS** makes ProFinder slip into the memory while you run whatever commands or programs that you want. Once you have finished, entering **Exit** will restore ProFinder.

■ **Select tagged files** allows you to change the display so that it only shows those files that have been tagged. Pressing the asterisk will return the display to normal.

■ **List all files** returns the full file display if you have been using a partial listing.

■ **File tag by wildcard** allows you to tag files selectively; for example, you can ask to tag only those files that have the extension .TXT by entering * . **TXT**.

■ **Retag** allows you to automatically apply the tag again to any files that have been untagged through using the file commands.

■ **Untag all** does just that, returning all files to normal.

ProFinder will allow you to look at any file and will display its contents in either ASCII or WordStar format. If, when you look at a file, the format is wrong, you can toggle between the two using **Ctrl-Q G**. In essence this facility resembles a mini text editor but without the ability to change text. It also uses many of the keystrokes used by WordStar, for instance **Ctrl-K B** to start a block. See the illustration below for a full list of the keystrokes available. You can move around the file in exactly the same way as in a WordStar document, and the bottom line of the screen also contains a list of the function key labels.

```
C:\WS5\DIARY.DOC                        ▓
                         Trip Diary

September 10

What  a  wonderful  city  London  is!  We've  been  here  two  days  and
have  been  literally  running  from  one  tour  to  another.   We're
pretty  exhausted,  and  look  forward  to  exploring  a  few  sights   on
our own.

This   morning  we  took  a  tour  that  began  at  Trafalgar  Square.    We
took   the   underground  (their  word  for  subway)  from  our  hotel.
We've   found   the   London underground to be a great  way  to  get
around   and   less   costly  than  taxis.  We  had  a  whirlwind  tour
seeing   Parliament,   the  Tower  of  London,  Tower  Bridge,  and   the
changing   of  the  guard  at  the  palace.  Most  impressive  were   the
crown  jewels  in  the  Tower  of  London.

We   have  bein  touring  so  much  that  this  afternoon,  we  decided   to
do  a  little  shopping.   We  went  to  one  of  the  world  famous  depart-
ment   stores.    The  enormity  of  the  place  was  overwhelming.    We
found   we  were  more  comfortable  shopping  inthe  smaller  shops.   I
bought  a  wool  scarf  and  a  tea  set.

F1Help  F2LocateF3Prev  F4Next  F5Write  F6Print  F7Begin F8End     F9Open  10Auto B
```

ProFinder View File Menu

As with the entire program, pressing **F1** will provide you with help, popping up a dialogue box that contains the available keys. In this instance the help is not particularly context-sensitive.

You can search for text within a file, as on the Main Menu, by using **F2** and then inputting up to three strings of text. The facility

317

SECTION 102
Viewing files

will also pop up another menu that allows you to set the parameters for the search. Once you have found the first string, pressing **F4** causes the program to find the second string; pressing the key again will find the last one.

Marking out blocks is done in the same way as in WordStar; **Ctrl-K B** sets the start-of-block marker, while **Ctrl-K K** applies the end of block. The program is also pre-programmed to allow you to use the alternative **F7** and **F8** keys respectively. You can also mark an entire line as a block by using **F10**.

Having marked a block you can then write it to another file on the disk, using **Ctrl-K W** or **F5**, by supplying a new filename. **Ctrl-K P** or **F6** allows you to print the block.

ProFinder will allow you to open additional windows – up to three of them – that contain different files but you cannot copy or move text between them. To close a window press **Esc** – not **Ctrl-K Q** – but make sure you have saved the file if you have made changes to it.

■ SECTION 103
Creating a menu

Using a menu to run your programs is something that many people do, or would like to do, but menu-driven programs are often complex and/or expensive. ProFinder provides an alternative. You can set up a complete series of menus that will allow you to run whatever programs you wish, subject only to the memory limitation.

Whenever you press **F10**, asking for a menu, ProFinder will look in the current directory first, before looking in the default directory. Because of this, you can store separate menus in every directory. The program comes complete with a sample menu which is stored in a file called USERMENU.PF. As it is an ASCII file it can be loaded into WordStar and changed – but open it as a non-document. The file looks like this:

```
>Sample Menu
Documents,      /k=":c{enter}{F3}\doc{enter}{F7}{enter}"
<------ Inset -------
Inset,          c:
                cd\inset
                inset
                pf ~d~p
Remove Inset,   c:
                cd\inset
                  ri
                pf ~d~p
<---- PC Outline ----
Normal version,c:
                cd\pco
                pco /r
                pf ~d~p
Small version,  c:
                cd\pco
                pco /r /m=20
                pf ~d~p
<------ Other -------
Lotus,          c:
                cd\lotus
                123
                pf ~d~p
Quit,           /m=quitmenu.pf
```

As it stands, the menu looks exceedingly complex and so it needs some explanation.

Creating a menu

The first line is merely the heading. The greater sign (>) informs ProFinder that it should display the contents of the line centred at the start of the menu.

Line 2 uses composite ProFinder functions and what this line does is this:

■ The **/k=** closes the menu and then performs the list of keystrokes that is contained within the quotes.

■ The : displays the current prompt while the **c{enter}** changes to drive C.

■ The directory prompt will appear on the screen and then **{F3}** clears it.

■ **\doc{enter}** changes the directory to \DOC – or tries to.

■ **{F7}** activates the Sort routine, while **{enter}** accepts the default order.

■ The files within the \DOC directory will then be displayed in the current order.

Within the command line, whatever is enclosed in the { } brackets is treated as a command. In the above instance the function keys, which themselves activate commands, are enclosed in these brackets, thus confirming their status. The standard MS-DOS command keys are also treated this way. Thus **{enter}** is the same as pressing **Enter**, **{esc}** is the same as pressing the **Esc** key. The program makes no distinction between upper and lower case.

The next line in the menu is a heading, denoted by the less than sign (<). Whatever appears after this character will be displayed as a heading on the menu and the cursor cannot move onto that line.

Those words which appear at the start of a line, like that on line 4 of the menu, will appear on the menu as keywords. You cannot use more than 30 characters for these. The indented lines control the actions of the keyword and they are separated from the keyword by a comma.

Thus the 'module' that begins with 'Inset' first logs onto drive C, then changes to the INSET directory and loads the program. Finally, it returns to ProFinder in the current drive, denoted by the ~d, and the current directory, shown by the ~p. *Inset* is the screen capture program that is supplied with Version 5.5 and beyond of WordStar.

The final line terminates the menu and then stores the current drive and directory information. The \m= is responsible for this. It tells ProFinder to keep the information in the file named after the equals sign.

To get the best from the menu ability of ProFinder you will need to create your own menus, so experiment and try it out.

APPENDICES

Summary of dot commands

The dot commands are a quick and simple way of creating on-screen and printing effects. Each command must be on a separate line and be the first, and only, string of characters.

.av *<note>*,**v**	Shows contents of *<note>* and asks for variable input when merge printing
.aw off	Turns the auto-alignment off
.aw on	Switches auto-alignment on
.bn *<number>*	Activates a sheet feeder
.bp off	Turns bidirectional printing for a daisywheel printer off
.bp on	Switches bidirectional printing on
.cb	Forces a column break
.cc *<number>*	Starts new column if less than the specified number of lines remain
.co *<number>*	Prints the specified number of columns
.co *<number1>*,*<number2>*	
	Prints *<number1>* columns, *<number2>* distance apart
.cp *<number>*	Begins new page if less than the specified number of lines remain, when in column mode
.cs	Clears screen for messages when printing
.cv *<note1>* *<note2>*	
	Prints note of type 1 as note of type 2
.cw *<value>*	Changes character pitch
.df *<filename>*	Uses data from filename for merge printing
.dm *<note>*	Contents of *<note>* appear on screen whilst document is being printed
.ei	End conditional merge printing statement (Merge Printing)

Summary of dot commands

.el	If last **.if** statement is false then do this (Merge Printing)
.e# <*number*>	Changes default endnote symbol to that of the ASCII code expressed in <*number*>
.fi <*filename*>	Inserts a file to allow either chaining or nesting when files are being printed.
.fm <*number*>	Prints footnotes <*number*> of lines below main document text
.fn e	Footnotes only appear on evenly-numbered pages
.fn o	Footnotes only appear on odd-numbered pages
.f1 <*note*>	Prints contents of <*note*> on footnote line 1
.f2 <*note*>	Prints contents of <*note*> on footnote line 2
.f3 <*note*>	Prints contents of <*note*> on footnote line 3
.f# <*number*>	Sets footnote symbol to character of ASCII code expressed in <*number*>
.go bottom	Go to end of document (Merge Printing)
.go top	Go to start of document (Merge Printing)
.hm <*number*>	Prints header notes <*number*> of lines above text
.hn e	Prints header notes on even pages only
.hn o	Prints header notes on odd pages only
.h1 <*text*>	Prints <*text*> as header note 1
.h2 <*text*>	Prints <*text*> as header note 2
.h3 <*text*>	Prints <*text*> as header note 3
.if <*condition*>	Sets conditions for merge printing
.ig <*note*>	Shows <*note*> as non-printing comment
.ix <*note*>	Uses <*note*> for index entry
.kr off	Turns automatic kerning off

Summary of dot commands

.kr on	Turns automatic kerning on
.la *<number>*	Selects a foreign dictionary
.lh *<value>*	Adjusts line height in terms of forty-eighths of an inch
.lm *<number>*	Sets left margin
.lq dis	Sets letter quality printing to discretionary
.lq off	Turns letter quality printing off
.lq on	Turns letter quality printing on
.ls *<number>*	Sets line spacing to value expressed in *<number>*
.l# 0	Turns line numbering off
.l# d	Makes line numbering continuous
.l# d/p *<number>*	
	Sets spacing for line numbers to value contained in *<number>*
.l# d/p 1/2, *<number>*	
	Places line numbers *<number>* columns to left of margin
.l# p	Restarts line numbering on each separate page
.ma *<v>=<e>*	Stores result of equation *<e>* in the variable *<v>* when merge printing
.mb *<number>*	Sets bottom margin to *<number>*
.mt *<number>*	Sets top margin to *<number>*
.oc off	Turns off automatic line centring
.oc on	Activates automatic line centring
.oj off	Turns right justification off
.oj on	Turns right justification on

■ APPENDIX I
Summary of dot commands

.op	Turns off page numbering
.pa	Sets page break
.pc 0	Prints page numbers in centre of last line
.pc <*number*>	Prints page numbers in column <*number*>
.pe	Prints endnotes immediately thereafter
.pf off	Disables variable alignment when merge printing
.pf on	Aligns variables when merge printing
.pg	Uses default page numbering
.pl <*number*>	Sets page length
.pm <*number*>	Indents paragraph to column <*number*>
.pn <*number*>	Sets page number to <*number*>
.po <*number*>	Sets page offset
.po e <*number*>	Offsets even pages by <*number*> columns
.po o <*number*>	Offsets odd pages by <*number*> columns
.pr or=l	Selects landscape mode
.pr or=p	Selects portrait mode
.ps off	Turns proportional spacing off
.ps on	Turns proportional spacing on
.p# <*number*>	Starts paragraph numbering at <*number*>
.p# <*number*>, <*style*>	
	Sets paragraph numbering and style
.rm <*number*>	Redefines right margin to <*number*>
.rp <*number*>	Specifies number of print runs
.rr <*number*>	Imposes one of the default ruler lines
.rv <*fields*>	Sets field names from database file for merge printing

■ APPENDIX I
Summary of dot commands

.rv*	Merge prints *dBASE* file using *dBASE* field names
.rv* \$<*number*>	Reads and merge prints column, or row, <*number*> from spreadsheet
.rv* \$<*number*>\$<*number*>	
	Reads cell expressed by numbers from spreadsheet when merge printing
.sr <*number*>	Adjusts sub/superscript displacement
.sv <*number*>,<*note*>	
	Replaces variable <*number*> with text from <*note*> when merge printing
.tb <*value(s)*>	Sets new tabulations, in columns or inches
.tc <*note*>	Uses contents of <*note*> for table of contents
.tc<*number*> <*note*>	
	Uses contents of <*note*> for table of contents <*number*>, which may be in the range 1 – 9
.uj dis	Sets micro-justification to discretionary
.uj off	Cancels micro-justification
.uj on	Activates micro-justification
.xe <*new setting*>	Redefines the custom print character **Ctrl-P E**
.xl <*new setting*>	Redefines the custom print character **Ctrl-P L**
.xq <*new setting*>	Redefines the custom print character **Ctrl-P Q**
.xw <*new setting*>	Redefines the custom print character **Ctrl-P W**
.xx <*new setting*>	Redefines the custom print character **Ctrl-P X**

The WordStar Professional Opening Menu contains a total of eighteen commands, all of which are to do with the control and management of entire files, rather than the text that they contain, though they also lead to the actual text manipulation screens. The available commands, all activated by a single key press, are:

A   **Additional**

Allows you to run one of the two associated programs – MailList or TelMerge – which form part of the WordStar suite. See Parts 6 and 7 respectively.

C   **Protect/unprotect a file**

Used to change the Read Only attribute of a single selected file. See Part 3, Section 35.

D   **Open a document**

Permits you to open a standard document – one that contains print control codes, other fonts, etc. – and then make changes to it. See Part 3, Section 34.

E   **Rename a file**

Similar to the MS-DOS command REN, and the same rules apply. It allows you to change the name and/or extension of a file. See Part 3, Section 35.

Esc   **Shorthand**

Allows you to change or delete the user-programmed keyboard macros. See Part 4, Section 62.

F   **Turn directory on/off**

A simple toggle switch that can be used to blank the directory display. See Part 3, Section 32.

APPENDIX II
Main Menu command keys

I Index a document

Allows you to create an index of a file, providing the document has been configured to allow this. See Part 5, Section 67.

J **Help**

Activates the on-line help facility, allowing you to obtain information on every aspect of the program's capabilities. See Part 3, Section 32.

K **Print from keyboard**

Allows you to send a line of print directly to the printer without opening a document. You send words to the printer one line at a time but the page will not be printed until you press **Ctrl-U**. You should note that the printed page does *not* conform to any page layout you may have set within Word-Star!

L **Change drive/directory**

Used to change to alternative drives and/or directories so that you may save or open different files. See Part 3, Section 33.

M **Merge print a file**

Having created a database, this option will be used to print out form letters which make use of the database contents. See Part 6, Section 76.

N **Open a nondocument**

Used to load and then change pure ASCII files – those without print controls – such as CONFIG.SYS. See Part 3, Section 34.

O **Copy a file**

Allows you to make a duplicate of a file. Note that you cannot place the copy anywhere other than in the current directory. See Part 3, Section 36.

P   **Print a file**

Outputs a file to a selected printer or to another file. See Part 3, Section 38.

R   **Run a DOS command**

Permits you to use any MS-DOS command or other program, providing it is available on the computer's path, while making Wordstar temporarily memory resident. See Part 3, Section 37.

S   **Speed write**

Opens an unnamed file. The name will be given to it when the file is saved. See Part 3, Section 34.

T   **Table of contents**

Used to create a table of contents of a document file, providing the file has been pre-configured to allow it. See Part 5, Section 68.

X   **Exit WordStar**

Terminates the program and returns you to the system prompt. The monitor display will be returned to normal providing you have selected the appropriate option in WSCHANGE. See Part 3, Section 32.

Y   **Delete a file**

Allows you to delete selected files, either individually or in groups, by using the MS-DOS wildcards. See Part 3, Section 36.

?   **Memory usage**

Gives you a detailed inventory of the memory as used by WordStar.

APPENDIX III
Block and Save Menu key commands

All of these commands are accessed, on the editing screen, by pressing **Ctrl-K** followed by the respective character below.

A   **Copy between windows**
Allows you to copy a pre-defined block of text from one window to another. See Part 4, Section 55.

B   **Begin block**
Sets or deletes the start-of-block marker at the current cursor position. See Part 4, Section 60.

C   **Copy**
Makes a copy of a previously-defined block to the current cursor position. See Part 4, Section 60.

D   **Save**
Saves the current document and returns to the Main Menu. See Part 4, Section 59.

E   **Rename**
Allows you to rename the current file or any other in the directory from within a document. See Part 4, Section 61.

F   **Run a DOS command**
Makes WordStar temporarily memory resident while you run any command or program available on the current path. See Part 4, Section 61.

G   **Move between windows**
Allows you to move a pre-defined block of text from one window to another. See Part 4, Section 55.

H   **Turn display off**
Hides the block markers and any text they contain. See Part 4, Section 60.

I   **Column replace toggle**

Causes copied or moved blocks to overwrite existing text instead of it being inserted. See Part 4, Section 60.

J   **Delete a file**

Allows you to delete any file from the current directory from within a document. See Part 4, Section 61.

K   **End block**

Sets the end-of-block marker at the current cursor position. See Part 4, Section 60.

L   **Change drive/directory**

Allows you to change the drive or directory you are currently logged onto from the editing screen. See Part 4, Section 61.

M   **Math**

Adds the numbers contained in the currently marked block and displays the answer. See Part 4, Section 60.

N   **Column toggle**

Switches you between column and standard mode for dealing with blocks of text. See Part 4, Section 60.

O   **Copy a file**

Makes a duplicate of any file from within the editing screen without having to return to the Main Menu. See Part 4, Section 61.

P   **Print a file**

Allows you to print any file in the current directory while you continue to work on the editing screen. See Part 4, Section 61.

Block and Save Menu key commands

Q   **Abandon changes**

Discards any and all changes made to a document and returns to the Main Menu. See Part 4, Section 55 and Section 60.

R   **Insert a file**

Reads a file from the current directory and appends it to the current document on the editing screen. See Part 4, Section 60.

S   **Save and resume**

Makes a backup copy of the current document in case of accidental machine failure and then returns to editing screen. See Part 4, Section 59.

T   **Save as**

Saves the current document to another file-name and returns to the Main Menu. See Part 4, Section 59.

V   **Move**

Moves the previously marked block to the current cursor position. See Part 4, Section 60.

W   **Write to disk**

Saves the currently marked block of text to a disk file. See Part 4, Section 60.

X   **Save and exit**

Saves the current document, giving it a filename if necessary, and then returns to the Main Menu. See Part 4, Section 55 and Section 59.

Y   **Delete**

Erases the currently marked block from the document. See Part 4, Section 60.

z   **Sort**

Rearranges the marked block in order based on the first letter of each line. See Part 4, Section 60.

0-9   **Set marker**

Inserts one of the text markers into the document; they are only valid while the document is on screen, i.e. they are lost when the text is saved. See Part 4, Section 60.

"   **Upper case**

Changes all the letters in the currently marked block to upper case, i.e. capitals. See Part 4, Section 60.

'   **Lower case**

Changes all the letters in the currently marked block to lower case. See Part 4, Section 60.

.   **Sentence**

Makes the words and characters in the currently marked block conform to the normal sentence rules. See Part 4, Section 60.

■ APPENDIX IV
On-screen Format key commands

All of these commands are activated, on the editing screen, by pressing **Ctrl-O** followed by the appropriate letter.

A **Toggle auto-align**

Used to switch the auto-alignment on or off.

B **Soft spaces dots**

Toggles the soft space characters on and off. See Part 4, Section 53.

C **Centre line**

Toggles the line centring. See Part 4, Section 52.

D **Print controls**

Used to remove the display of the print controls. The switch toggles between them being active or passive. See Part 4, Section 53.

E **Enter soft hyphen**

Enters a hyphen – one that will only appear if it is at the end of the line. Used to hyphenate words that may extend past the right margin.

F **Paragraph styles**

Brings up a separate menu that will allow you to manipulate or select a paragraph style.

G **Temporary indent**

Sets the paragraph indentation for the duration of that paragraph. See Part 4, Section 52.

H **Auto-hyphenation**

If switched on then words which extend past the right margin will be split by a hyphen so that the text can be justified.

■ APPENDIX IV
On-screen Format key commands

I   **Set/clear tabs**

Allows you to change the default tab settings. See Part 4, Section 50.

J   **Justification**

Toggles the justification switch so that the text will be spread to fill the margins, or not. See Part 4, Section 53.

K   **Open or switch window**

Allows to you to open a second window, containing another document, or move between the two of them. See Part 4, Section 55.

L   **Left margin**

Changes the setting for the left-hand margin. See Part 4, Section 50.

M   **Size window**

Adjusts the size of the second window by defining how many lines it will occupy. See Part 4, Section 55.

N   **Notes**

Allows you to create notations that will apply to the text. See Part 4, Section 56 and Part 5, Section 67.

O   **Ruler to text**

Places the ruler line directly into the text. See Part 4, Section 51.

P   **Page preview**

Activates the Page Preview sub-program that will allow you to examine your document in a WYSIWYG environment. See Part 4, Section 54.

R   **Right margin**

Allows you to adjust the default right-hand margin. See Part 4, Section 50.

S   **Line spacing**

Changes the default line spacing in the range 1 to 9. See Part 4, Section 53.

T   **Ruler toggle**

Switches the ruler line, at the head of the screen, on or off. See Part 4, Section 51.

U   **Columns**

An effective shortcut that allows you to create columns easily. Entering the number of columns, the space between them and the value for the right-hand margin inserts the relevant dot commands in the document for you.

V   **Vertically centre**

Centres the text on a page so that it will appear in the middle of it; blank lines will be added to the beginning and end to make it fit. See Part 4, Section 53.

W   **Word wrap toggle**

Turns the right margin on or off. If off then text will continue to be added to the line instead of scrolling to the next one. See Part 4, Section 53.

X   **Margin release**

Releases both the left and right margins.

Z   **Paragraph number**

Allows you to number the paragraphs to make a structured document.

■ APPENDIX IV
On-screen Format key commands

]   **Right flush**
            Right justifies whatever is on the current line. Note
            that the entire line, and not just a part of it, will be
            justified.

?   **Memory usage**
            Identical to pressing ? from the Opening Menu.

■ APPENDIX V
Print Controls key commands

These keys are used primarily to set the print control codes. The commands are activated by pressing **Ctrl-P** followed by the appropriate letter.

A   **Alternate**

Sets the pre-defined alternative font so that all characters entered thereafter will be printed in this font. See Part 5, Section 64.

B   **Bold**

Used to set a marker that begins or ends the bold printing effect. See Part 5, Section 65.

C   **Pause**

Causes the printer to pause when it reaches this statement. See Part 5, Section 69.

D   **Double strike**

Sets the marker which defines the text that will be printed with double strike. See Part 5, Section 65.

E   **Custom**

A user-defined and customised printer control code. See Part 5, Section 69.

F   **Phantom space**

Used with daisywheel printers to produce a space. See Part 5, Section 69.

G   **Phantom rubout**

Used with daisywheel printers to produce a special character. See Part 5, Section 69.

H   **Overprint**

Superimposes one character onto another. See Part 5, Section 69.

APPENDIX V
Print Controls key commands

I   **8-column tab**

Moves the cursor eight places to the right, regardless of the pre-set tabs. See Part 5, Section 69.

K   **Indexing**

Used to mark a word or phrase within the text as an index entry. Used prior to running the index generation from the Main Menu. See Part 5, Section 67.

N   **Normal font**

Cancels any previously set font, but not printing effect; restores the default set within WSCHANGE. See Part 5, Section 64.

O   **Binding space**

Ensures that two words are treated as a single entity. See Part 5, Section 69.

Q   **Custom**

A user-defined and customised printer control code. See Part 5, Section 69.

R   **Custom**

A user-defined and customised printer control code. See Part 5, Section 69.

S   **Underline**

Sets the markers used to enclose the text that will be underlined. See Part 5, Section 65.

T   **Superscript**

Sets the markers used to enclose text that will be printed in superscript, i.e. above that standard text line. See Part 5, Section 65.

U   **Null**

Not used but will generate a ^U within the text.

Useful for placing in front of dots if they are liable to end up on the beginning of a line where they would be treated as dot commands without this.

V   **Subscript**

Sets the markers used to enclose text that will be printed as subscript, i.e. below the standard text line. See Part 5, Section 65.

W   **Custom**

A user-defined and customised printer control code. See Part 5, Section 69.

X   **Strikeout**

Marks the text that will be struck through when it is printed using the character preset in WSCHANGE. See Part 5, Section 65.

Y   **Italics**

Sets the markers used to enclose text that will be printed in italics, i.e. sloping text. See Part 5, Section 65.

0   **Extended characters**

Brings down a menu containing all the IBM extended ASCII characters and their appropriate codes. Entering a code will then place the relevant character into the text at the cursor position. See Part 4, Section 41.

=   **Select font**

Allows you to change the current font to any of those available within the printer definition menu. See Part 5, Section 64.

-   **Select colour**

Allows you to change the colour of the text that will

be printed, providing your printer is capable of doing so. See Part 5, Section 64.

? **Select printer**

Chooses one of the available printers and assign it permanently to the current document. See Part 5, Section 63.

* **Graphics tag**

Marks the position of the upper left-hand corner of a graphic, which must be in PIX format, that you want to include in the document. To print the picture you must have Inset loaded.

& **Start Inset**

Activates Inset so that you can capture or create an image for later use.

■ APPENDIX VI
Quick Menu key commands

All of these commands are activated by pressing **Ctrl-Q** followed by the pertinent letter.

A   **Find/replace**
Allows you to search for and then replace any word, or string of words, up to 68 characters long, with another string. See Part 4, Section 48.

B   **Beginning of block**
Will move the cursor to the start-of-block marker, providing one exists. See Part 4, Section 49.

C   **End of file**
Moves the cursor directly to the last possible position on a document, i.e. to the end. See Part 4, Section 40.

D   **End of line**
Moves the cursor to the extreme right-hand edge of the current line. See Part 4, Section 40.

Del   **Delete line to left**
Erases all characters from the cursor position to the beginning of the line. See Part 4, Section 45.

E   **Upper left**
Moves the cursor to the top left-hand corner of the editing screen. See Part 4, Section 40.

F   **Find text**
Allows you to input a word or phrase which the computer will then search for and move the cursor to. See Part 4, Section 47.

G   **Character forward**
Will move the cursor from its current position

towards the end of the file until it reaches the selected character. See Part 4, Section 49.

H   **Character back**

Moves the cursor from its current position back towards the beginning until it finds the selected character. See Part 4, Section 49.

I   **Page/line**

Allows you to select and then move directly to a selected page. The cursor will position itself at the top left-hand corner of the page. See Part 4, Section 49.

J   **Thesaurus**

Activates the thesaurus, which will provide synonyms for the word above the cursor. See Part 4, Section 44.

K   **End of block**

Will move the cursor to the end-of-block marker, providing one exists. See Part 4, Section 49.

L   **Spell check rest**

Activates the spelling checker which will check all the spellings from the current cursor position to the end of the document. See Part 4, Section 42.

M   **Math**

Activates the in-built calculator. See Part 4, Section 46.

N   **Check word**

Allows you to verify the spelling of an individual word without having to spell-check the entire document. See Part 4, Section 43.

O   **Enter word**

Spell-checks an individual word before entering it into the text of the document. See Part 4, Section 43.

P   **Previous**

Moves the cursor to the position it occupied prior to your issuing the last command.

Q   **Repeat**

Causes the next key press to be repeated indefinitely until it is interrupted.

R   **Beginning of file**

Moves the cursor directly to the top left-hand corner of the file. See Part 4, Section 40.

S   **Beginning of line**

Moves the cursor to the left-hand edge of the current line. See Part 4, Section 40.

T   **Delete to character**

Will delete everything from the cursor position to the selected character. See Part 4, Section 45.

U   **Align document**

Used to align the text within a document, primarily after a find and replace, so that it matches the margins. See Part 4, Section 45.

V   **Previous find**

Moves the cursor to the location of the last find/replace that was carried out; alternatively it will move it to the location of a previously moved block.

W   **Scroll up**
Causes the display to scroll up one line at a time.
See Part 4, Section 40.

X   **Lower right**
Moves the cursor to the bottom right-hand corner
of the screen – or as near as it can get. See Part 4,
Section 40.

Y   **Delete line right**
Deletes all the characters on the current line from
the cursor position to the right-hand edge of that
line. See Part 4, Section 45.

Z   **Scroll down**
Causes the display to scroll down one line at a time.
See Part 4, Section 40.

0-9   **Marker**
Moves the cursor directly to a preset marker. See
Part 4, Section 49.

?   **Character count**
Gives a report on the number of bytes used from the
beginning of the document to the current cursor
position.

=   **Find next font**
Moves the cursor to the next specified font, providing it exists. See Part 4, Section 49.

APPENDIX VII
WordStar error messages

In general, WordStar Professional is very user-friendly and many of the error messages that it produces are fairly straightforward and self-explanatory. However some of them require a little elucidation. This list is not complete but covers the more commonly encountered errors.

A filename is required

Possible cause: You are trying to open a document without specifying a filename.

Cure: Either enter a filename from the keyboard or use the cursor keys to select a file from the directory.

A word is too long to fit in the margins

Possible cause: The margins have been changed and the document reformatted. The result is that a word on the line no longer fits between the margins.

Cure: Hyphenate the word or change the margins to allow for it.

Arithmetic error

Possible cause: The calculation is invalid, e.g. you are trying to divide by zero.

Cure: Check the equation and if necessary sub-divide it and do the parts separately to find the fault.

Can't delete or rename the file being edited

Possible cause: You are trying to delete the file which is currently being edited.

Cure: None – this file cannot be deleted or renamed. You must save or it abandon it first.

WordStar error messages

Can't edit temporary file

Possible cause: You are trying to load a temporary file, e.g. into another window.

Cure: None – you cannot edit any file that has an extension starting with '.$'.

Can't find COMMAND.COM

Possible cause: The system file COMMAND.COM is not available on your path.

Cure: Check that the program is on the path using WSCHANGE, i.e. ensure that Wordstar has your computer's configuration properly set.

Can't find that file. Create a new one (Y/N)?

Possible cause: You have tried to open a non-existent file.

Cure: Select **Y** to create a new file, **N** to re-input the filename.

Can't move to undefined marker

Possible cause: You have used **Ctrl-Q** *<number>* without having set a marker.

Cure: Set the marker(s) using **Ctrl-K** *<number>*

Can't update dictionary

Possible cause: The personal dictionary has reached the limits of its preset memory allocation.

Cure: Change the amount of memory allocated in WSCHANGE.

Changed have been made. Abandon anyway (Y/N)?

Possible cause: You have asked to discard a document to which changes have been made since it was loaded.

Cure: Pressing **Y** allows the abandonment, **N** cancels the operation and allows you to save the file.

Cursor is not on a note

Possible cause: You have tried to change a note without the cursor being on the marker of that note.

Cure: Press **Esc**, move the cursor to the note marker and try again.

Drive is write protected

Possible cause: The disk you want to use has the write protection covered or it is a fully-sleeved cover.

Cure: Remove the tab or use another disk.

End of block is at or before the start of block

Possible cause: You have tried to perform a block operation but do not have the block markers set correctly.

Cure: Set the markers in the correct positions.

End of block not below and to the right of start of block

Possible cause: Appears only in column mode. The end of block marker must be in a column to the right of the first marker.

Cure: Either move the marker or change back from column mode using **Ctrl-K N**.

Equation is too complex

Possible cause: WordStar cannot perform your calculation.

Cure: Break the equation into parts and do each separately.

File access denied by DOS

Possible cause: You are trying to create a file bearing the same name as one of the reserved MS-DOS words, e.g. PRN or AUX.

Cure: Rename the file using a non-reserved word.

File already exists. Overwrite (Y/N) or append (A)?

Possible cause: You used **Ctrl-K T** to save a file and the name you have entered is the name of an existing file.

Cure: Pressing **Y** will cause the new file to overwrite the old one, **N** cancels the operation, and **A** adds the new file to the end of the existing one.

File error

Possible cause: Appears if there is an undefinable error with your disk, e.g. it may be full and thus not have room for your file to be saved. Usually WordStar will be able to give you more specific information than this, but it retains this error message as a final catch-all.

Cure: Cancel the current operation and check the free space on your disk.

File won't rename

Possible cause: You have tried to rename a file to the same name as a hidden or system file.

Cure: Use a different name.

Help is not available

Possible causes: The WSHELP.OVR file is missing; there is insufficient memory available; you have turned the help facility off.

Cure: Check that the overlay file exists, unload any TSR programs, check that the correct level of help is set by using **Ctrl-J Ctrl-J** and also check the settings in WSCHANGE.

Incorrect printer name

Possible cause: You have input the wrong name on the printer menu.

Cure: Re-enter the correct name.

Insufficient memory for background printing

Possible cause: All the available memory is being used for other purposes.

Cure: Save the document and then print it from the Main Menu.

Line too short to use as a ruler

Possible cause: The line you specified contains less than two characters.

Cure: Increase the number of characters.

Merge print information missing

Possible cause: You have omitted a field name or a dot command from the document being merge printed.

Cure: Check the document contains all the necessary information.

■ APPENDIX VII
WordStar error messages

Mismatched parentheses

Possible cause: You have used nested brackets in an equation and they do not balance.

Cure: Check or re-enter the calculation.

No block defined yet

Possible cause: You have tried to perform a block operation without setting the block markers.

Cure: Set the markers and then retry the operation.

No numbers in block to add or subtract

Possible cause: You have used the key sequence **Ctrl-K M** but the block does not contain any figures.

Cure: None – the maths feature only works with numbers.

No second window

Possible cause: You have tried to use a block operation, e.g. **Ctrl-K A**, to another window that is not open.

Cure: None – open the window first.

Not a valid directory path

Possible cause: The path you have specified is misspelled or incomplete.

Cure: Re-enter the information.

Not enough memory to continue

Possible cause: You have allocated nearly all the memory to TSRs so that there is now insufficient for WordStar to run correctly.

Cure: Unload the TSRs and start again.

APPENDIX VII
WordStar error messages

Not enough space to store shorthand macro

Possible cause: You have tried to create a macro but you are already using all the memory allocation for storing them.

Cure: Increase the memory by using WSCHANGE or delete some of the existing macros.

Printer may not be ready. Press C to continue

Possible cause: The printer may be turned off, off-line, out of paper or otherwise disabled.

Cure: Check the printer, paper and ribbon and then press C.

Second window is in use

Possible cause: You are trying to create a note with two windows open.

Cure: Close one window and then retry. (Equally you cannot run Page Preview if you have two windows open.)

Too large to undo later. Undo anyway (Y/N)?

Possible cause: The block of text you are trying to delete contains more characters than can be held in the unerase buffer.

Cure: Either delete the block in sections; save the block and then delete it; or continue – but then you will be unable to restore the block.

APPENDIX VIII
ASCII codes

Dec	Hex	Char	Dec	Hex	Char	Dec	Hex	Char	Dec	Hex	Char
0	00	NUL	32	20	Space	64	40	@	96	60	`
1	01	SOH	33	21	!	65	41	A	97	61	a
2	02	STX	34	22	"	66	42	B	98	62	b
3	03	ETX	35	23	#	67	43	C	99	63	c
4	04	EOT	36	24	$	68	44	D	100	64	d
5	05	ENQ	37	25	%	69	45	E	101	65	e
6	06	ACK	38	26	&	70	46	F	102	66	f
7	07	BEL	39	27	'	71	47	G	103	67	g
8	08	BS	40	28	(	72	48	H	104	68	h
9	09	HT	41	29	)	73	49	I	105	69	i
10	0A	LF	42	2A	*	74	4A	J	106	6A	j
11	0B	VT	43	2B	+	75	4B	K	107	6B	k
12	0C	FF	44	2C	,	76	4C	L	108	6C	l
13	0D	CR	45	2D	-	77	4D	M	109	6D	m
14	0E	SO	46	2E	.	78	4E	N	110	6E	n
15	0F	SI	47	2F	/	79	4F	O	111	6F	o
16	10	DLE	48	30	0	80	50	P	112	70	p
17	11	DC1	49	31	1	81	51	Q	113	71	q
18	12	DC2	50	32	2	82	52	R	114	72	r
19	13	DC3	51	33	3	83	53	S	115	73	s
20	14	DC4	52	34	4	84	54	T	116	74	t
21	15	NAK	53	35	5	85	55	U	117	75	u
22	16	SYN	54	36	6	86	56	V	118	76	v
23	17	ETB	55	37	7	87	57	W	119	77	w
24	18	CAN	56	38	8	88	58	X	120	78	x
25	19	EM	57	39	9	89	59	Y	121	79	y
26	1A	SUB	58	3A	:	90	5A	Z	122	7A	z
27	1B	ESC	59	3B	;	91	5B	[	123	7B	{
28	1C	FS	60	3C	<	92	5C	\	124	7C	¦
29	1D	GS	61	3D	=	93	5D	]	125	7D	}
30	1E	RS	62	3E	>	94	5E	^	126	7E	~
31	1F	US	63	3F	?	95	5F	_	127	7F	Δ

Extended ASCII codes

Dec	Hex	Char	Dec	Hex	Char	Dec	Hex	Char	Dec	Hex	Char
128	80	Ç	160	A0	á	192	C0	L	224	E0	α
129	81	ü	161	A1	í	193	C1	⊥	225	E1	β
130	82	é	162	A2	ó	194	C2	T	226	E2	Γ
131	83	â	163	A3	ú	195	C3	├	227	E3	π
132	84	ä	164	A4	ñ	196	C4	─	228	E4	Σ
133	85	à	165	A5	Ñ	197	C5	┼	229	E5	σ
134	86	å	166	A6	ª	198	C6	╞	230	E6	μ
135	87	ç	167	A7	º	199	C7	╟	231	E7	τ
136	88	ê	168	A8	¿	200	C8	╚	232	E8	Φ
137	89	ë	169	A9	⌐	201	C9	╔	233	E9	θ
138	8A	è	170	AA	¬	202	CA	╩	234	EA	Ω
139	8B	ï	171	AB	½	203	CB	╦	235	EB	δ
140	8C	î	172	AC	¼	204	CC	╠	236	EC	∞
141	8D	ì	173	AD	¡	205	CD	═	237	ED	ø
142	8E	Ä	174	AE	«	206	CE	╬	238	EE	∈
143	8F	Å	175	AF	»	207	CF	╧	239	EF	∩
144	90	É	176	B0	░	208	D0	╨	240	F0	≡
145	91	æ	177	B1	▒	209	D1	╤	241	F1	±
146	92	Æ	178	B2	▓	210	D2	╥	242	F2	≥
147	93	ô	179	B3	│	211	D3	╙	243	F3	≤
148	94	ö	180	B4	┤	212	D4	╘	244	F4	⌠
149	95	ò	181	B5	╡	213	D5	╒	245	F5	⌡
150	96	û	182	B6	╢	214	D6	╓	246	F6	÷
151	97	ù	183	B7	╖	215	D7	╫	247	F7	≈
152	98	ÿ	184	B8	╕	216	D8	╪	248	F8	°
153	99	Ö	185	B9	╣	217	D9	┘	249	F9	·
154	9A	Ü	186	BA	║	218	DA	┌	250	FA	·
155	9B	¢	187	BB	╗	219	DB	█	251	FB	√
156	9C	£	188	BC	╝	220	DC	▄	252	FC	ⁿ
157	9D	¥	189	BD	╜	221	DD	▌	253	FD	²
158	9E	₧	190	BE	╛	222	DE	▐	254	FE	■
159	9F	ƒ	191	BF	┐	223	DF	▀	255	FF	

■ APPENDIX X
Pitch and point

The size of the characters you produce will depend on the type of printer that you are using. Dot matrix printers, without exception, and daisywheel printers to a lesser extent, base their printed character size on **pitch**. This is a measure of the number of characters that can be printed in one inch across the width of the paper. The pitch size is actually the number of characters within that space. It is based on the letter O which is taken to be the average size of all the characters, which is why wider letters like W and M will sometimes impinge on the letters to either side of them in the printed text. Thus 10-pitch means you can print ten characters to the inch, 12-pitch is twelve per inch and so on. Therefore the higher the pitch value the smaller the characters.

Ordinary laser printers, on the other hand, base their printed character size on **points**. A point is $1/72$ of an inch and it refers to the height of the character block. It also influences the width of the characters but to a much lesser extent. Thus 12-point means that the characters are $12/72$, or $1/6$ of an inch high, so you can print six lines to an inch down the length of the paper – which is the normal default for most printers anyway. On the other hand 36-point, being $36/72$ or $1/2$ inch, means that you can only print two lines to the inch down the paper. Therefore the higher the point value, the larger the characters and so you can print less of them in the same space. (You can also define point sizes, but not pitch, in fractions – e.g. 12.6 – but that gets really confusing. Things work better if you stick to whole sizes rather than divisions of them.)

However, that is not the end of the matter. Neither the pitch nor the point sizes refer to the actual characters, although to all intents and purposes you can treat them as if they do. Both sizes are a hangover from the days when printers set type using little lead character blocks. The sizes actually refer to these rather than the symbols they contain because the blocks contained a built-in separator – a blank space above and below the characters – to allow the proper spacing of the letters or symbols. You will also notice that the sizes are defined in inches. On either side of the character is a blank area which ensures that the characters do not butt up tight to each other. The spaces above and below the letter or number are to prevent the character from hitting the symbols on the lines above and below. The spaces – both types – are more or less constant on the lead blocks, regardless of which letter is being used.

However, on a computer this is not the case. All characters on any computer occupy the same character area – e.g. a block of 9 pixels by 9 – and the letters and symbols are distorted to make them fit into that block. Thus the spacing around the characters will vary from letter to letter and symbol to symbol. This is why, when you look at text on the screen, the lines are separated by only a single pixel or two. But when you come to print it out the text will normally be separated properly because the printer uses a different resolution and different character blocks.

Even though a letter is regarded as 10-point the actual character might only physically occupy 70% of this. Equally, while the height of the entire block might be 36 points the letter only occupies 27 points, or 75% of the total height. And then, just to confuse matters further, different typefaces use different amounts of blank space around their characters. Thus if you are using Courier, the figures above might be correct but if you change to Times Roman then the actual character size may be 65% and 60% for instance. The size of the characters on their blocks cannot be changed, it is pre-programmed by the font designers. This is why you can suddenly find that changing the typeface of a single line makes an enormous difference to your layout. You might expect the characters to stay the same size but they don't and all the rest of the text flows to accommodate the new size.

■ APPENDIX X
Pitch and point

One final point. Blank spaces and carriage returns are also characters and the rules about sizes apply to them too. Thus you can tighten up a document by reducing the point size of the lines in between paragraphs. Equally, you can spread the paragraphs by increasing the point size where you do not want to add a complete line. WordStar, when used with any of the laser printers it supports, works on point sizes – never on pitch, which only applies to dot matrix printers – and so all the characters that it is capable of producing are based on this.

Answers to the Money Puzzle

The Money Puzzle, used throughout this book as the example on the editing screen, was especially created for this purpose. For anyone who is interested here are the answers to the questions. Yes, I know the puns are awful!

a) An old form of transport: *A penny farthing bicycle (1¼d)*

b) Move up and down, in water perhaps: *To bob (2/-)*

c) Mars, Jupiter and Venus are .....: *Three far things (¾d)*

d) A type of pig: *Guinea (£1/1/-)*

e) Underwear for a one-legged woman: *Half a knicker (10/-)*

f) A section of a regal head-dress: *Half a crown (2/6)*

g) An unwell decapod mollusc: *Sick squid (£6/-/-)*

h) A stone: *Fourteen pounds (£14/-/-)*

i) He turns skin into leather: *A tanner (6d)*

j) A type of singing voice: *Tenor (£10/-/-)*

k) A section of a primate's limb: *An ape knee (½d)*

If you add up the amounts from each answer you will find that you have a total of Thirty-One Pounds, Sixteen Shillings, Two and a Half Pence.

APPENDIX XII
Map to WSCHANGE options

A CONSOLE

A Monitor

A Monitor selection

  A IBM PC compatible (inc EGA,VGA)
  B IBM PC CGA compatible
  C IBM PC ROM compatible
  D IBM PC EGA compatible, 43 lines
  E IBM PC VGA compatible, 50 lines
  F Reset all IBM scrn, fn key defaults

B Monitor name

C Screen sizing

  A Height
  B Width
  C Horizontal scroll width

B Function keys

C Video attributes

A Select colours individually
B Colour display default
C Monochrome display default
D Shipped default

D Monitor patches

A Special characters

  A Del display string
  B Soft hyphen display string
  C Begin block marker
  D End block marker
  E Box drawing characters
  F Tab (ASCII 09) mask

B Cursor control

  A Cursor movement delay
  B Delay value for auto-realignment
  C Cursor sizes

C Video attributes

  A Video attribute subroutine
  B Colours
  C Reverse bright/dim

D Save colours

E Cursor size for mono monitors

  A Thin cursor during insert mode
  B Block cursor during insert mode
  C Thin cursor during overtype mode
  D Block cursor during overtype mode
  E Thin cursor after WordStar
  F Block cursor after WordStar

F Cursor size for all other monitors

  A Thin cursor during insert mode
  B Block cursor during insert mode
  C Thin cursor during overtype mode
  D Block cursor during overtype mode
  E Thin cursor after WordStar
  F Block cursor after WordStar

E Keyboard patches

A Function Keys

  A Size/delay for function key burst
  B Function key burst lead-in char
  C Edit Menu translation table
  D Opening Menu translation table
  E Prompts translation table
  F Type ahead flush control
  G Onscreen function labels

B Keyboard repeat rates

  A Short delay before inserting
  B Long delay before inserting
  C Fast rate for inserting text
  D Slow rate for inserting text
  E Short delay before deleting
  F Long delay before deleting
  G Fast rate for deleting text
  H Slow rate for deleting text

C Save function keys

■ APPENDIX XII
Map to WSCHANGE options

B PRINTER

A Choose a default printer

B Change printer name sign-on

C Printing defaults

Printing defaults Menu #1

A Print nondocument as standard
B Bidirectional printing
C Letter quality printing (NLQ)
D Microjustification
E Underline blanks
F Proportional spacing
G Normal character font
H Alternative character font
I Strikeout character
J Line height (1440ths/inch)
K Sub/superscript roll (1440th/in)

Printing defaults Menu #2

A Print page numbers
B Kerning
C Load Inset at print-time

D Printer interface

A Printer busy handshaking

  A Busy test for output to printer
  B Long busy timeout(msec,0=dis)

B Printer subroutines

  A Initialisation subroutine
  B Un-initialisation subroutine
  C Output status subroutine
  D Character output subroutine
  E Input status subroutine
  F Character input subroutine
  G Printer patch area

C Background printing

  A Concurrent printing
  B Beep if printer wait condition

C COMPUTER

A Disk drives

  A Valid disk drives
  B Delay disk access if typing

B Operating system

A Single-user system
B Multi-user system
C IBM compatibility

  A IBM compatible ROM BIOS
  B IBM counter/timer for beeping
  C Put characters directly in video RAM
  D INT 1C time interrupt
  E Hardware cursor movement

C Memory usage

Memory usage Menu #1

A WordStar RAM resident (help off)
B Entire main dict. to RAM if room
C Speller, thes, hyph memory usage

  A All share memory
  B Speller, thes. share, hyph. separate
  C Speller, hyph. share, thes. separate
  D Each in separate memory

D Main spelling buffer (kbytes)
E Personal dict. memory (kbytes)
F Message & menus buffer (records)
G Text spillover, 0=auto (records)
H Shorthand buffer size (records)
I Dot cmnd buffer, RR, etc. (bytes)

Memory usage Menu #2

A Mem. alloc. for unerase buffer
B Mem. alloc. for editor (kbytes)
C Header and footer size (bytes)
D Memory for merge print (kbytes)
E Number of menu font defns
F Number of font family defns
G No. of prop. space data tables

H PDF buffer size (records)
I Footnote buffer size (records)
J Endnote buffer size (records)

D WordStar files

WordStar files Menu #1

A Define default search path

  A Define default search path 1
  B Define default search path 2
  C Define default search path 3
  D Define default search path 4
  E Define default search path 5
  F Define default search path 6
  G Define default search path 7
  H Define default search path 8
  I Define default search path 9

B Reassign drive, path all WS files
C Messages and menus file
D Indexer exclusion list file
E Shorthand storage file
F Help overlay
G Paragraph styles library file
H TelMerge from Additional Menu
I MailList from Additional Menu

WordStar files Menu #2

A Spelling checker overlay
B Main spelling dictionary file
C Personal spelling dictionary file
D Foreign language dict. (if req.)
E Thesaurus overlay file
F Thesaurus dictionary
G Thesaurus definitions overlay
H Advance Page Preview work files
I Advanced Page Preview file
J Location FONTID.CTL for Page Prev

WordStar files Menu #3

A Hyphenation overlay
B Main data file for hyphenation
C Index file for hyphenation

D Printer description files
E Printer overlay files
F Print from keyboard template file
G Inset program print-time loading
H Graphics files directory display
I Graphics files file extension

WordStar files Menu #4

A Backup file type
B Temporary text file type
C Temporary text file type
D Temporary block file type
E Newspaper column file type
F Endnote file type
G Footnote file type
H Workfile for paragraph styles
I Messages buffer size (records)
J Make backup files when saving

E Directory display

A Display file directory
B Directory in alphabetical order
C File types excluded from directory
D Filenames that are shown
E Initial directory log-on
F Show space remaining on disk
G Show size of each file
H Show files when change drv/dir
I Display dir. at filename prompts

F Computer patches

A Initialisation string
B Un-initialisation string
C Initialisation subroutine
D Un-initialisation subroutine
E General patch area
F Printer patch area
G Extra patch area
H Multi-user control
I WordStar control

D WORDSTAR

A Page layout

A Page size and margins

- A Page length
- B Top margin
- C Bottom margin
- D Header margin
- E Footer margin
- F Page offset on even page
- G Page offset on odd page
- H Left margin
- I Right margin
- J Paragraph margin (-1 for none)

B Headers and footers (page nos.)

- A Print page numbers
- B Position of page no. (-1=centre)
- C Initial page number

C Tabs

- A Regular tab stops
- B Decimal tab stops

D Footnotes and endnotes

Footnotes & endnotes Menu #1

A Footnote font and style

- A *Footnote font*
- B *Default ruler to use*
- C *Default colour to use*

B Footnote repeating character table

C Footnote reference mark in text

- A *Attribute*
- B *Leading character*
- C *Trailing character*

D Footnote reference mark in note

- A *Attribute*
- B *Leading character*
- C *Trailing character*

E Footnote tag type

- A *Type of reference mark*
- B *Restart each pg. or increase seq.*

F Footnote separator

G Footnote continuation text

H Footnote position

I Running footnote format

J Footnote VMI lines

- A *VMI between lines (1440ths/inch)*
- B *VMI for each footnote line*
- C *VMI between text & separator line*
- D *VMI between separator & first line*

K Footnote file type

L Footnote buffer size (records)

Footnotes & endnotes Menu #2

A Endnote font and style

- A *Endnote font*
- B *Default ruler to use*
- C *Default colour to use*

B Endnote repeating character table

C Endnote reference mark in text

- A *Attributes*
- B *Leading character*
- C *Trailing character*

D Endnote reference mark in note

- A *Attributes*
- B *Leading character*
- C *Trailing character*

E Endnote tag type

F Endnote VMI text lines separation

- A *VMI between notes*
- B *VMI for each endnote line*

G Endnote file type

H Endnote buffer size (records)

E Stored ruler lines

A Default ruler line

- A *Left margin*
- B *Right margin*
- C *Paragraph margin*
- D *Regular tab stops*
- E *Decimal tab stops*

B 1st stored ruler line

- A *Left margin*

B *Right margin*
C *Paragraph margin*
D *Regular tab stops*
E *Decimal tab stops*

C 2nd stored ruler line

A *Left margin*
B *Right margin*
C *Paragraph margin*
D *Regular tab stops*
E *Decimal tab stops*

D 3rd stored ruler line

A *Left margin*
B *Right margin*
C *Paragraph margin*
D *Regular tab stops*
E *Decimal tab stops*

E 4th stored ruler line
A *Left margin*
B *Right margin*
C *Paragraph margin*
D *Regular tab stops*
E *Decimal tab stops*

F 5th stored ruler line

A *Left margin*
B *Right margin*
C *Paragraph margin*
D *Regular tab stops*
E *Decimal tab stops*

G 6th stored ruler line

A *Left margin*
B *Right margin*
C *Paragraph margin*
D *Regular tab stops*
E *Decimal tab stops*

H 7th stored ruler line

A *Left margin*
B *Right margin*
C *Paragraph margin*
D *Regular tab stops*
E *Decimal tab stops*

I 8th stored ruler line

A *Left margin*
B *Right margin*
C *Paragraph margin*
D *Regular tab stops*
E *Decimal tab stops*

J 9th stored ruler line

A *Left margin*
B *Right margin*
C *Paragraph margin*
D *Regular tab stops*
E *Decimal tab stops*

F Paragraph styles

A Library of paragraph styles
B Default paragraph style
C Temporary file extension
D Storage buffer size

G Units of measurement

A Horizontal unit
B Vertical unit
C Line height unit
D Font size unit
E Unit for all measurements

B Editing settings

A Edit screen, help level

Edit screen Menu #1

A Help level
B Display fn. keys at help level 4
C Status line
D Status line filler character
E Soft space display
F Soft space character
G Page break character
H Binding space character
I Snaking column character
J Column break character
K Dot leader character
L Print control display

Edit screen Menu #2

A Ruler line

APPENDIX XII
Map to WSCHANGE options

B Default onscreen fn. key labels
C HMI (1800ths) units for ruler line
D VMI (1440ths) units for line height
E Hard return ending character
F Soft return ending character
G Long line character
H End of file character
I Overprint line character

Edit screen Menu #3

A Line feed character
B Form feed character
C Page break character
D Column break character
E Window separator character
F Dot command character
G Dot command at start of page
H Merge print dot command char.
I Unknown dot command character

B Typing

A Word wrap at right margin
B Insert characters
C Fast typing display pause
D Fast typing page/line/col. delay
E Disk access pause
F Automatic backspace characters
G Scroll speed

C Paragraph alignment

A Right-justification
B Line spacing
C Auto-hyphenation
D Chars. before auto-hyphenation
E Auto-align
F Delay value for auto-alignment
G Watch progress of ^QU alignment

D Blocks

A Column mode
B Column replace mode
C Beginning block marker
D Ending block marker

E Erase and unerase

A Max. chars. that can be unerased

B Unerase single character erasures
C Del erases to left (not at cursor)
D Erasing and cursor type ahead

F Lines and characters

Line and characters Menu #1

A Characters that are part of a word
B Characters for moving across words
C Soft space display
D Soft space character
E Page break character
F Binding space character
G Snaking column character
H Column break line character
I Dot leader character
J Thousands number separator
K Decimal point

Lines and characters Menu #2

A Hard return character
B Soft return character
C Long line character
D End of file character
E Overprint line character
F Line feed character
G Form feed character
G Page break character
H Column break character
I Window separator character

Lines and characters Menu #3

A Dot command character
B Dot command at start of page
C Merge print dot command char.
D Unknown dot command character

G Find and replace

A Default find and replace options

H WordStar compatibility

A ^H moves left (not erase left)
B ^6 hard to soft CR/auto-align
C Del erase left (not at cursor)
D Cursor stays in col. 1 at marker
E No extra soft lines at para. end
F Esc acts like ^R and

G   Automatically fill out last record
H   ^QX goes to right side of screen
I   Classic commands at Open. Menu
J   Dot commands auto. put into file

I   Paragraph numbering

    A   Paragraph numbering style
    B   Para. numbering separator at end
    C   Outline style numbering

J   Line numbering

    A   Line numbering font
    B   Continuous line numbering
    C   Line spacing between line nos.
    D   Left margin for line number
    E   Left margin char. for line number
    F   Right margin for line number
    G   Right margin char. for line no.
    H   Space between no., left marg. char

C   Other features

A   Spelling check

    A   Spelling check overlay
    B   Main spelling dictionary file
    C   Thesaurus overlay file
    D   Personal spelling dictionary file
    E   Dictionary usage

       A   *Swap dictionary/program disk*
       B   *Personal dict. on dictionary disk*
       C   *Personal dict. on working disk*
       D   *Entire main dict. to RAM if room*
       E   *Main spelling buffer (kbytes)*
       F   *Always ask for personal dict.*
       G   *Definitions during spell session*

    F   Main spelling buffer (kbytes)
    G   Personal dict. memory (kbytes)
    H   Smallest word checked
    I   Turn spelling check on or off
    J   Check for double word
    K   Watch progress of spelling check

B   Nondocument mode

    A   Nondoc. file when in cmd. line
    B   Print nondocument as default

C   ^B and ^QU strip MSB of chars.
D   Tabs and auto-indent by file type

C   Indexing

    A   General exclusion list file
    B   Normally index every word

D   Shorthand (macros)

    A   Shorthand storage file
    B   Storage buffer size (records)
    C   Format for today's date
    D   Format for current time
    E   Dollar format for numbers

E   Merge printing

    A   Separator between data items
    B   Variable name indicator
    C   Date format for &@& variable
    D   Time format for &!& variable

F   Character conversion patches

    A   Uppercase table
    B   Lowercase table
    C   Collating sequence table
    D   Keystroke code translation

G   Miscellaneous

    A   Sign-on message
    B   Longest delay (sign-on)
    C   Medium delay (menus)
    D   Shortest delay (doc align)
    E   Erasing and cursor type ahead
    F   ^N split line (or hard RET to soft)
    G   Window prompt for doc/nondoc
    H   Size of other window
    I   Auto-backup
    J   Go to top of page
    K   Language default
    L   Current code page support

E PATCHING

A Auto-patcher

B Save settings

C Reset all settings

Index

Index

Index

Index

Index

Index

Index

Index

Index

Index

Index

Index

Index

Index

Index